Culture as Comfort
Many Things You Know About Culture
(But Might Not Realize)

Sarah J. Mahler

Florida International University
Global & Sociocultural Studies

Boston   Columbus   Indianapolis   New York   San Francisco   Upper Saddle River
Amsterdam   Cape Town   Dubai   London   Madrid   Milan   Munich   Paris   Montreal   Toronto
Delhi   Mexico City   Sao Paulo   Sydney   Hong Kong   Seoul   Singapore   Taipei   Tokyo

Editorial Director: Craig Campanella
Publisher: Nancy Roberts
Associate Editor: Nicole Conforti
Editorial Asssitant: Molly White
Associate Managing Editor: Bayani Mendoza de Leon
Project Manager: Anne Ricigliano
Marketing Director: Brandy Dawson
Marketing Manager: Kate Mitchell
Marketing Assistant: Paige Patunus
Project Coordination, Text Design, and Electronic Page Makeup: Laserwords Maine, Inc
Senior Manufacturing Buyer: Alan Fischer
Cover Art Director: Bruce Kenselaar
Image Permission Coordinator: Beth Brenzel
Image Researcher: Krystyna Sperka Borgen
Text Rights Clearance Editor: Jane Scelta
Permissions Project Manager/Specialist: Craig Jones
Cover Art: © Jo Anne Pedro

Credits and acknowledgments borrowed from other sources and reproduced, with permission, in this textbook appear on page 137.

Library of Congress Cataloging-in-Publication Data is available on request from the Library of Congress.

1 2 3 4 5 6 7 8 9 10—STP Courier—15 14 13 12

ISBN 10:   0-205-88000-2
ISBN 13: 978-0-205-88000-3

Inspired by Sophia
Matured with Miguel
Entrusted to You

CONTENTS

PREFACE

TO *CULTURE AS COMFORT'S* READERS

Imagine you have been working to achieve a dream for twenty years. That is exactly what this book's publication and that fact that you are reading it signifies for me. Bringing to public view the ideas in this book has long been my personal as well as professional passion. The road to this point has not been easy; it has been a prolonged personal odyssey. I am very grateful to Pearson for publishing *Culture as Comfort* because for almost a year, various publishers I spoke with were enthusiastic about the content but still reluctant to write me a contract. It was not for the usual reasons publishers reject manuscripts—poor market potential, bad fit with press, or bad reviews. This book's reviews were overwhelmingly glowing. Its problem was that it's a very atypical book and publisher after publisher didn't know what to do with it. Why? Books fit known genres and markets so when a new manuscript comes along, it is assessed along those criteria. *Culture as Comfort* did not fit any one genre: It's not a true textbook nor is it exactly a supplemental book (like an ethnography or a case study). It's also not a book steeped in theoretical language that is typically assigned to graduate students. It's also not a typical trade book, a nonfiction book written for non-academic readers. So what *is* this book?

Culture as Comfort is my best attempt at making visible for as many people as possible what is so hard to really see—culture. The book itself is the first big step toward this goal. (It is not the only important step; I am developing other aspects and applications of the approach I provide here on my website cultureascomfort.com). Why do I say that it is really hard to see culture? As I explain in the book, we learn so much of what we call culture so early on in life that "it" resides largely in our subconscious. Thus, we rarely view what we think and do as cultural—at least not until we find ourselves outside of our cultural comforts. Instead, we take culture for granted as the way things are—as normality.

Why might it be worthwhile putting so much effort into helping people see culture? I believe how we now tend to view culture gets in the way of truly understanding "it." For instance, we speak about culture as some*thing* we "have" but we rarely consider how we acquire "it" or even what we do with "it." This book addresses how people learn cultural ideas and practices so that readers begin to see culture as a *continual process of doing* more than as a possession. It is my firm conviction and a major motivator for devoting years of my life to this project that by shifting our primary way of seeing culture from thing-like (possession) to processes we go through and participate in (actions and thoughts) we will spend more time continuing to expand our cultural comfort zones than to defend those we "have" against others. My hope is that in reading and thinking about this book, you will begin to see what you already know and typically feel (culture as comfort) and this will embolden you to *embrace your cultural discomforts* as well as your comforts.

I wrote above that this book is oriented toward as wide an audience as possible. Doing so is rare among academics. Why? In my career, scholars are rewarded for publishing, but not much for publishing this type of book. We are expected to do research that fosters new knowledge and to present this knowledge, in the appropriate technical language, to critical review by other scholars in our subfield. *Culture as Comfort* does draw upon a wide array of scholarly knowledge but, although quite a few of the ideas presented are new, they are not based on any research I am doing to specifically address how people learn culture. Rather, I synthesize others' research and present it as nontechnically as possible along with my own ideas and insights. Additionally, I wrote the book with many personal stories and anecdotes that would rarely appear in typical scholarship because they would make scientific research appear subjective. Adding them to the manuscript helps explain why *Culture as Comfort* does not fit the standard publication boxes most known to publishers—fiction (stories) or nonfiction (textbooks, memoirs, biographies, studies, etc.). I am quite convinced, and research documents the insight as well, that most of us learn best through stories not abstract information. People with incredible abilities to memorize such things as lists of numbers often recall information by making up stories about it. The stories in this book are real, not made up; I include them in hopes that they help make the information both enjoyable and easier to recall.

In sum, I hope that you not only enjoy learning many things that you already know about culture but might not realize, but that you also enjoy the learning process.

TO MY COLLEAGUES IN ACADEMIA IN PARTICULAR

This book is driven by academic questions that I have been working on since adolescence when I began to ask the very questions I try to answer here, but it is not a book written for a typical academic audience. It *is* written to be scholarly, but it is not intended to fit the classic scholarly genre of writing. That is a very fine line to walk and therefore I want to explain my intentions very directly. Thank you for taking the time to read this.

Most of us academics, I am quite sure, regularly traverse the huge gap between the way we present the same material (whether through the written word or by lecture) to our peers versus how we present it to our students, particularly to undergrads. We have to shift our use of jargon, our level of detail, and our means of delivery to bridge the gap. There are variations, of course, in how we go about code switching from classroom to conference but the key is that we recognize that audience matters. While conceiving of this book, which was written after I wrote a much longer, more complex version and was asked to scale it back for a more undergraduate readership, I kept my audience in mind as consistently as I recommend to my PhD students that they never forget their problem statement. I tell them to tape that statement above their work area so they never lose sight—literally—of their purpose. My goal with this book is to bring fundamental lessons about what it is to be human to the widest audience possible. This has meant making some tradeoffs that I address now.

CROSSING-DISCIPLINES WITH ACCURACY Publishing across disciplinary lines is dangerous; publishing across many disciplinary lines in few of which the author enjoys expertise constitutes near academic suicide. People who spend their lives becoming experts tend to defend their academic turf against those who tread upon it without the proper authority and there is good, scholarly reason to do so. But this comes at a cost. Knowledge *becomes* disciplinary and therefore bounded. As with most everything else, it is people who impose the categorical order upon the world that we use, defend, and reproduce. Yet understanding the human condition in particular requires a wide angle and a nearly Renaissance person's command of information and analytical tools. In short, I am arguing that as much as the important criterion of expertise tends to push us academics into smaller and smaller subfields there is a need to synthesize information across a wide array of scholarly inquiry. Syntheses, however, rarely get published unless as review articles because they do not typically include original data. And cross-disciplinary syntheses are very risky as they hold the high potential of not only making generalizations instead of particular claims but of generalizing beyond one's expertise. The detractions are many and the rewards are few, so, in my experience, we shy away from what I am doing here—even without going further afield by writing syntheses for a general audience. Yet, I have long felt that there is a growing need to translate what we do into people's vernaculars. So much of what people do in life is driven by assumptions about the human condition that are rarely, if ever, taken to task. It is high time that many mistaken assumptions be challenged. To do so, I feel, requires transdisciplinary work and translation.

Translation, however, should not mean lowering standards of accuracy. Toward that end, in preparing for and writing *Culture as Comfort* I have spent years pouring through vast literatures trying to the best of my ability to understand them within their own contexts, culling accurate material that reflects our state-of-the-art understanding of different areas, fully knowledgeable of the fact that these are multiple, dynamic areas of contested knowledge which I cannot do full justice to in any book, let alone a book like this one. But I have tried and I have also sought the expertise of scholars across different disciplines to check my work, identify any inaccuracies, and suggest useful alternatives and information. Moreover, my publisher added another layer of factual oversight through their editorial work and by hiring specialists to read through the material. That said, I am sure that colleagues in academia will find fault with some of the information I marshal to make my claims. I take responsibility for inaccuracies but request that matters of clarification and debate spill over into the blog and wiki I have created for this book's ideas at cultureascomfort.com. The book is intended to stimulate wide and even wild conversations and those tools are there to foster them.

CRAZY CONJECTURES? Although most of what appears in *Culture as Comfort* rests upon a scholarly foundation, it did not originate there. The inspiration was both much more mundane and quotidian. The idea popped into my head when beginning to teach Introduction to Anthropology during my first semester as a professor and, coincidentally, when my daughter, Sophia, was a young infant. The happenstance of trying to reconcile what my textbook had to say about culture with what I was observing in my child set me thinking in wholly new directions not only about culture but also about anthropology. Why did so few anthropologists study how children learn culture even though learning culture is one of the fundamental characteristics of culture we always have our students learn? That serendipitous time in my life—no doubt inflected by months of poor sleep as well—stimulated my interest in how people learn culture. This inquietude never left me even as I progressed along in my career in a pretty traditional way. I did not study enculturation because my expertise was in migration studies, but I formulated ideas about enculturation, let them gestate in my mind, and tested them out on my students for over a decade before beginning to see whether anyone else had written or was researching on the topic. Whenever I could, I read both within and beyond anthropological literatures to see what others' ideas and findings included.

To cut to the chase, I found that a lot of my crazy initial conjectures were not only affirmed by the literature, but that I was probably making some connections others were not even seeing. I still feel this way, although the work by other scholars has advanced so amazingly that there are only a few of these crazy conjectures left. The rest of the gaps are rapidly being filled in where only conjecture had been. Why publish them in a book intended for undergraduates and a broad lay audience, then, instead of in peer-reviewed articles where they can be debated? I have two responses which I hope are satisfactory but which I suspect may not be for some. First, this book makes high-level claims that are overwhelmingly substantiated by others but without going into the level of detail others provide and which would be required for peer-review. For instance, I argue that neural pathways in the brain reflect a person's experience in the world but I do not elaborate on the roles of different parts of the brain and their purposes nor on the impact of neurotransmitters. I also argue that people create, learn, and perpetuate cultural patterns (order) which is not too controversial since Clifford Geertz long ago wrote that people spin their own webs of meaning. However, I dedicate more time and energy in explaining culture as order and also argue that this makes much of social life predictable (at least within our cultural competencies). Being able to correctly interpret others and largely predict what they will do and think lowers the stress, I add, on the brain's computing power. It is a good, energy efficient strategy to have the brain not compute everyone and everything anew with each encounter but to store packets of information and use them to make instantaneous inferences from past experience about the present and future. That synthesis is not one I have seen anyone else write. I may be wrong with my synthesis and a few other crazy conjectures but speculation, as neuroscientist Ramachandran (2001: xvii) argues, "is nothing to be ashamed of: every virgin area of scientific inquiry must first be explored in this way. . . . We need to roll out our best hypotheses, hunches, and hare-brained, half-baked intentions, and then rack our brains for ways to test them."

DISCONNECTED DOTS   I can well imagine (and hope) that some of my colleagues reading this book will connect the dots between what I write (and what neuroanthropology, cognitive anthropology, neuroscience, cultural psychology, and other fields I touch upon are finding) and the concepts, theories, and theoretical debates that so many of us have been grappling with over our careers. And yet I rarely, if ever, connect those dots in the text. Why? Isn't social science truly, if almost never stated as such, the study of the patterns we observe in people and then theorizing why what we do is patterned? If so, then knowing how infants and young children learn socially produced and communicated patterns relates to famous scholars' attempts to explain them with such abstract concepts as "social facts," "habitus" and "structuration." All of this work helps connect the proverbial social science dots between "structure" and "agency." Yes, I definitely see these dots as connected. But they are not connections with meaning to the audience I am most trying to reach with this book, though I am very happy if the book is read by people who are anxious to connect these particular dots. And if you belong to this latter group, then please go right ahead connecting these dots and sharing your insights with the rest of us. Somewhat similarly, those of you familiar with the psychology literature might think to yourself that when I say culture is about comfort you think "cognitive consonance" and when I say discomfort you think "dissonance." Those are also dots that can be connected, but, again, I do not hear anyone in the supermarket talking about being cognitively dissonant and I'm not sure that this term would ever make it into everyday language. Comfort and discomfort just convey the ideas in ways that most of us can relate to more easily.

I also see this book as provoking some controversy among scholars regarding the old "Culture of Poverty" debates. This is not my intention but I anticipate that some will claim that my book blames victims because it argues that people learn the cultural practices around them and tend to reproduce them. That's a pretty standard statement but it can be used to argue that the poor reproduce the so-called culture of poverty. This is one of the reasons why it is so important to also examine the arguments in the book regarding how the genesis of cultural practices creates similarities and at the same time differences within and across peoples but that difference, per se, is not sufficient to produce social hierarchies. In short, I have taken pains *not* to blame only the disadvantaged for their condition in life but to lay greater responsibility on the shoulders of the advantaged. Everyone, however, is responsible for cultural reproduction and, to a lesser degree, cultural innovation; the problem is that we rarely see what we take for granted. We don't typically see our culture because it just is normal to us. This book, then works toward making these processes more transparent in the hopes that people will become more empowered to broaden their comfort zones to the degree possible. Some people are in a more advantaged position to expand more than others but we can all expand.

My goal in writing this book, then, is not really to advance social science among scholars but to get general audience readers to experience an Aha! moment in which they say to themselves something like, "I never thought about that!" In other words, most of us never stop to think about the fact that what we do as people is patterned and why. We don't need to because we've learned the patterns so early on that they reside in our subconscious understanding—and for good reason. We have other things to do with our conscious reasoning! But never thinking about how we become similar to those with whom we share "our" culture leaves us susceptible not only to ethnocentrism (which is part of the human condition) but, more importantly, to xenophobia. And those isms and phobias have remedies but to remedy them we need to see what usually is hidden. Connecting those culture-as-comfort dots *is* what I want to accomplish with this book and thus other dots are left unconnected intentionally because they would distract from my larger purpose.

APPLYING ANTHROPOLOGY Where I went to graduate school (and my experience was not unique), applied anthropology was treated as less prestigious than basic science anthropology. I have come to appreciate and practice both in the course of my career. This particular book, however, is designed to use academic insights to promote meaningful applications more than anything else I have done to date. I see the applications of the lessons about culture in this book as endless and hope that my scholarly peers will embrace this potentiality along with me. I believe strongly that we can and should make anthropology increasingly relevant to all students and all fields. We can do this in many ways; the way I promote it in this book is by aiding people from all walks of life to see culture more readily and in so doing become more culturally empowered to bridge themselves to others more than building boundaries to keep them out. I hope you will join me and bring your students along too. This book is only one step in that direction.

ACKNOWLEDGMENTS

It's been twenty years (I always know the number of years because it reflects my daughter, Sophia's, age) and there are many, many people who have helped me along this journey whom I wish to thank. I will try to mention everyone, but to those I inadvertently leave out, please accept my apologies in advance. I'm really bad at recall, particularly with names.

Sophia is so central to this book that I am going to break tradition in how most people write acknowledgments by thanking her and other family members first. She not only inspired me to write this book by showing me how babies inquire about culture, but she has accompanied me every step of the way providing support and love but also challenges and moments of discomfort. All of these have been important but maybe the highlight was when she told me about stumbling in her Introduction to Anthropology course in college when asked to define "culture" on an exam. "Mom," she related, "I froze because I couldn't answer the question the way I knew the professor wanted me to!"

Family members, my parents and brothers in particular, but also my step-children and -grandchildren have been supportive over the many years of gestating this book. However, no one person has been more insistent that I put aside distractions, get the book done, and then the word out that it was finally ready than my husband, Miguel. Everyone needs someone who so completely believes in you that they never let you fall without insisting that you pick yourself up. "Mike" is that person to me, my greatest cheerleader. Thanks for always being there for me.

Most of us realize that the cohort of students with whom you go through school, especially if as in graduate school the experience is very taxing, tend to be friends for life. You've shared scholarly rites of passage together and they bond you tightly. That has been true for me. My cohort from grad school at Columbia not only kept me going during those hard years of work, but has been supporting me ever since. First, special thanks to those of you who have read and given me feedback on the whole manuscript and in some cases variations of it—Jean Scandlyn, Nia Georges, and Maxine Weisgrau. Thanks to Robin Nagel who tried to get her literary agent interested. No luck. Hopefully agents will read this and be more willing to get out of their boxes! Thanks to friendship and comic relief from Steven Rubenstein and kudos to my other classmates too. A profound and special thank you is indeed needed for Mayor Maurice Ferré. Maurice insisted that this book would be a winner and has championed my writing it to the exclusion of all other "distractions" and academic encounters. Many colleagues of mine at FIU read some or all of the manuscript giving me critical cross-disciplinary feedback, in particular Laura Ogden, Bob Lickliter, Anthony Dick, Shannon Pruden, Markus Thiel, Chuck Bleiker, Lynne Barrett, and Rebecca Friedman while others including Alex Stepick, Maria Aysa-Lastra, Dennis Wiedman, and Vrushali Patil attended my debut presentation and helped me see connections I needed to make. There are many other colleagues who have been supportive in spirit including Rick Tardanico, Doug Kincaid, Hugh Gladwin, and Juliet Erazo. My home at FIU in Global and Sociocultural Studies has been a great place to nurture these ideas and so thanks to all of you as well as many other colleagues and staff at FIU—in particular the staff of my former international center: Myriam Rios, Cristyn Casey, Christine Caly-Sanchez, Majelissa Luna, and Pedro Botta, among others. They always smiled when I stole a few hours from the bureaucracy to work on "my project." Shout out to Emilio Williams for connecting with me, reading the manuscript and being among the first to apply it to his grandson, his students, and in his everyday life. Thanks to Mark Cassini for his intercultural communication reading perspective, to sponsors of my first book tour (prepublication) in Portugal and Spain—Tobias Schumacher, Beatriz Padilla, Rosa Aparicio, Liliana Suárez, Lorenzo Chacón, Silvia Carrasco, and Raúl Hernández.

Over the course of my career I have enjoyed working with many undergraduate and graduate students and hearing from them about their experiences with "Dr. M" and her "purple pen treatment." My first cohort of PhD students formed themselves into what they called "Team Mahler" and they have been enormously supportive of me and this project over the years. Particular thanks to members Jasney Cogua-Lopez, Anne Braseby, Sharon Placide, Tricia Vanderkooy, Francisco Sastre, Tekla Nicholas, Cynthia Malakasis, Mayurakshi Chaudhuri, Dusan Ugrina, Nadia Riazati and Alejandro Angee. "Keep paying it forward!"

I owe a great debt to numerous people for steering this book through the turbulent waters of publishing. I wish to thank them in chronological order because without the earliest fans I might have given up. Gary Ferraro mentored me early on about audience and publishers. Christa Erml has been not only a great critic and researcher but also a great fan. Richard Robbins read the original, longer manuscript and immediately "got it" but also realized I needed to recast it for undergraduates and the general public. I did and it has made a huge difference. June Belkin-Dietrich and especially Anna Pagano copy-edited and fact checked superbly. Amy Serrano and Associates have been helping me get my words out and organizing and launching my social media. At Pearson I am grateful to Nancy Roberts, my acquisitions editor, for making sure this one did not get away and to Dickson Musselwhite for listening when I most needed it. My production and marketing teams of Nicole Conforti, Kate Mitchell, Amy Saucier, Bayani DeLeon, Thomas Scalzo, Krystyna Sperka Borgen, Molly White, and Rachel Comerford (apologies to others behind the scenes who I have not included) have been terrific. Special thanks to Jo Ann Pedro for designing my website logo, the book cover and another graphic.

Thank you to those who have already invited me to speak about the book and to those many more whom I shall meet in the future. In your hands is the kernel of what I hope will grow into a full-fledged change in the way people think about culture and go about doing culture.

Although this book germinated many seasons ago, it would not have matured as much without the indirect stewardship from dozens of scholars who probably do not know how important their work has been in general and to me in particular. When I first began thinking about what would become *Culture as Comfort*, the subfields from which I drew much of my own knowledge about the brain and learning in early childhood such as cultural psychology, neuroscience, neuroanthropology, and the anthropology of children and childhood were themselves in their infancy. The diligence of a generation or more of scholars has vastly improved our knowledge and I am proud to make a bit of a contribution alongside them. I cannot mention them all for lack of space (I hope I've done better in the bibliography!) but want to mention, in particular, anthropologists Mary Douglas, Robert A. LeVine, David Lancy, David M. Rosen, Rachael Stryker, Melvin Konner, Sarah Blaffer Hrdy, Daniel Lende, Greg Downey, Susan Shepler, and Alma Gottlieb; psychologists and/or neuroscientists Barbara S. Rogoff, Martyn Barrett, Harry C. Triandis, Susan T. Fiske, Paul Bloom, VS Ramachandran, and Eleanor E. Maccoby; sociologists Douglas S. Massey, Joe E. Fagin, and Deborah Van Ausdale; and last, but definitely not least, geographer David Sibley. At this time I wish to acknowledge and thank the dozen or so peer reviewers of the manuscript whose comments have enabled me to make important improvements and correct inaccuracies: Janet Altamirano, Wharton County Junior College and University of Houston Downtown; Ronald Bolender, Mount Vernon Nazarene University; Keri Brondo, University of Memphis; Walter Calgaro, Prairie State College; Heide Castaneda, University of South Florida; Pearce Paul Creasman, University of Arizona; Alyssa Forcehimes, University of New Mexico; Cynthia Fowler, Wofford College; Vance Geiger, University of Central Florida; Katrina Kardiasmenos, Bowie State University; Andrew Kinkella, Moorpark College; Jonathan Marion, California State University San Marcos; Jason Miller, University of South Florida; Mark Peterson, Miami University; Michael Polich, McHenry County College; Joanna Salapska-Gelleri, Florida Gulf Coast University; Stanley Walling, Community College of Philadelphia; and Leanna Wolfe, Los Angeles Valley College. I take full responsibility for any errors that remain.

Behind every successful man, the saying goes, is a supportive woman. Behind every successful woman, I argue, are a whole bunch of supportive women and probably quite a few men (and children) too. That's certainly been my case. I apologize for not naming everyone but several groups have encouraged me for many years during this project. They include my oldest and most loyal friends (Debbie Hungerford Shirt, Sophia Chang, Barb Fitton Hauss, Amy Hertz, Amy Nishida, Rachel Trachten, Deanne Tucker, Kristen Costello, Judy Weiss, Susan Zoroff, Sonia Dueño, Elizabeth Campbell and I'm sure I've forgotten someone!), Priscilla's Group of Miami women leaders (Carolyn Rose-Avila, Margaret Starner, Peggy Maisel, Stephanie Layton, and Dorrit Smetana Marks in particular). Lastly, I wish to honor someone whom I have not seen since college but who helped me learn that I could embrace being discomforted (instead of feeling humiliated by it) and that cultivating creative discomforts is a worthwhile enterprise for us all. Thanks, Roger, wherever you may be.

What Is Culture?
What Is Culture to You?

*I don't know how many times I've wished that I'd never heard that
damned word.*

—Raymond Williams, speaking about "culture"
(Kuper 1999: 1)

This book is about "culture." You probably hear or say this word at least a couple of times each day, but have you ever stopped to think a bit about what the word "culture" means? What does "culture" mean to you? What pops into your mind when you hear the word "culture"? Before you continue reading this book, please take a few moments now to jot down your thoughts and ideas about culture in the space provided on the next page. Nothing to fear; this isn't a quiz or a measure of how much you know already. It's just one of a number of times in this book that you will be asked to participate in activities that get you grappling with the ideas covered here. Since I will likely introduce you to new ways to understand culture, having you record your thoughts about this concept before you go any further will help you if your thinking has changed later on and, if so, how. You're unlikely to recall your starting point unless you record it. So you are asked to write your thoughts down now. You will encounter these Planned Pauses throughout the book. Unlike in other texts in which the exercises occur at the end of the chapter, Planned Pauses occur when the moment is right for you to pause your reading, think about what you've been learning and apply that knowledge. So in the Planned Pause area provided please write down whatever comes into your mind when you think about "culture." Take as long as you wish.

Please keep these initial ideas in mind as you read this chapter. Consider this the starting point in what I hope will be an interesting journey and one that, much like the classic journeys in literary works such as the *Odyssey* and the *Iliad*, will be a journey of critical discoveries. The journey in this case is to see culture differently and, in so doing, to become much more in charge of your cultural life and destiny.

PLANNED PAUSE 1-1

WHAT I THINK OF WHEN I HEAR THE WORD "CULTURE"

Instructions: *In the blank space below write down your immediate response to the question posed: "What Do You Think Of When You Hear The Word 'Culture'?"*

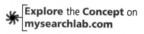

Explore the **Concept** on
mysearchlab.com

DO WE INHERIT CULTURE? WHAT ROLE DOES BIOLOGY PLAY, IF ANY?

No two people will jot down exactly the same ideas in the previous exercise; even professional anthropologists, who specialize in studying cultures, have different notions of what we think culture is. However, there is at least one fundamental characteristic of culture that pretty much all anthropologists and other social scientists agree upon: *People learn culture; we are not born with culture.* Do you agree? Is culture something you are born with or something you learn? You may feel somewhat ambivalent about your answer because many of us think of culture as part of our inheritance from our family, something that is passed down to us from generation to generation, kind of like our genes. But you would probably agree that there is a big difference between why your nose is shaped the way it is and why you speak your native language. The first is definitely more biological (although your nose could have had a few accidents that changed what might have been its shape) while the second you recognize is clearly something you learned. You did not arrive into this world speaking a language and you weren't born knowing how to greet someone.

Yet for many of us there is a very strong urge to hold on to the idea that culture is inherited. After all, we learn culture from our families so it can feel like it's biological in some sense. We also think of people being born not only into different cultures, but also into different races and sexes. There's definitely something biological about these in that we identify people of different ethnicities and sexes by physical clues; however, while we may be born male or female, does that mean we know at birth how we are supposed to act if we're boys or girls? Many people feel that we are born into religions in ways similar to being born male or female. But are we born knowing the prayers to say or the appropriate ways to behave in our religious tradition? No. We learn these. So, back to the basic question: Are we born with culture or do we learn it? What's more important, nature or nurture? Nature versus nurture has long been a big debate so if you're still struggling with the question, that's good. There is no doubt that we have had to evolve *biologically* into a species that depends very highly on learned behaviors and less on innate behaviors. We evolved certain abilities that enable us to learn culture and we are not completely divorced from our environment; especially in an age of global warming, we know that we also affect our environment. Nature and nurture interact in complicated ways, which I address to some degree in the coming chapters, but *we do not inherit culture biologically*. That's a key point. We do not inherit very many specific ways of thinking and behaving biologically, yet we do learn culture, but how? It may help to consider the following situation. Suppose there is a childless couple who wishes to adopt. The couple cannot find any children locally so they decide to adopt a baby from overseas. Will that baby grow up with the culture of his homeland or his adoptive land? If his parents make absolutely no effort to teach him about "his" native culture, will he have any idea how to speak or behave there if he returns?

Thinking about this hypothetical situation hopefully will convince you that despite a lot of confusing biological ideas about where we get culture, we do not inherit it genetically. We have to learn it. The hypothetical is also a great example of a fundamental point I will make in the book, which is that people are incredibly adaptable. Whatever culture is, "it" enables us to adapt to life with any group of people in any place in the world where people survive. We have a tremendous capacity for flexibility, but we enjoy it primarily very early in our lives. That is, as we learn culture, we lose some of this birthright flexibility. We lose flexibility—but never all of it—as we acquire the cultural practices, patterns, ideas, beliefs, and so on of the people who transmit them to us. And as we learn those ways of life in early childhood, we quickly act and think very much like our culture "teachers." By the time we enter kindergarten we have become really expert in our culture. We may not know how to read a book but we can read others' faces. We may not know how to count numbers, but we know whom we can count on (trust) and can identify people who don't do things as we do (people who are not "us"). We know almost nothing about geography—the different continents and countries—but we know where we belong and where we feel we don't belong.

Every one of us reading this book has learned culture; we've all been through the processes involved and we've become quite expert at navigating the many cultural spaces of our lives (home, school, work, restaurants, movie theaters, clubs, places of worship/religions, sports, etc.). So what do you remember about learning your culture? Think hard for a few moments back to when you were 5 years old or younger. What memories can you recall that involve learning to adapt to your cultural environment?

If you've had a hard time with this question, you are not alone. Why? Well, we learn a huge amount of culture while we are just infants and toddlers. Most of us have few, if any, memories from that period of our lives; yet that's exactly when we are learning culture by leaps and bounds. Early childhood is when we learn language, but do you have any memories about learning specific words and when you started speaking in sentences? I certainly don't. Whatever I know from that time is from the stories I've heard about myself from my family members. No wonder culture has this mysterious quality; we learn it but we do not recall much, if anything, about learning it. We are good at it, yet we typically have a hard time identifying much about our culture above and beyond the basics like foods, major holiday traditions, and language—at least, until we meet someone whose cultural practices are very different from our own. That means that we don't "see" our own culture very easily unless we either leave and go somewhere where the people's way of life differs from our own, or we meet people with cultural differences even within our own society.

So, what *is* culture? This question has been asked by generations of scholars; at one time over a half-century ago two anthropologists surveyed a wide variety of definitions in use and published a book entirely devoted to this question (Kroeber & Kluckhohn 1963), but that hardly settled the matter. Hopefully by the time you finish reading this book and doing the short exercises in it, you will feel much more able to respond to this question yourself. For me, culture is not one *thing* or even many *things*; it's a word that people invented to signify a wide array of ideas and processes. When we use the word "culture" we use it as a conceptual shortcut; instead of really having to talk about all these different ideas that are included within the word "culture," we just say the word and go on our merry way. But when we *don't* stop to take a good, long, hard look at this word, we just help to perpetuate that shortcut. We actually take shortcuts with many concepts, for example, "identity," "globalization," and "personality." Each of these has a lot of meanings and uses. When we say these words we can avoid having to deal with that complexity; we don't stop to understand what each truly means. I actually like the fact that we experience some confusion with these big terms because confusion invites people to clarify what's going on. In the case of the term "culture," however, the fact that more and more people use this word to mean more and more "things" just creates more and more confusion. And when that happens, it is a good idea to try to break through the confusion and create greater clarity (see also Domínguez Duque et al. 2010). That's a main mission for writing this book.

I am by far not the first person to tackle this "culture" job. However, I am among the first to tackle it by helping us understand what culture "is" by showing how and why we learn culture early in life *so that we can see how we continue to learn culturally throughout life.* My goal is to not only help you better understand the concept of culture but for you to use this knowledge innovatively in your own lives. To be able to harness culture to your own needs (and, hopefully, for the greater good as well), you must see and examine consciously what we rarely actually see—our own culture. As you'll soon find out, we learn culture before we are aware of the processes and outcomes involved and, in so doing, we do not see ourselves as having a particular culture; we take what we think and say and do as normal. It's so cultural, I often say, it's natural. It's second nature. No wonder we think that culture is somehow biologically inherited!

REDISCOVERING CULTURE FOR THE VERY FIRST TIME

Now that you have recorded your own ideas on culture and you have tried to recall learning culture as a child, I think it is worth taking a look at the term's origins and different meanings. Why do that? Don't we all know what culture means? We use the word nearly every day. Well, a goal of mine is to be more mindful as we go about doing culture so I think getting more background could be illuminating. If you encounter an unfamiliar word, you could look it up in a dictionary. Now although culture is familiar word, there might be meanings that you are unfamiliar with, so please read through the definitions I found for the "culture" entry on dictionary.com below. Record which meanings, if any, you didn't know and which get you thinking about culture in new ways.

Culture:

1. the quality in a person or society that arises from a concern for what is regarded as excellent in arts, letters, manners, scholarly pursuits, etc.

2. that which is excellent in the arts, manners, etc.

3. a particular form or stage of civilization, as that of a certain nation or period: *Greek culture.*

4. development or improvement of the mind by education or training.

5. the behaviors and beliefs characteristic of a particular social, ethnic, or age group: *the youth culture; the drug culture.*

6. *Anthropology.* the sum total of ways of living built up by a group of human beings and transmitted from one generation to another.

7. *Biology.*
   a. the cultivation of microorganisms, as bacteria, or of tissues, for scientific study, medicinal use, etc.
   b. the product or growth resulting from such cultivation.

8. the act or practice of cultivating the soil; tillage.

9. the raising of plants or animals, especially with a view to their improvement.

10. the product or growth resulting from such cultivation.

I remember consulting the dictionary some time ago and finding the "Biology" meaning, number 7 above. A light bulb went off in my head. I'd never thought of culture as what you grow in a petri dish—a bacteria culture—but I certainly knew that meaning from science classes. Does this or any other meaning of culture you found get you asking where the word culture comes from? If so, then you'll really enjoy learning more about the term's history a bit later in this book. Culture definitely has an interesting story of its own that few people know, one that will potentially change the way you see culture forever. Before going into the etymology (origins) of the word, however, it's important to do a little more analysis of these definitions. Toward that end, I've devised a simple activity I'd like you to do now. Go through the different definitions and see if you can group them into which ones are similar to others and which ones seem to be very different from the others. You should come up with a few groupings of definitions. (Hint: The italicized words in the dictionary entry above might help you.)

When I do this activity, I come up with four groups.

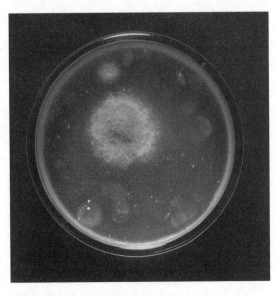

Yeast Being Cultured in a Petri Dish. Does this Type of Culture Occur to You When You Hear the Word "Culture"?

My first grouping includes definitions 1, 2, and 4. I put them together because to me these definitions refer to people who are "cultured." People often speak about someone who has good manners, who knows a lot about art, and so on, as "cultured." Sometimes you might hear someone comment about a sloppy eater as being "uncultured." Another way that this meaning for culture appears is in references to "popular" or "low" culture (the art, music, books, etc. that everyday people enjoy) versus "high" culture (the art, music, books, etc. that a society's elite patronize).

The second of my groupings includes just definition 3. To me, this refers not to individuals but to their society. This meaning of culture is used to measure societies on a scale between civilized/cultured and barbaric/uncultured. So societies that are very "developed" are often referred to as being civilized or cultured, while those seen as "backward," "undeveloped" or even "developing" are often referred to as uncivilized or uncultured. (By the way, I am not saying *I* feel this way; it's just that I've heard the term "culture" used in these ways.)

My third grouping includes definitions 5 and 6, which are the traditional anthropological ones, although dictionary.com identifies only the sixth meaning this way. That is, anthropologists use the term "culture" to mean the way of life of a people. The difference between definition 5 and definition 6 is that the first typically refers to a "subculture" while 6 refers to a culture as a whole. If this is confusing, it should be. What part of a culture is a subculture? When does a subculture become a culture? You get the idea. Our terms often confuse us more than they help us explain or understand phenomena.

The last grouping of dictionary meanings I created contains the rest of the definitions. They are the oddballs—at least at first glance. They all refer to *cultivating* bacteria, plants, and even animals and seem to have nothing to do with people. Hopefully, you got the same light bulb or "a-ha" moment when you saw these definitions that I did. You probably have seen what petri dishes look like in biology lab—the containers used to grow cultures of bacteria, fungi, and so on. And you surely are familiar with the term "agriculture"; perhaps you know its cousin terms for growing food in water (aquaculture) and small gardens (horticulture). In all probability you never associated these culture words with human culture, but they actually are related. Culture makes its first appearance as a word between the years 1400 and 1450. Back then, in Latin, it only referred to cultivating land, to tilling the soil. Yes, that's right. The word started out as agri*culture* and only later was applied to people. How did it make the jump to people? If you know a bit about its history, you start rediscovering the word "culture."

"Culture" derives from the Latin word *colere* (pronounced "*cóllar*-ay"), which was used among Latin-speaking European peoples in the late Middle Ages (Kuper 1999). *Colere* is a verb. That is really important since "culture" now, as we know, is almost always used as a noun. So *colere* was the verb rural peoples would have used frequently but narrowly to talk about farming. Most people at that time earned their living by cultivating the land, growing their own food. That sense of the word is also preserved today in the terms "horticulture" and "aquaculture" as mentioned above, but also in things such as "viticulture" (vineyards) and "cultured milk" (yogurt and cheese). Please note, however, that each of these terms is a noun, not a verb, and that if we ever use those terms now, most likely we do so without linking them mentally to the more common sense of their root word "culture"; that is, to human culture. We hear "agriculture" but we do not associate that "culture" with human culture. We are even less likely to think of scientists' "cultivation" of bacteria in laboratory dishes (bacteria cultures) as related somehow to our culture, yet they share the same linguistic root.

No matter how unrelated a petri dish may seem to a ballet production, agriculture and human culture *are* intimately linked. We can see this relationship when we understand *colere* as signifying the human manipulation of nature toward a particular end—originally toward the growing of food and the breeding of animals. For most of human existence on Earth, for hundreds of thousands of years at least, people survived by hunting and gathering our food, by food foraging. Starting only about 10,000 years ago we began to farm, to cultivate, and this involved manipulating nature much more than before. Tracing the term "culture" back to its original meaning, *colere*, reveals that culture is best understood as a verb—to cultivate (i.e., to manipulate or transform).

However, it is not a stretch to see how human manipulation of nature is akin to human manipulation of ourselves. When we cultivate we create something—typically food, but also things such as cultured pearls. Pearls occur naturally but very rarely. Because people value pearls, we cultivate more of them by inserting grains of sand into oysters. We manipulate natural processes to culture (cultivate) something. We manipulate not only other species, but we also cultivate ourselves. For example, it is not unusual to hear people talk about cultivating our talents when talking about music, art, and theater. And when we participate in these we might feel more cultured. When we emphasize the result of a process, we make culture seem less like a process (for which a verb is a good descriptor) and more like an outcome (for which a noun is better). In other words, we typically don't think of cultivating ourselves (or that we learn culture) but we refer to ourselves as having been cultivated—as being "cultured." I know this may seem like a linguistic trick, but really understanding where the word "culture" comes from helps us understand why there are so many ways we use the term, many of which we use without realizing. This is why I call this section of the chapter "Rediscovering Culture for the Very First Time."

"Culture" is a noun, which obscures the fact that it really is about process, in this case the process of learning the particular ways of people around oneself. People learn culture—we learn "it" through interacting with other people and we continue to practice our cultural abilities throughout life. Culture, then, should be understood as in constant motion. But the noun "culture" and the ways we tend to refer to it make it appear as something we have rather than the ways we interact and interpret each other. We acquire cultural abilities as very young children. By the time we are even aware of this learning, however, we have become so thoroughly accustomed to patterns of thinking and behaving that we rarely, if ever, see ourselves as cultural products, as having been cultivated in particular cultural ways. And because we learn culture so early in life, we don't actually think about what we do as cultural; we just feel that it's *normal*—after all, it comes naturally to us. We have a hard time saying what our culture *is*, though we can describe some of its characteristics. Yet we feel culture deeply rooted in us; it is something we hold onto and we are reluctant to alter because, well, it is our *nature*. Oops, I mean, our *culture*. Well, therein lies at least part of the problem . . .

So, let me take a moment to summarize what I hope you will have learned from this exploration into the dictionary definitions of culture. One dictionary definition relates the word to its origins as a verb for cultivating food through the manipulation of plants and animals. Another definition reveals that this cultivation is not just any type of food production; rather, it refers to selective breeding. That is, culture is not only about human manipulation of nature; it is also about humans *improving* upon nature. We cultivate drought- and pest-resistant crops and we breed dogs to do specific tasks that are useful to us. We make them into something better (for us) than was originally offered by nature. The term "culture," then, implies a very subtle yet very powerful underlying notion of *directed* change, of improvement,

An Advertisement for "Culture" or "Culchah"?

of evolution or progress. This applies to us as well as to animals and plants. That is, we cultivate ourselves through doing culture. A third common definition we find for culture refers to how we not only improve upon nature, but also improve ourselves. We cultivate ourselves and when we do, we too become "cultured." This meaning for culture usually does not refer to learning culture, broadly speaking; it conveys the idea that people can become culturally refined. That is, when individuals are cultured, they are viewed as having achieved higher social status than unrefined, "uncultured" people. When culture refers to refinement and we describe refined people as, for example, patronizing the arts, the word "culture" is often written with a capital *C*. "Arts and Culture," "Cultural events," and "Ministry of Culture" are typical expressions for this use of the word. Some people even pronounce the word differently when referring to Culture over culture as "culchah." To be "culchahed" is to be someone who has devoted a lot of time to cultivating her talents in music, art, theater, and so on, not someone who has spent her life cultivating her talents typing, working in a factory, or farming. We all learn culture, but only some are viewed as being "culchahed."

When whole societies view themselves (or are viewed) as more refined, evolved, civilized, developed, and so on, then what is commonly referred to as being "cultured" for individuals turns into a scale for measuring human progress or social evolution with more so-called developed nations located at the higher end of the scale and so-called developing nations further to the other side. I don't want you to think I am asserting that human society evolves from simple to complex, uncultured to cultured, from undeveloped to more developed, because I find these ideas problematic. I do want you, however, to both see and understand how these ideas about social evolution are subtly asserted whenever societies are classified as more "cultured," developed, and so on, than others.

Finally, there is the other dictionary definition for culture: when the word is used just to signify a particular way of life. If I speak about my culture I typically refer not to the plants I have in my garden, the number of sculptures I have on display, or the petri dish experiment I left in the laboratory. What I mean is how I, and others, share a similar language, customs, ways of thinking and acting, and so on. Again, however, please note that this common use of the term emphasizes culture more as a *thing* than as a process. We speak of having a culture. Sometimes we talk about "losing" our culture, especially if we are immigrants to a new country. Occasionally, people talk about learning a new culture when they live abroad for a long time, but most people never talk about learning their native culture. One of the principal reasons for this is that we cannot remember learning culture, and thus it seems more "thing-like" than a process of learning.

One definition for culture that you might have expected to find in the dictionary but that does not appear, at least in my entry, is culture as in artifacts. Don't people make things that reflect their culture (and which we often sell as representing a culture)? Food is an excellent example. We strongly associate certain foods with certain peoples and thus with "cultures" but we also use clothing and jewelry and bodily decorations, as well as music styles, to help us identify different so-called cultures and we compare architectural and artistic styles for the same reason. Are these material things not culture? They certainly are produced by people and reflect their cultural comforts, so, yes, they need to be understood as cultural. But for the purposes of this book in which the fundamental starting point is infants learning to relate to other people, I will emphasize culture as interpersonal and thus relational more than I will talk about material culture. Similarly, while some people are interested in the information people produce and pass along to others from generation to generation (such as knowledge of herbs good for treating wounds, how to build shelter, how to play a particular instrument, how to manipulate an avatar on a computer screen, philosophical positions, etc.) (Boyd & Richerson 2005), and I, too, find this very important and valuable, my focus in this book, is on how people learn to relate to one another beginning in infancy. I then take this understanding about culture as *learned patterns of behavior and thought* and examine what this relational perspective adds to our understanding of the human condition. However, in this book I do not address how children learn their society's "values." Values is another really complex concept we rarely take time to examine thoroughly. We just hear the word and think we know what it means. I do, however, describe how we learn cultural practices and ideas in general—processes of learning that apply to values as well as to more observable behaviors such as how people greet one another or adorn their bodies.

TAKING STOCK: WHAT HAVE YOU LEARNED SO FAR?

This book is probably a bit unusual from others you may have read in the past or may be reading now. It does not have you do application exercises at the end of the chapters, but instead in the middle of the chapters and at times when they are hopefully most useful to you. This is one of those times, a Planned Pause to have you respond to what you have been reading. This particular Planned Pause is called "How I View 'Culture' Now" because it asks you to reflect upon what you've just read. Please take a few moments now to think about what you wrote down when you first started reading this book about your own thoughts on culture. Now compare what you wrote about culture then with what you have learned about culture to this point. Do you see culture now exactly as you wrote about it earlier, or has your perspective shifted? If it has shifted, what do you see now that you didn't see before?

PLANNED PAUSE 1-2

HOW I VIEW "CULTURE" NOW

Instructions: *In the space provided immediately below, write a short paragraph or two describing how your ideas about culture have shifted and/or have been enhanced by reading this chapter. Be specific. Refer to information in the chapter.*

Explore the **Concept** on
mysearchlab.com

Now that you have had a chance to think about how your understanding of culture may have shifted so far, I will be up front with you about what I *hope* you have learned. I certainly hope that you have learned that we use the word "culture" in a wide variety of ways. Of course, you already knew this because, most likely in your everyday speech, you have used most (if not all) of the dictionary meanings for culture. That is why the subtitle to this book is "Many Things You Know About Culture (But Might Not Realize)." We have knowledge that lies beyond our conscious awareness. We typically *do* culture appropriately in our social circumstances, but that does not necessarily mean that we are really aware of what we do and why we do it. So, one of my objectives is to bring to a more conscious level your understanding of culture. That way, when you hear others use the term, you can do so with a more critical eye. When you, yourself, use the term you can use it more powerfully as well. Culture is by far not the only very complex concept we use in everyday speech to convey a variety of meanings; we have a lot of other concepts such as "justice," "power," "religion," and so on. Scholars dedicate their careers to studying these concepts and trying to make sense of them. However, culture—despite being one of the most important concepts people use all the time—has unfortunately been examined much less than other concepts. We study much more the similarities and differences *between* what we call cultures (but what probably should be called groups or peoples) than where the word "culture" comes from and what we use it to signify. Quite some time ago, I asked myself, "Why is this so?" That question is what started my journey toward writing this book. During the "Taking Stock" exercise a moment ago, did you come up with something about culture that you didn't know before? Were you at all surprised about where the word comes from and why we use it in so many ways? I certainly hope so. Recall the ideas about culture you wrote about at the beginning of this chapter. Have they shifted at all?

The point I want to emphasize going forward is how much we humans have to learn and therefore why we take shortcuts. We are born with the capacity to learn culture, to learn languages and ways of believing and behaving, but we are not born already knowing all this. During early infancy what we have come to call culture is etched into us as we participate in learning what we are expected to do, say, and believe. Another way of thinking about this is that babies are born into complex social worlds that they know nothing about. They have to become integrated into their societies; no one is born knowing what he or she should say, do, or think in order to be able to communicate with others and feel that he or she belongs to that society. It might even be helpful to use the analogy of immigrants arriving to a new country where they don't know the language, customs, beliefs, and so on. Immigrants, however, typically arrive after they have become integrated into their own societies, whereas babies arrive never having been integrated into any society. And they have to learn a lot of basic skills that newborns from other species already "know"—such as how to move their arms and legs in order to walk, feed, or grab things. Human infants are incredible because they arrive into the world so helpless and so dependent upon others to nurture them in almost every way. It's no wonder that we have such long childhoods as there is a lot to learn. What I find fascinating is not so much that we learn so many different abilities and we learn them very quickly but, rather, the fact that as adults we recall little to nothing about the processes of learning from our earliest years.

I now end this chapter with a very straightforward goal for you, one that I hope you share as you continue to read this book. I would like you to *stop thinking about culture as something you have and move toward thinking about culture as how we humans relate to one another so that we can understand, interpret, and, to a large extent, predict each other's behavior.* That is, we *do* culture, we don't *have* culture. Without this ability to understand others, and given that we enjoy relatively few genetically programmed behaviors that condition most species' lives, we would live in a world of chaos where everyone would behave independently and thus unpredictably. We would have to use so much of our mental abilities just to try to figure out what everyone else was doing that we would be overwhelmed, worried, and anxious all the time. Instead, we are a cultural species. As babies and toddlers we rapidly learn that human life, though complex and certainly variable from person to person, is highly patterned. Children pick up these patterns so fast that often they only have to experience something once to understand it, subconsciously, as "the way things are." They have to learn so many things quickly to be able to behave and think according to the people around them. Otherwise, they would be frightened most of the time—just as young children frequently feel anxious when they meet strangers or encounter new foods—and live poised on psychiatric meltdown day in and day out due to the uncertainty. Of course, the fact that youngsters learn and apply their knowledge so fast means that by the time they enter kindergarten, they have mastered much if not most cultural knowledge *and as a consequence* severely reduced their cultural flexibility. During these middle years of childhood, kids are typically rule enforcers. They spend a lot of time not crossing culturally created lines. Boys don't want to do girl things and vice versa. And, perhaps surprising to many readers, children by this age have learned quite a bit about the social hierarchies operative in their societies. They not only understand them, but they apply them to each other in ways that can appear cruel to adults—such as a 5-year-old refusing to play with a 4-year-old because she is younger, or black children being called "dirty" by nonblack children.

We all play a part in how our and others' children learn culture, but to date we largely have been unaware of how our actions have been shaped, even hampered, by our notions of culture and our limited attention to how we acquire and do culture. We should make it our goal to change our cultural awareness and skills so that we can be more creative and empowered as cultural beings and teachers.

We Weren't Born to Be Random: Culture as Comfort

> *Humans, having freed themselves from the limitations formerly imposed by biology, have burdened themselves with many more.*
>
> —*Edward T. Hall (1990: 43)*

Now that you are more familiar with where the concept of culture comes from—its different meanings and so on—it is time to jump right into the main purpose of this book: explaining how and why we learn culture and what knowing more about that means for our lives. To figure out how we learn culture, we have to think about what we are born with. Think about any newborns you have met in your life. What can they do without anyone's help? Are they born complete blank slates, or do they arrive equipped with some innate abilities? Take a moment now to contemplate your responses to these important questions before going on to read the rest of this chapter.

As you may know, human infants are born with fewer survival skills than those of many other species. They cannot move around, feed, or clean themselves, and certainly cannot escape danger. Human babies are born completely dependent upon others for survival and lack even basic abilities such as being able to see distances, regulate their body temperature, or move their arms and legs intentionally. Compared to newborns from other species who typically acquire these abilities in hours, days, or weeks after birth, human babies take months. As I explain later, human infants are actually born very immature in order for their heads to fit through the birth canal (Dunbar 2010). We do, however, arrive with a very powerful tool for survival: our capacity—indeed our drive—to learn culture—and this capacity is rooted in our biology. However, "culture is neither nature nor nurture, but some of both. It combines inheritance and learning in a way that cannot be parsed into genes or environment" (Richerson & Boyd 2005: 11). We have evolved powerful brains that enable us to speak language, interpret each others' symbols, interact in patterned ways that distinguish our group from another's, and all the other abilities involved with what we lump together as "culture." Much, but certainly not all, of this development takes place in early childhood, from birth to about kindergarten. In short, we are not born with culture, but must acquire it quickly very early on in life. We learn so much cultural knowledge during these years, yet, as adults, we can remember little to nothing about these lessons. No wonder culture has a mysterious quality; no wonder it seems as if we inherit culture from our genes.

Children are born with little cultural knowledge but with an infinite ability to learn. I say "little" because it turns out that in the womb toward the end of their gestation, babies are already beginning to acquire cultural preferences. For instance, they hear people speaking and begin to process the sounds that will become their native language (Bader-Rusch 2003: 101). They can recognize the voice of their mother and others whom they have heard speaking regularly (Small 1998). Recently, I went to the hospital to meet one of my student's babies who was born eight weeks premature. The tiny boy, named Felipe, was on a respirator to help him breathe and it was irritating him. But whenever he heard his father or mother's voice he showed great excitement by kicking his spindly legs and thrashing his tiny arms, even though there was plenty of other noise and commotion in the intensive care area. So, little Felipe clearly had begun to learn things about his family while in the womb; but compared to the huge amount of cultural knowledge he would learn after birth, what he acquired in utero is miniscule. Felipe's responses are a good reminder as well that people learn to relate to each other in ways specific to our group, not in ways specific to our species. Babies come into the world having to learn not only basic functions and survival tools, but also the ways of the people they grow up around. As children learn these ways, as they become socially integrated, they grow comfortable in the cultural environments they are exposed to and frequently fearful of unfamiliar environments. Think back for a moment about experiences you have had with small children. Have you ever seen them shrink from unknown people—what some psychologists refer to as "stranger anxiety" (Hahn-Holbrook, Holbrook, & Bering 2010). Most likely you have had this type of experience with a toddler. She will hug her parent's leg when she meets you because she doesn't know you. She, to jump ahead a moment, can't interpret you yet and, thus, *predict* what you'll do. She doesn't

Mom, Who Is That?

know you as well as she knows her caregivers. Therefore, she cannot immediately read your body language and categorize you as friend or foe. So she clings to familiar people and shows anxiety with those who are unfamiliar. That's the very crux of human life—and of my approach to culture.

SEEING CULTURE THROUGH A DIFFERENT LENS

If we are not born with a cultural imprint, what *are* we born with that helps us to know how to behave in different circumstances? This is an important question, one for which there are no sure answers, but there are vigorous debates. What we know is that we are born with just a few genetically programmed behaviors that do not appear to be influenced much by experience; these are typically called reflexes and instincts. We have some unconditional reflexes such as blinking when something comes toward our eye or recoiling when we touch something hot. And we have a few "chain reflexes" such as sucking and breathing, which we usually do without consciously controlling them. The term "instincts" is often used to signify more complex behaviors than reflexes; the word is a shortcut to avoid big controversies over what people (or other species) can and cannot change about ourselves, what we are programmed to do versus what results from the interaction between genetic predispositions and developmental experiences. Bird migration patterns and nest-building behaviors are good examples of bird "instincts." Birds of the same species do not migrate to the exact location nor do they build exact replicas of each other's nests, but the patterns are very similar. In everyday speech, it is common to hear people making references to people's "instincts" and to doing things "instinctively," but this is often misleading. For example, imagine a journalist interviewing a runner about her performance in a particular race and the runner responds, "I don't think about it. It's just instinctive." What the runner means is that she does not have to *consciously* think about what she does. She has become an expert in the particular context of running, so most of what she does is subconscious. That is different from an instinct because instincts are behavior patterns common to all members of a species. Arguably a good example of an instinct among humans is precisely our drive to find patterns, to find social order in the world around us. The beauty of this instinct, however, is that it does *not* produce identical behavior but, in contrast, allows us to adapt to widely ranging environmental and social conditions.

Instincts and reflexes are a smaller percentage of our genetic predispositions than for most species that depend on them overwhelmingly for survival; the vast majority of species on Earth have little to no childhood learning period but must be able to survive with minimal assistance from the moment they are born (van der Elst 2003). Human children, in contrast, spend many years learning how to live as those around them. Why?

Humans have evolved to depend less on the genetically programmed, highly inflexible behaviors called instincts and depend more on the plastic, flexible, learned behaviors we have come to call culture. That does *not* mean genes play no role in our lives; genes are critical in all species' existence. We just have evolved genetically to depend much more than other species upon *learning* and this makes us more flexible. Species whose young learn how to behave after birth are better able to survive changing environments; species ruled by programmed, innate behaviors are at a greater risk of extinction when their life circumstances change. At some point in our evolutionary past, it must have been better for our survival to trade the predictability and constancy of instincts and reflexes for culture. Biological anthropologists and other scientists debate this point, but the current wisdom is that around 300,000 years ago, dramatic and frequent fluctuations in the climate of certain areas of Africa were probably the instigator (Boyd & Richardson 2005). Most of our human ancestors lived there, and they either adapted to these rapid changes through natural selection or died out. At some point around this time, a group or perhaps groups of our ancestors evolved in a slightly different direction due to the pressures on their survival from all these changes in climate. They became smarter and more adaptable than humans before them; they were better at culture than the others. These ancestors—our own species of *Homo sapiens*—then began leaving Africa, adapting to climates all around the world and out-competing other humans they encountered along the way. There are important lessons from this research on our evolution for our understanding of culture.

So what is culture? A solid, commonsense definition for culture is "socially learned and transmitted information" (Brown 2008: 5). While this definition is broad enough to include certain activities that have been observed among non-human species (such as chimpanzees, elephants, porpoises and even whales), in this book I consider only culture among people. From the definition, then, culture is about interpersonal relations. It's about learning how to conduct ourselves in ways that others can interpret and understand. However, I emphasize that we don't really think consciously about doing culture; rather, we *feel* culture. When we are socially integrated to the point where we both understand others and they understand us (not just in terms of spoken language but also our gestures, expressions, etc.), we "know" this by feeling comfortable. Thus, while culture is about knowing particular ways of thinking and doing; we don't think about what we do culturally on a day-in-and-day-out basis. We just do what is normal for us and when we do, we *feel* comfortable. A strange thing about culture, however, is that we rarely are aware of feeling comfortable when we're in our cultural comfort zones; rather, we are much more likely to feel our cultural *discomforts*. What's a cultural discomfort? You might know what I mean through the expression "feeling like a fish out of water." When was a time in your life that you felt that you did not understand others around you? Typically this happens when we go into an unfamiliar social context. In a moment you will do a Planned Pause about such an experience and what it was like for you. What did you feel? Explain what happened, how you felt strange, and then reflect for a moment on *what* probably caused you to feel cultural discomfort.

When we're outside our cultural comfort zones, we typically feel uneasy, awkward, stressed, anxious, and sometimes afraid. When that happens, I suggest checking in with your "cultural discomforts." Feel anxious in a particular setting? You are probably moving into a cultural space you're either not familiar with or one where you aren't culturally fluent. You don't know exactly how to behave, so you probably watch others around you quite closely. Maybe you become a "fly on the wall," observing others but only as you wait for a good opportunity to fly away. When we feel cultural discomforts we often feel foolish or even stupid. We don't know how to act like the people around us. Why are we/they different? Next time you experience a cultural discomfort, focus first on how you feel and *what* it is specifically that you don't know that makes you feel uneasy. Are people speaking a language you do not understand, and thus you fear they might be making comments or even jokes about you? Or are they speaking the same language as you but using some jargon you do not know? Maybe you understand what they say but do not recognize things they are doing, such as their gestures, the way they are dressed, or their jokes? When you've learned some of the differences between what you do and what they do, focus in on someone you can observe who seems completely at ease in that environment. This person is probably culturally fluent in that context (while you are not). Study that person and observe how he or she acts with ease. You'll learn the most about this "culture" by observing people who navigate it easily *and* by figuring out why you don't.

PLANNED PAUSE 2-1

CHECKING IN WITH MY CULTURAL DISCOMFORTS

Instructions: *Identify an experience in your life during which you felt awkward because you did not know the culture of the people around you. You felt like a fish out of water. Write a paragraph describing the experience and then a second paragraph analyzing it. For the analysis explain* **why** *you felt strange. Also explain what happened. Did you stay and adapt or leave? Did the other people try to help you integrate (feel comfortable) in that environment? Why or why not?*

Explore the **Concept** on
mysearchlab.com

Now, on the other hand, whenever you feel confident and at ease, *you* are probably in the center of one of the cultural spaces of your life where you have a lot of experience. You're in a cultural comfort zone. You just don't think about it that much because you are comfortable. You only take notice when you feel uncomfortable, and everyone else does too. That's the way culture is; we do not pay attention to that which for us is normal; we pay most attention to that which is different. This is why we all become ethnocentrists. Yes, we *all* learn to see the world through the particular lenses of our society. We don't typically see our behaviors and habits as just as strange as those of others; rather, we see what we do as normal and what others do as different or, perhaps, strange or even wrong. We just do not tend to think about this consciously. That is why being around small children is so refreshing; they have yet to learn the higher-order social filtering that older children and adults apply. They just call it like they see it. A case in point is my 5-year-old niece, Katie. We were playing with her bilingual (Spanish-English) doll, Dora, recently. When its talk button is pushed, the doll alternates between languages. Katie only knows English. When the doll spoke in Spanish once, I repeated the words in Spanish and then said to Katie, "Dora speaks Spanish." Katie didn't miss a beat and responded, "Yeah, but she speaks regular [i.e., normal] like us too." Katie has a profoundly strong sense of her cultural patterns—and they are not just any patterns, they are what's normal and comfortable *in her life*. Her mind is perfectly capable of continuing to learn new languages and a whole host of cultural knowledge, but she's already happily ensconced in her cultural comfort zones. In short, become more aware of what you take for normal because it is much more likely to be particular to you and others like you than to be normal for our entire species.

So now reflect back on the experience you wrote about a few moments ago. You wrote about feeling like a fish out of water, like you were outside your cultural comfort zone. Would you like to return to that same feeling? My experience with most people, myself included, is that we avoid feeling culturally uncomfortable. We *say* we like new experiences and meeting new people, but we rarely go outside our cultural comfort zones without being pushed to do so. Why? Because when we're outside our sphere of competence we feel awkward, clumsy, even dumb. People, especially adults, don't like to feel these feelings. We are supposed to be experts, not newbies. So what do we do? We avoid cultural discomforts. There are, of course, some individuals, and even some classes of people (such as cultural anthropologists like myself who spend large quantities of time studying people whose comfort zones are way different from ours), who don't mind cultural discomforts and perhaps even enjoy them. That is fine once you have already mastered a set of culturally appropriate knowledge and behaviors that allow you to survive and feel confident in your context. However, that's not the situation of newborn babies.

Imagine cultural discomfort in the extreme. An easy way to comprehend this feeling is to picture yourself suddenly being dropped off on a completely different planet, with creatures that communicate with each other and seem to understand and obey each other, but in ways that are incomprehensible to you. How would you feel? Probably scared out of your wits! Your mind would be racing: What will these creatures do to me? Will I survive? You are at their complete mercy and have no way of negotiating with them. You cannot read their gestures or their facial expressions to tell if they are serious, joking, or something else altogether. Of course as an adult being dropped off into a new context, you would be *aware* of the differences because you have known a world where you fit in. You could, for example, try to figure out these creatures' way of life. You could see if some of them are in charge, interpret how they treat others, and then guess what they might do with you. You could look and see if they have any behaviors, such as a smile (assuming they have faces), that appear to have equivalents in human society and then guess how to behave in ways that will—hopefully—spare your life.

SEEING CULTURE THROUGH AN INFANT'S EYES

Now transport your thoughts to newborn babies. When a baby is born he arrives into an unknown world and is at the complete mercy…of strangers! He has no knowledge of another culture for comparison and few genetically programmed skills to help him survive. Survival is about learning to behave according to the ways of his caregivers. He has absolutely no other choice. Luckily, babies are born to interact (Bloom 2010; Fogel 1993; Giddens 1979; Gopnik 2009; LeVine & Norman 2001; Raeff & Benson 2003; Todorove et al. 2011; Tomasello 1999); some even go so far as to characterize people as "interaction engines" (Levinson 2006). That makes sense since we are, after all, a social species. Humans take social interaction to a new

Human Interaction Engines: Toddlers.

level, however. We must be hypersocial in order to learn the vast amount of knowledge necessary to operate in the many different, and changing, cultural environments that humans occupy.

If you think about it, you'll likely agree that babies have an enormously complex task that they accomplish in only months—figuring out the social system around them. They have to interpret facial expressions, body language (such as how far apart people should be physically when speaking and how to sit "properly"), and spoken language; they need to learn all the routines of daily life and, arguably most important, whom to trust and whom not to trust. Moreover, each new place and interaction (a store, the doctor's office, a visit to relatives, etc.) adds more complexity to what babies must learn. What are the cultural rules governing this space? Are they the same as those at home or are they different? Do the people behave similarly to or differently from people I already know? Do they seem nice or should I fear them?

At the same time they are collecting cultural experiences, babies must also develop their ability to control their muscles, to direct their hand–eye coordination, and a host of other physiological tasks. No wonder brain activity consumes 60 percent of babies' energy and they sleep through most of their early weeks and months. They need time to process and store all their learning in their brains (Meltzoff et al. 2009). Studies show that by age 2, children are only on about the same level as 2-year-old chimpanzees and other apes in their understanding of their spatial and physical worlds, but they are much further ahead in social skills such as learning, communicating, and reading others' intentions (Dunbar 2008; James 2008; Tomasello 2008). Some even argue that the social skills needed to live in groups (e.g., knowing about each other, realizing that others think differently, and even being able to tell stories that communicate broader social lessons) provided evolutionary forces that expanded the brain—particularly the frontal lobes of the neocortex, the outermost layer of the brain. As we acquire these social skills, we learn to relate, as we commonly hear people say, "instinctively," with others; that is, behaving without thinking consciously about how to behave—as in the case of the runner discussed earlier. But this is not the realm of true instincts; our language just confuses us. Rather, when we do not have to think consciously about how to act, we are in our cultural comfort zones. Young children are least shy around those with whom they feel comfortable. They are most shy when they interact with new people, whose behavior they are not yet able to understand and therefore predict.

As we interact, we practice our social skills and become more expert and more comfortable. The great irony of a cultural species, however, is that as we become more comfortable in particular cultural contexts and traits, we lose some of our infinite birthright flexibility. This is the most fundamental and profound of human dilemmas:

Humans' Fundamental Cultural Dilemma: Growing up human requires us to arrive into the world completely ready to learn any cultural practices, yet, over the course of our lives, we learn to navigate specific cultural spaces. As we learn to navigate these spaces, we grow comfortable in them and with the people who share them with us. Simultaneously and unintentionally, we build and retain borders around our cultural comfort zones that we rarely cross. Other people do the same so that we end up with differences that are real, that we not only act upon but feel, but that we have also created. That is, these differences are not set in stone—but they feel to us as if they were. In short, we are born without cultural blinders but we quickly and inevitably acquire them. We must travel from infinite cultural possibilities into narrower cultural realities. We unintentionally trade flexibility for predictability and uncertainty for comfort.

Culture, then, is about comfort.

When using this phrase, I specifically do *not* want to leave you with the impression that becoming culturally comfortable is the same as being *right* or *moral*. I am not talking about right and wrong; rather, I'm referring to how we become comfortable with particular practices and beliefs because we are exposed to them early in life. People can and do become comfortable behaving and thinking in ways that others may find objectionable; simple examples include preferential treatment of boys over girls or physical punishment of children who misbehave. These occur in many societies and are viewed as "normal" (i.e., culturally comfortable) and also as morally appropriate whereas other societies can and do find them objectionable on cultural and/or moral grounds. This book is not about morality; I mention morality here only because as I explain how we become culturally comfortable I know some readers might think this justifies any culturally comforting practices. I *am* a cultural relativist in that I argue that people's practices should be viewed and understood within their cultural context before they are judged; but I am not an extreme relativist who finds no practices objectionable.

As creatures of comfort, children as well as adults shy away from uncomfortable situations. Young children are more flexible because their cultural comforts are still not firmly established and, quite literally, etched into their brains. Adults are still flexible but, as the saying goes, it is harder to get old dogs to learn new tricks. There are physiological as well as psychological and emotional reasons for this, as you'll see shortly. In the next section, you will see how this inevitable yet unintentional trade-off—cultural flexibility for cultural order—takes place.

FROM NEWBORN NOVICE TO TRAINED TODDLER: ACQUIRING CULTURAL COMFORT

Over a century ago, psychologist William James wrote that babies leave the womb only to be thrust violently into "one great blooming, buzzing confusion." As you will see, he was both right and wrong. What he meant was that newborns abandon the dark, tight, sensory-limiting space of the womb for the bright, open, and sensory-stimulating space of society. We swaddle them to recreate the physical comforts of the womb and we surround them with dependable caregivers whose repeated actions begin the process of culturally ordering this vast social space. Children arrive into this social space prepared in several fundamental ways to become culturally competent. As discussed earlier, children are born with some predispositions or "readinesses" to interact with others, to look for and infer

Babies Learn By Observing Others.

patterns from what they observe so they become selective in what they pay attention to, and to store these patterns in their brains (Bjorklund 2000; Enfield & Levinson 2006; Haith & Benson 1998; LeVine & Norman 2001; Martin, Ruble, & Szkrybalo 2002; Rogoff 2003; Saffran et al. 1996). From my perspective, the key piece of information here is that social life is patterned, not random, so babies are born to detect and reproduce these patterns. *Humans' behavior is patterned and is thus highly intelligible and predictable, but we have to learn these patterns.* (Hence, the world is not exactly the "blooming, buzzing confusion" that William James portrayed.)

How do infants become experts so quickly? How do they go from newborn neophytes to elementary school experts? This is a very complex process or set of processes that researchers are only beginning to understand. The publications on this fascinating topic are growing astronomically within academic circles. The information being produced is too vast, and is often presented in too-technical language, to cover here. Therefore, I do not go into great detail about the literature in this area, for it would take volumes. Rather, what I will do is reference the findings that are widely accepted and, to my mind, most important without using technical terms or academic language. After boiling down a lot of material I have come up with five critical puzzle pieces to understanding how and why we learn culture. Before I list them and then discuss them in some depth, I openly add in a caveat to say I do not research babies myself and thus am synthesizing others' research. Moreover, I interpret their work through an anthropological lens most scholars studying how we learn culture (i.e., enculturation) do not use. Therefore, the way I understand the research and fit together the pieces of this interesting puzzle reflects my own theorizing. Scholars formulate theories as we try to understand phenomena. Given the new and dynamic nature of research and information in the areas I synthesize, what I argue may be even more speculative than usual, although it is informed speculation. Speculation, as neuroscientist Ramachandran (2011: xvii) argues, "is nothing to be ashamed of: every virgin area of scientific inquiry must first be explored in this way. . . . We need to roll out our best hypotheses, hunches, and hare-brained, half-baked intentions, and then rack our brains for ways to test them." With a few notable exceptions such as (Domínguez et al. 2009; Domínguez et al. 2010; Lancy 2010; Lende & Downey 2011; LeVine & New 2008), anthropology has not been at the forefront of understanding enculturation since the 1970s. I believe anthropology's broad understanding of the human condition can add more to this inquiry.

In this book my goal is to relate how people learn in general to the specifics of learning culture. Researchers address aspects of learning culture such as learning gender, race, and nationality, but what I am aiming for is a more basic, more general model of how we learn what we call culture. Here is my argument in five pieces that I fit into the overall puzzle I've been studying about how people learn culture. At this point in the book I make my case outright but as I go forward I explain each in greater depth. Some of my assertions parallel those of other scholars and some, especially in the area of theory of mind, vary from others' ideas. In sum, the following is how I've synthesized and interpreted a wide variety of scholarship and translated it into language that I hope is accessible to you:

1. Babies are biologically predisposed to interact with others and also to look for those interactions to be patterned (Gopnik 2009; Martin et al. 2002; Rogoff 2003; Todorov et al. 2011). That is, people evolved as a social species in which interaction varies greatly from group to group, so we are born to interact but have to learn how to interact in the ways particular to those around us.

2. Babies' social interactions with caregivers are replicated into everyday routines that organize their social world into patterns (so, indeed, babies find what they are looking for) and these are stored in the brain as nerve connections (e.g., Bruner et al. 1966; Eliot 1999; Gopnik 2009; Kitayama & Uskul 2011).

3. Patterned interactions with others, coupled with what have come to be called "mirror neurons" in our brains, generate babies' ability to understand that others have different perspectives. Without this ability, we could not interpret others' behaviors and empathize with them (what psychologists and neuroscientists frequently term "theory of mind") (Brooks 2011; Domínguez et al. 2009; Ramachandran 2011; Rizzolatti et al. 1996; Tomasello 1999). To me, however, being able to interpret and empathize with others serves a more critical function—that of being able to predict others and thus trust them. When we trust people, we can, albeit unconsciously, predict how they will behave and when we share culture we also are able to subconsciously predict their behavior.

4. When we can predict others, this reduces the brain's cognitive load as a baby or an adult does not have to calculate every observation anew (e.g., "Is this new person going to be nice to me or a danger to me?"), which would take up a lot of the brain's energy and effort (Donald 1991; Fiske & Taylor 2008).

5. Trust is felt emotionally as comfort. This last piece is the thesis of this book and reflects my particular perspective and contribution to the overall project of understanding what culture is and how we learn it. Researchers are discovering that we really do *feel* comfort because under certain conditions our brains release chemicals called neurotransmitters (e.g., oxytocin and vasopressin) that create in us the sensation of comfort. Trust is not just any emotional comfort, however. It is emotional comfort that reflects cultural patterns.

CONSTRUCTING THE PUZZLE OF HOW BABIES LEARN CULTURE

Let's look at these different puzzle pieces and how they fit together in greater depth.

The first essential piece to fit into the puzzle is the understanding that humans are predisposed to interact (Boyd & Richerson 2006; Gopnik 2009; Hrdy 2009). This is our biological inheritance and the foundation upon which we build cultural interactions. Overwhelmingly, babies are born to interact socially, although we do not all interact to the same degree. For example, it is commonly recognized now that the social abilities of people with autism are compromised in complex and varying ways (Ramachandran 2011; Trevarthen et al. 1998). Moreover, with some people we interact intensely and with others we interact more sporadically. Intensive interaction between babies and their primary caregivers is commonly referred to as "attachment" (Bowlby 1988; Harwood, Miller, & Irizarry 1995; Konner 2004; LeVine & New 2008). The idea is that babies become so close emotionally to some people with whom they interact that this is similar to being physically attached. Monkeys and apes are born able to attach to their mothers physically by clinging to their bodies (Small 1998). They spend their infancy physically as well as emotionally attached. Human babies cannot cling physically to their mothers as strongly, but they still attach psychologically and emotionally. Physical touch as well as social interaction are key to human attachment. Since the 1960s when John Bowlby first introduced the concept of attachment, psychologists have come to argue that human babies must bond with at least one other person in order to develop normally. Among anthropologists who study baby–caregiver relations cross-culturally, the universality of attachment is debated, particularly the assumption that babies attach overwhelmingly to their mothers (Lancy 2010; LeVine & Norman 2008; Stryker 2010). In many if not most societies, babies are cared for by many people in the course of a day (Weisner and Gallimore 1977). Thus, attachments are likely to be multiple. To my mind, the important issue is not how many people a baby interacts with or whether this constitutes attachment. Rather, the key is that babies learn through intense interactivity with others how to interpret and predict those people's behavior, and this ability to predict them—instead of having to interpret each person anew every time the baby comes into contact with that person—produces psychological and emotional comfort—trust. Newborns are completely dependent upon others for their survival, but it is by internalizing daily routines with others that they come to feel comfort rather than fear. What kinds of routines help produce cultural comforts?

The second piece to the puzzle of learning culture is how repeated activities in everyday life—routines or, in anthropological terms, rituals—between babies and caregivers create *culturally specific* social contexts of predictability. The first routines are very small-scale social interactions between baby and interactors—the rituals of feeding, bathing, dressing and changing, being picked up and carried, being burped and rocked to sleep, and so on. Although these activities are common to most societies, *how* they take place (and with what materials) varies greatly, thereby producing culturally specific rituals. For example, in her ethnography on raising babies among the Beng people of the Ivory Coast in West Africa, anthropologist Alma Gottlieb (2004: 107–112) details the elaborate bathing and dressing rituals mothers go through with their infants every day. Each morning before dawn and before they breastfeed their babies, mothers heat water and prepare an enema to train the babies to defecate at this time. Then the infants are bathed, followed by each mother carefully cleaning and polishing her baby's jewelry items (bracelets, necklaces, anklets, etc.). Next, she applies lotion to sooth the baby's skin and then uses mixtures of medicinal leaves to paint protective designs on the baby's head and body. I did not go to such lengths when my daughter, Sophie, was an infant but I did bathe, dress, and feed her in similar ways most of the time.

These routines, these sequences that are repeated similarly time and again, create in the infant what some researchers refer to as "participatory cognition" (Fogel 1993: 122–129). This means that we learn and remember through participating directly in activities with others. Even very young infants perceive these sequences as patterned. The patterned interactions of life's small routines add up to knowledge, predictability, and comfort—culture. For example, a baby kicks his feet and, just by luck, they hit a dangling mobile hanging overhead. The next time he sees the mobile he "knows" to kick it again. Babies learn most, however, when they interact with other people. Imagine a very young infant lying on her back and her mother grasping her hands to pull her up into a sitting or standing position. The first time this happens, the baby's head flops backward because she doesn't expect this to happen to her; she struggles to pull her heavy head up so that it catches up to her body. The next time, however, the baby recognizes the interaction, reacts to the soft tug on her arms, and pulls on her mother's hands in order to assist movement and lift her head up. This is sometimes referred to as "co-regulation," a term that researcher Alan Fogel (1993) uses to convey how we interact through mutually adjusting to each other. If the baby struggles to pull up, her mother either waits for her to finish her co-regulation or gives her some support behind her head or back. This microsocial interaction is about learning to mutually adjust to each other; these adjustments take some effort each time the activity is repeated until the baby knows exactly what to do. Ah, mini cultural competence! Moreover, these behaviors become so routine that neither the baby nor the mother has to think about them. Instead, they are carved into the circuitry of their brains. Multiply this process by thousands of different repeated activities and you get a sense of how we learn culture.

Hopefully you will be aware of an unusual yet commonsensical approach to learning communicated in the past few paragraphs. I am by far not the first person to point out that we humans learn primarily through interactions with others, rather than just listening to others and copying what they say or do. We learn primarily through participation—a realization made quite some time ago by the famous Russian psychologist Lev S. Vygotsky, not through having someone lecture to us. Particularly for those readers who either sit in lecture halls a lot or teach students, this finding will make total common sense and not be earth-shattering. What I believe *is* radical, however, is our newfound ability to understand how our interactions build our brain circuitry and how this constructs what we commonly call culture. This is the arena of neuroscience, particularly social neuroscience (Todorov et al. 2011). So, learning is not just social; it is also environmental, physiological, psychological, and emotional. As we interact with our physical and social environments, these repeated activities become wired into our brains over time (Kitayama & Uskul 2011). (Some psychologists refer to certain learned information as "procedural memory" in that we package together a set of information about how to do something and then just access that procedure when we need to.) Once the circuits are built strongly, we typically go on automatic, losing direct awareness of these activities. We aren't born with much brain wiring, but we need to build nerve connections to survive in our social surroundings. As we learn routines we feel them as comfort and trust; we can predict what people will do based on past experiences. While this is especially the case with those we know, we also subconsciously expect that other people will behave similarly. This is what figuring out the cultural patterns of our social world is all about—making subconscious inferences from our direct experiences to everyone and everything else. This mechanism begins to explain how cultural competence quickly becomes cultural ruts that are hard to break out of—a point I will return to soon.

It is through mutually choreographing the small routines of early life, these most intimate of cultural spaces occupied by baby and closest caregivers, that familiarity grows. These are the routines that young children love. Have you ever noticed how toddlers enjoy doing the same activity over and over and over again without getting bored? Have you ever wondered why they never seem to tire of watching the same movie or reading the same book or hearing you repeat the same story? You get bored to tears but the kids love that story! And they never tire of singing the same songs or playing the same games. Whenever I'm around preschoolers I teach them a game involving a little song I sing while tickling their back. Kids love this game and invariably ask me to repeat it over and over again. Recently, I played with a 3-year-old and she loved it so much that she occupied me for nearly an hour; each time I finished she'd wink and say, "Again!" When videos and DVDs came along, children started to watch movies and TV shows over and over at home. I recall Sophie was 2 years old when the movie *The Lion King* came out. There was great public concern that the death of the baby lion's father would be scary for young children, so many parents, including myself, watched the video with our children the first time and maybe several times after that. But as the kids watched for the fifth and then the tenth and then the one hundredth time, we no longer worried because the scene was no longer new. The death now was not shocking but predictable, normalized through repetition. Why would this be important? For a small child whose daily life will involve novel and thus potentially scary events, something that is repeated over and over provides just the right opportunity to figure it out. Most importantly, it becomes predictable. In the case of *The Lion King,* the kids learned what would happen and it was no longer scary to them. The novelty had become routine.

The third piece of the puzzle about learning culture, then, is that familiar routines teach children how to interpret others and, in so doing, help the children to predict subconsciously what others will do. A classic type of routine is imitation or mimicry. Young children, as you may well know from personal experience, are experts at copying what they see others do. Some time ago, psychologist Andrew Meltzoff found that even minutes after birth babies can imitate what they see, such as someone sticking out his tongue. This type of data is strongly suggestive that the ability to mimic is innate. But that is not the whole story by any means. Starting as early as nine months, children are able to actually understand that other people think differently than they do. As mentioned earlier, this ability is often referred to by scholars studying this really dynamic field as theory of mind because children learn other people's models of the way the world is, other people's ways of thinking and doing, and then model themselves after these others' behaviors. This, of course, is critical to cross-cultural learning but young children are primarily learning that other people *around them* do not think or act exactly the same as they do. This ability to see others as different

Babies Love to Imitate.

from us is the foundation for self-awareness (Goleman 2006; Ramachandran 2011). How do you know who you are unless you know who you are not? We are both similar and yet different. Similarity is critical to emotional connections with others. This seems to be the rationale behind the metaphor of the mirror used with mirror neurons. As we look at others particular neurons in our brains, the mirror neurons, fire as if we, ourselves, were doing what they are doing (or thinking). In the ongoing and fascinating research on mirror neurons in the past decade and a half or so, one key finding is that our brain's mirror neurons will fire when we watch someone else doing something, *as if we were doing it ourselves* (Pascual-Leone et al. 2005). We "feel" others' pain emotionally even if we do not physically. We, thus, can relate more appropriately to others. When the mirror neuron circuits in the parts of the brain where social learning is most active malfunction, however, the result is various forms of autism (Ramachandran 2011: 141).

Researchers associate mirror neurons with humans' enhanced ability to mimic and understand what others do (model their behavior and even recognize their intentions) (e.g., Domínguez et al. 2009). Other species have mirror neurons so these neurons are not unique to our species—in fact, they were first identified among macaque monkeys (since doing experiments on human brains is highly regulated), but our species has not only more such neurons but also connects them into mirror neuron circuits that involve more of our brain areas than other species. In short, we are definitely superior in these abilities and research seems to document that we have abilities other species do not. And there are infinite applications of these abilities, particularly our ability to understand others' intentions—important to everything from engaging in warfare to formulating chess strategies to recognizing when a child is going to do something dangerous.

The way I understand the importance of mirror neurons, however, is a bit different than that of neuroscientists and other researchers. For me, the key is not empathy nor ability to imitate—although these are very important—but predictability. When we understand others and model ourselves after them, we have a formula for shared cultural comforts. But what is missing is the fact that we humans live in three time dimensions: past, present and future. Although our interest in the future varies a lot among peoples, we are all aware of the future and to greater and lesser degrees obsess over it. Why? We know it exists but we cannot control it—at least not fully. What we cannot control yet which influences us can cause us a great deal of stress and this is not helpful to our brains, particularly, I argue, the brains of young children, which are absorbed in very complex learning processes. So, for me, culture provides a great deal of predictability. When people act and think in predictable ways to those around us, our brains do not have to spend a lot of energy interpreting them. Rather, we "know" what they are doing and likely to do. In this way predictability is a cornerstone of trust, and thus of culture as comfort. Given that most of what people do is patterned, the key is to identify these patterns and then to store them in our brains as cultural knowledge.

Cultural learning, then, depends on turning "new" into "known." That which is known is stored in memory circuits as predictable. For example, once you observe a tossed ball fall to the ground, the next time you expect it to behave the same way. It is thus predictable. Luckily, children are extremely adept at this type of learning and they need to be good at turning new into known. They pay attention most to what is new or novel, at least until it becomes predictable. Since we are not born with many biologically innate routines, the everyday life of newborns is full of novel experiences, but only for a short while. Research with infants documents how remarkably quickly babies identify patterns in behavior; they are what we could call "pattern hungry." For example, the video series *The Baby Human*

(2003) documents how researchers do experiments with infants as young as a few months old. The researchers measure how fast babies learn patterned events by showing them an activity several times. A typical activity would be to place infants a few months old in front of a puppet theater where they watch a puppet pick up a block and move it from one location to another. The babies focus their attention intently at first because this is a novel thing to observe. However, after the activity has been repeated a couple of times the babies lose interest; they have learned that pattern. Once they uncover a routine they become bored. They know what to expect. When the puppet appears again, they look away. But when the activity is changed such that the results are not the same, the baby shows puzzlement, interest. For example, the puppet moves the object to the opposite side of the stage from before. You can imagine the baby realizing, "Oh, this is new!" so she pays attention.

BRAIN ACTIVITY: CONVERTING THE NEW INTO THE KNOWN

Novelty is thus the counterpart to routine. Even adults are most interested in what's new; we are bombarded with information all day long but what do we pay attention to? The "news." What is newsworthy? Ironically, what typically makes the news is *atypical*. Most people don't murder but most murders make the news. People are generally law abiding, but news programs focus on crimes. So whether we are babies or seniors, we are disproportionately interested in what's new and largely ignore what is routine. This is an important trait because recognizing newness is critical to learning culture whether as a child or an adult.

Fortunately for us, our brains convert the novel into the known very quickly. If that were not true, our brains would have to go through many more calculations than they do even when we encounter someone or something known. Imagine if you had to figure out who a person was each time you met her; imagine if you had to go through all the cultural calculations to figure out if this is a person whom you could trust. That would take huge amounts of the brain's calculating effort—just like it does with very young children. As I explain in more detail later in this chapter, repeated experiences get stored in our memory so that we do not have to recalculate everything the next time we encounter something similar. That is, our brains take a shortcut to where we stored the memory about that similar experience. This saves us from dedicating so much energy and brain computing time to this task. Since the brain siphons off a disproportionate share of energy, taking shortcuts is important and would have been a key evolutionary advantage. This is the fourth puzzle piece to learning culture. Without knowing it, our brains recognize the similarity and jump to what we "know" about it. Novelty has become knowledge (and, as you might have guessed, this is why we so easily stereotype as well). We know how to act and think in the ways that others can interpret and that make us all feel comfortable. This is how we get to emotional comfort through cultural acquisition, the fifth and final piece of the puzzle I'm putting together here.

Of course, learning culture is not equally easy for all of us. Autistic children are among those who struggle most. If your child is autistic, this perspective on culture could be particularly useful. There is no one type of autism. Although children with autism enjoy varying degrees of sociability along the autism spectrum, they commonly have a hard time understanding that other people do not think exactly as they do—theory of mind—which most nonautistic children begin to develop by the end of their first year (Tomasello 1999). Children with autism, for example, almost never invent imaginary companions like nonautistic children do. These imaginary companions help kids learn to think from others' perspectives (Gopnik 2009). Their brains do not process social information in the same way people without autism do (Ratey 2002; Tomasello 1999; Trevarthen et al. 1998). They seem to have greater difficulties cutting through all the information coming at them in order to detect and store social patterns. In some cases, such as among the small percentage of people with autism who are savants, their brains focus on one area, producing incredible numeric, artistic, memory, or other abilities, but they cannot engage in social interactions that most people handle with no problem. Perhaps the most famous savant is the character played by the actor Dustin Hoffman in the film *Rain Man*, a man who cannot hold a conversation with someone but can instantly do complex mathematical feats. This makes sense in the context of what you have been learning here: learning to interpret other people takes a lot of brain power. Children without autism learn this skill for those with whom they come to share culture early in life and then apply the shortcuts or schemas to new people they meet and to those they know. Children with autism, however, appear to lack this ability and thus, for them, each new face is another interpretive task to tackle. Something too exhausting to handle repeatedly and thus often it is better to avoid eye contact. Providing simple, very recognizable patterned behaviors appears to be useful, particularly for facial expressions. I have heard from parents of children with autism that their kids enjoy Japanese anime movies and the television program *Thomas the Tank Engine* precisely because the characters' emotions are very starkly displayed and thus easier to interpret than most humans' faces. This anecdotal information is confirmed by some scholars. Rendering faces and facial expressions more intelligible through exaggeration or simplification is often done for young infants. Where I live children's toys often have simple, exaggerated facial features (e.g., Mickey Mouse and face-oriented mobiles) and adults—at least in the United States—often smile more intensively than normal when interacting with infants and speak with simpler, exaggerated tones (what is often referred to as "Motherese"). I argue that such culture work helps babies identify patterns faster and thus aids them to find comfort in reading others' expressions correctly.

As we appreciate how important detecting, interpreting, practicing, and imposing patterns are to our sense of comfort, we gain new insight into how to handle the special

Thomas the Tank Engine and Friend: Note Their Easy-to-Interpret Facial Expressions.

challenges autistic children and their families face. This is one concrete application of viewing culture as comfort. Now take a moment and reflect on what you have learned in this chapter and the book so far, and consider how it might affect the ways in which you interact with young children in the future. How might this awareness affect your parenting or your understanding of how you were parented?

LEARNING CULTURE IS NOT MEMORIZATION: CULTURE IS CREATIVE BUT ALSO ORDERLY

While it is true that most babies discern patterns in others' behavior, they do not simply memorize and repeat what they have experienced. Yes, they do imitate others but they do not only repeat what others do. They learn culture as patterns, as the rules to their social order, but they do not stop with repeating these patterns (imitation). Rather, they also learn to apply them in new ways. That's a mouthful so let me turn to concrete examples. One excellent example is how children learn language. It's easy to think that children learn language by memorizing what they hear. This makes sense as children are often taught words this way. A parent points to an object and pronounces its name, and then encourages the child to repeat what was said. Some time ago, however, linguists, most notably Noam Chomsky, observed that young children do *not* learn language merely through memorization of what they have heard. Yes, they memorize words' pronunciation and meanings but they learn grammar by detecting its rules (patterns) and applying these rules to generate sentences that they have never heard before. The evidence against memorization and for learning and applying the rules of language is easily seen in the "mistakes" young children frequently make when, in English and other languages, they use irregular verbs and plurals. A toddler is often heard making a mistake such as by saying, "Mama, I saw two sheeps!" or "Daddy, I goed to school today!" These examples illustrate how children learn the rule (to make a plural in English add an *s* to the end of a noun) and do not just memorize what they hear others say (in which case they would say "sheep" and not "sheeps"). Research indicates that babies in the womb are already learning the cadences, the regularities, if not yet the grammar of their parents' native language(s), and that when they are born, they can already discern this language from unfamiliar languages to which they are exposed (Mehler et al. 1978; Small 1998; Werker et al. 1981). For example, in an experiment by Mehler et al. (1978) newborns were allowed to suck on a pacifier wired to a tape recorder and the babies were given headphones to listen to people speaking. If a baby sucked for a particular amount of time, the voice of the baby's mother reading a story would come through the headphones; if the baby sucked a short time then another voice read the story. Babies quickly learned the patterns and sucked longer to hear their mothers' voice. Clearly, in the womb they could differentiate among voices and begin to detect patterns in spoken language. They recognized the sounds associated with their mothers' speech but also were even picking up the more subtle patterns to what will become their native language such as intonations and grammatical rules. Additional experiments by Mehler and colleagues show newborns will suck their pacifiers harder if exposed to people speaking the native language correctly versus just saying words in random order or speaking a language the infants were not exposed to in the womb. All of this is foundational to their being able to speak the language later. They pay attention to and learn the simple rules first (e.g., how to conjugate regular verbs but not necessarily the irregular ones; how plurals are formed in most cases). Then, they apply these rules when they speak.

So very early in life, we learn specific words and what they signify such as "ball" and "spoon" and "mommy." We also learn that putting words together into sentences is not random but patterned. We learn and apply grammatical rules (although we don't know grammar consciously until we are taught it in school). When we have words and grammar, we can start making sentences we have never heard. Even the earliest sentences that toddlers speak are not mere repetitions of sentences they have heard; they use their language tools to create their own sentences (Gopnik 2009). So we are both creatures of habit and habit creators.

Creativity is extremely important for adapting to changing life circumstances—we can invent new ways to do things; we can figure out ways to solve problems that arise during our lives. This is one of the reasons why young children play and experiment; they try different ways to do things in order to learn how they work (Gopnik 2009: 88). However, our ability to innovate and change is tempered by the comfort of the known. We can change, but change is increasingly difficult as we grow comfortable culturally. In fact, every day we participate in reinforcing our cultural comforts but, on average, much less frequently in changing them. Why?

I answer this question by pointing out that while we need to be able to innovate and change, to survive from birth we must integrate into the social world into which we are born. Social integration is built upon repeated routines, upon patterns in what people say, think, and do. When we learn these we integrate socially—we become like those around us—and we experience our integration as comfort. Comfort derives from "knowing" what to do, what's right and wrong in our social world, so that we actually don't have to figure it out consciously. Early on, as we've seen with children and language, we figure out first the main rules; later on we learn the more subtle rules and the exceptions to rules. And as we learn the rules we apply them. Young children actually apply rules more rigidly than they exist in "real" life. They are little rule enforcers.

Finding the patterning in human interactions (cultural routines and the familiarity, comfort, and predictability they bring with them) is so important to the human experience (and to human survival, I would add) that children have been shown to actually *impose* patterns when they are missing or ambiguous. A classic case of this is children's experiences with pidgins. "Pidgin" is the term used to describe a mixture of two languages that results when adults who speak different languages are in prolonged contact and need some limited means of communication for activities such as trading (Bickerton 1981; Ramachandran 2011; Senghas 1995). Adult speakers blend the two languages in a hodgepodge of communication styles that suffices for getting things done. But for children exposed to a pidgin, this linguistic mixing is too haphazard, too unpatterned; they need rules that are black versus white before they can learn that much of life is gray. The work of various scholars indicates that when exposed to the vagueness of pidgins, children spontaneously develop rule-based grammars and transform the pidgin into what is referred to as a "creole language," or a full-fledged language with its own grammatical rules. They create clear-cut rules where pidgin offers ambiguous rules and they impose this clarity in the form of a new language.

From disorder we create order. We subconsciously trade flexibility for predictability, for the comfort that comes with order. Still don't believe me? Let me provide you with a classic example—sex.

For reasons that are still somewhat mysterious, people do not have a sexual season like almost all other animals have. Among dogs, the sexual season is referred to as "going into heat." Humans, however, can have sexual relations any time of the day, month, or year whereas almost all other species engage in sexual activity only during specific periods when females are fertile. So, what do we do with all this flexibility? We impose lots of rules upon it. We define when it is appropriate to have sex (such as after marriage, after menstruation but not during, etc.), who can have sex (such as restricting children and teenagers from engaging in it), where it is appropriate to have sex (certainly not in the classroom with everyone present, etc.), and so on. The cultural rules governing sexual activity vary widely from society to society, but every people imposes rules onto humans' biological flexibility for having sex. *That's the critical lesson of culture. We create our own order, but there is a trade-off with flexibility.* As we order ourselves culturally and find comfort therein, we lose some but not all of our flexibility. In short, and to repeat the quote by the famous anthropologist Edward T. Hall (1990: 43) that appeared at the beginning of this chapter, "Humans, having freed themselves from the limitations formerly imposed by biology, have burdened themselves with many more."

Conclusion

Learning culture, then, is about seeking, finding, reproducing, inventing, and imposing order onto human life. We evolved biologically to enable great cultural flexibility; that is, we were born to be flexible but we weren't born to be random. People create social order and young children must learn this social order by interacting with others. This is essentially what I understand culture to be—our ability to create and impose order on the social world we live in. This does not mean we are liberated totally from our biology, our genes, but we have a great deal of input into how we interact with our biology and our environment. Humans are born with incredible abilities to adapt to any circumstances, but we are born so dependent we could not survive without others' assistance. These others behave in patterned ways that babies are born to detect, learn, and apply. We thus are obligated to interact with others and play by their rules. (Yes, this means that power is intimately related to culture.) It makes sense, then, that even beginning in the womb we are learning these rules. In early childhood we concentrate on perfecting the simple rules and it is only after we gain competencies that we begin to experiment a bit beyond the rules, particularly with people whom we trust. Know any toddlers? They are rule lovers.

As a toddler, Sophie helped me see the importance of patterned or rule-based behavior among young children deeply involved in learning culture and in becoming socially integrated. One example was when she complained extensively about one of her schoolmates in daycare.

His name was Hans and he was the child of a Chinese mother and a Dutch father. It took him a bit longer than the monolingual kids to speak, but by age 3 or so, he was able to speak three languages and speak each to the correct person. Hans loved playing dress-up and his favorite item was a tutu donated by one of the teachers who had been a dancer. Each day he would pull the tutu off of the dress-up clothing rack and put it on. He then would wear it all day. This upset Sophie and the other girls to no end because it did not fit what they felt boys should wear. At home, Sophie complained repeatedly that "Boys do not wear dresses!" She refused to approve of his behavior until the last year of daycare when her understanding of the rules of gender had become more sophisticated than simple black and white.

Another highly rule-bound context Sophie and her friends were involved with for hours each day at preschool was an elaborate game they called "family." As its name suggests, this game consisted of playing the roles of parents and children in a family. The kids refused to allow any gender switching; only boys could be daddies and sons, and girls were limited to the roles of mommies or daughters. When I asked Sophie why girls could not be fathers or brothers, she would answer matter-of-factly that this was impossible. Girls are girls and boys are boys. She also refused to wear anything but dresses during her daycare years—but this changed immediately when she entered kindergarten. For her and for many children, breaking rules and accommodating ambiguity could only be attempted *after* mastering the rules. As parents know, children save their worst behavior (which often involves breaking the rules) for their parents. This is because children place the most trust in the people they are closest to; children can risk offending those people because they know they won't be "excommunicated" from their comfort zones for their actions. A total stranger is much riskier, at least until the child can see that the stranger behaves in *normal* (interpretable, predictable) ways, much like other people he knows. But how easily can children make these determinations?

While this chapter has focused on how we learn cultural order and find comfort in that order because, subconsciously, it makes most social interactions predictable, I do not want to imply that all human activities are oriented toward reproducing the social order. Yes, when people experience disorder (as with pidgin languages or times of war), we often impose order by inventing new rule-bound behaviors. We see this with children's play as well. But we are also endowed with incredible creative abilities such as our imaginations. We can speak sentences we have never heard before, imagine worlds we have never seen, invent new ways to do things, and so on. We can also continue to learn culturally even as we view ourselves as having a particular culture. We retain cultural flexibilities, but we are also very much creatures of habit and comfort. This is, to my mind, the greatest conundrum of the human condition.

This chapter has focused on the fact that as humans, we are not born with culture but must learn a huge amount of culturally specific knowledge to survive and thrive among those in our society. We are born very plastic and so can be molded—and mold ourselves—into any cultural shape; yet, as we take shape we trade much of this plasticity, this cultural flexibility, for the

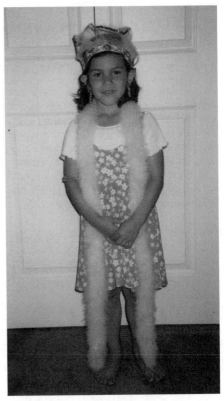

Sophie Performing Preschool Gender.

comforts of being formed. An obvious lesson in all of this is the impact of early infancy and childhood experiences on who we later become. Now it is appropriate to take some time to apply your newly acquired "culture as comfort" knowledge to real life. How can this knowledge be put into practice to help your life or another person's? Why is taking this new culture as comfort perspective useful?

PLANNED PAUSE 2-2

APPLYING CULTURE AS COMFORT TO REAL LIFE

Instructions: *Imagine that you are a cultural expert in a particular social environment tasked with helping some people who are not. Describe below in your first paragraph this social environment—a context that is familiar to you but which is unlikely to be familiar to everyone (such as your workplace, a particular hobby you participate in, a sporting event you attend, or even eating a meal with your family). Why is this context culturally comforting to you? In a second paragraph, explain how what is culturally comfortable for you is likely to be uncomfortable to others* **and** *provide two suggestions for how you could assist newcomers feel culturally comfortable in this context. Make sure you refer to the concepts and ideas developed in this book.*

Culture as Comfort Is the Way Our Brains Develop Too

Children are…"irrepressible taxonomizers."

—*Bloom (2009)*

As you understand culture better *not as a thing you have* but as ways of thinking and doing that you share with others, you hopefully will come to the conclusion that we *do* culture more than we *have* culture. We do culture to ourselves and to others, even though we are almost completely unaware of the daily culture work we do. Therefore, it's not so easy to figure out how we do culture. First, we need to know that what we're doing is cultural not natural. The best approach I have found is to look for patterns, for regularities in what we think, say, and do. Culture is not idiosyncratic to individuals; it is shared. We do culture similarly to others, but we typically don't think about what we do because it just comes to us "naturally." To begin to get more of an awareness of what you do culturally, I'll point you in a direction that should be pretty easy to grasp: doing social status. People are very attentive to how we stack up against each other, and thus it makes sense that we pay a lot of attention to how we show each other our social status. And, although people pretty much everywhere care about their social status, the hierarchies vary enormously from society to society and even within a society's groups. Toddlers negotiate social status around different criteria than those that are important to elementary school–age kids; their criteria, in turn, differ from those of teens, young adults, working adults, and retirees. So, take a moment now and think of how you show others your social status. Do you pay attention to what you wear, with whom you interact, what you own, where you go on weekends, who you friend on Facebook, and so on? Most likely you do a lot of different things to negotiate your status and what you do varies depending on whom you're with and where you are. So, for Planned Pause 3-1, think about the situations you have been in *during the last 24 hours* and respond to the following questions: What might you do in a similar circumstance now that you are more conscious about *doing* social status? What do others do to negotiate their social status that really bothers you? Why? Address these questions in the Planned Pause 3-1.

PLANNED PAUSE 3-1

"THE WAYS I DO MY SOCIAL STATUS"

Instructions: *People* **do** *different social statuses. We are not born knowing how to act male or female; act as a teenager or an adult; act out a race or ethnic or national identity; act high class, working or middle class; act appropriately for a particular job or occupation, and so on.*

Part 1: Choose **one** *of your social statuses (sometimes referred to as "identities") but* **not** *gender—which will be covered in another planned pause—and describe in detail the ways that you performed this status vis-à-vis others during a particular scenario or context* **you experienced in the past 24 hours.**

Part 2: Now write another paragraph discussing how you could perform your chosen social status more effectively in the same context you described above. That is, if you could start that experience over, what might you do differently—knowing what you now know about culture as comfort?

Explore the **Concept** on
mysearchlab.com

As you negotiate your social status, this is just one of an enormous number of ways that you *do* culture in your everyday life. There are so many ways we all do culture that it would be almost impossible for us to be consciously aware of each of them; it would take up just too much brain power. Recall from Chapter 2 that our brains use a lot of energy already so it makes sense that we would look for ways to save energy. And this is exactly what happens. As we learn culture in early life, we store in our minds not only what we do routinely so we don't have to think about it, but we also store how to interpret others' actions. This way we just respond appropriately without having to think about it. We have a very fitting phrase for this; we talk about doing what comes "naturally" even though it's cultural. No wonder it's so hard to understand culture; we usually don't think consciously about what we do unless we feel cultural discomforts when we step beyond our normal, everyday experiences. When we attend someone else's place of worship where the rituals are unfamiliar, travel far away from home, start a new job, or even have a meal at someone's home where they eat different foods than we are used to, we feel ourselves having to cross out of our cultural comfort zones. Yes, we like new experiences—we pay attention to what's new—but not so much when they make us feel awkward, anxious, uncomfortable, or even stupid. New experiences can cause uneasiness and most of us dislike feeling this way.

BUILDING OUR BRAINS' CULTURAL CIRCUITRY

We should not be blamed for avoiding cultural challenges (at least until you finish this book). It is actually very human to do so. And there *is* a physiological reason for this too. Scientists studying the brain know that it is contains billions of neurons, and each neuron can grow as many as 10,000 connections (called synapses) to other neurons. Multiply 100 billion or so neurons by 10,000 connections each and you get something like 40 quadrillion possible connections in our brains (Goleman 2006: 157; Ratey 2002: 9). We are not born with all those connections, however. We are born with almost all the neurons we will ever have, but not so with synapses. They multiply and connect based on our experiences in life. No wonder the brain grows incredibly fast early in life, more than doubling its size by age two and by almost another 50 percent by adulthood (Goleman 2006: 152). In just one area of the brain over a half *million* new synapses are produced in *one second* in babies between two and four months of age (Seung 2012: 107). This massive increase in synapse connections and lengthening of the neurons, etc. does take up space and space is not infinite even though young children's skulls do grow. Fortunately there is a way to ensure that space is used efficiently. How? Well, the brain retains synapses that are most useful and prunes away those which are not. Neurons activated together over and over will grow tighter connections and these circuits will get stronger and stronger, becoming akin to highways versus narrow roads. Particularly important are the highway-like nerve bundles that connect different regions of the brain that function together—such as the various areas associated with language (Seung 2012). In other words, "neurons that fire together wire together." However, connections that take up precious brain space without being used often enough get pruned; some estimate the loss at 20 billion (yes, *billion*) synapses pruned every day (Begley 2007: 76-7; Ratey 2001; Siegler 1996: 42). Pruning is an appropriate metaphor because the brain's wiring looks quite similar to very bushy plants. The bushy foliage blocks sunlight from piercing the underbrush and allowing for new growth below. So, the brain's infrequently used synapse connections can get in the way of those we need and those we may need to develop. The solution is to prune away the clutter. Exactly how and why this takes place is still under study. At this point, however, the research definitely helps us understand better what we know through personal experience— that habits are easy to maintain and hard to change (just blame those neuron circuits!); that adults do not seem to learn nearly as quickly as children; and that trying to do something we could do well early in life but stopped at some point (like playing a sport or an instrument) takes time and effort in order to do well again.

There are other factors in our brain's physiology that help explain why

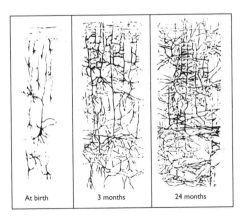

At birth   3 months   24 months

FIGURE 3.1 The Rapidly Increasing Neural Connections in an Infant's Brain.

the patterns we acquire in early childhood become so deep and enduring—such as myelination—but detailing all this can get very technical. The main point to focus on is that our brains are most malleable as infants and young children. That does *not* mean, however, that "Old dogs can't learn new tricks." People often say this phrase, but it is inaccurate. A better phrase would be, "Old dogs can learn new tricks but it's harder for an old dog than for a young dog." Don't ignore this hugely important point. We can and do continue to learn throughout life; we can and do build new synapses and even new brain circuits. We can also reconnect, rewire, re-emphasize (reweight) and even regenerate previously pruned synapses when needed such as after a brain injury (Seung 2012). Many books encourage us to keep our brains active by engaging with new people and participating in new activities as well as by eating right for the brain (e.g., Amen 1998; Begley 2007).

As you better understand the brain's physiology you should also be gaining greater insight into why we tend to gravitate toward our cultural comforts. Even if we do continue to learn new tricks as we get older, we primarily just go along in life practicing our old tricks—our cultural competencies. We do not even have to think about doing them because they are so familiar they come to us "naturally." As we learn cultural patterns, they become wired into our brains so that we can reproduce them as if flying a plane on autopilot. We are not aware of what we do as cultural unless and until we encounter people whose patterns differ. We notice the differences because our brains focus their computing power on what is new, while what is known has become automatic. So, as I stated at the beginning of this section of the book, we should not be blamed for avoiding situations involving cultural differences. Now that you know what causes "culture shock" you will hopefully become more empowered to deal with it differently. The next time you find yourself feeling discomforted, ask yourself to evaluate whether the discomfort arises from someone behaving in a way that does not fit your cultural comforts—your subconscious expectation for how life is patterned.

That so much of what we do culturally is not controlled consciously may be a hard fact to accept for some of you reading this book. We like to think of ourselves as largely in control of what we think and do but if you stop and think about it, you will be doing precisely what in day-to-day life we basically cannot do—stop the action so we can process it consciously. Just image trying to concentrate on telling your legs to walk and you will get an idea of how important it is that so much of our cultural patterns are done on autopilot. We do not really process all information anew but process it categorically. This makes our brains efficient while simultaneously making culture seem almost magical. When trying to explain this to people, I find it useful to talk about the famous computer Watson. In 2011, a contest was held on the game show *Jeopardy!* between a computer named Watson, built by IBM, and the game's best human contestants of all time. Watson defeated his adversaries handily. The computer won by searching 15 terabytes of stored information (encyclopedias, all websites on the Internet, digitized books, etc.) in a split second and comparing their information to the information in the *Jeopardy!* question. Watson didn't *know* the right answer but could calculate what was statistically (categorically) the most likely answer. During the show, these statistics were shown to viewers. The computer occasionally came up with wrong answers. A case in point was Watson's response "What is Toronto?" to a question under the category of "U.S. cities." This is a mistake few human contestants would make, but Watson's calculation was based on the clue not the category name.

Now, take this understanding of how Watson works and apply it to the human brain. Watson devoted all its computing power to *one* calculation at a time; people have to calculate many things simultaneously. Imagine you are walking down a busy sidewalk; your brain has to compute your physical movements in tandem with calculating many others' movements

The Computer "Watson" Winning *Jeopardy!* Against Its Human Competitors.

in order for you to avoid hitting them. As you do all this, you might also be talking to someone. You're talking and occasionally looking at that person to analyze her face and figure out what she's feeling. This is a very realistic scenario and not even all that complicated for us humans. But think about the computing power it would take for your brain to figure all the things it needs to keep track of in a split second *and* continue to calculate all those things as you walk along for minutes or hours. It has to be very taxing. But do you feel exhausted from walking 10 minutes in this type of situation? Probably not—especially if you are used to it. If we are used to it, it means that the circuits in our brains for what we are doing have been strengthened through past experience. Practice makes perfect, so to speak. But where do we get the practice and how does that relate to emotions?

As you now know, we practice from our earliest moments of infancy, and as we repeat experiences they become stored in our brain as neural circuits. One of the most complex knowledge areas to learn is emotions, for there are numerous muscles in the human face that can convey thousands of different emotions. Quite a few years ago, cross-cultural psychologist Paul Ekman studied different peoples around the world to see what emotions everyone recognizes regardless of their cultural contexts; he photographed them with expressions on their faces and holding signs signifying those expressions in English. He then studied the characteristics of these expressions and found out that everyone can produce and understand a very short list of just a few universal emotions (see Ekman and Friesen 2003). Although this is an active field of study and so it is difficult to make conclusions, it seems that we are born with the ability to interpret these fundamental emotions such as surprise, fear and anger. But we have to learn through experience to interpret *all the other emotions* that people in our society express. In other words, the vast majority of facial expressions that convey emotion are cultural, not universal. Interpreting these emotions as they are expressed by the face, voice and body takes a lot of experience. So how do we learn to interpret this information so well? Recent research suggests that we may learn them much like Watson was programmed, that is, categorically. Computers using artificial intelligence like Watson are fed associations and then use those to make new inferences, or predictions. For example, two teenagers working on getting computers to recognize human emotions programmed

Research Shows that All People Can Produce and Interpret Certain Universal Emotions—For Example, Anger, Disgust, Surprise, Fear, Happiness, Contempt and Sadness. How Many of these Expressions Can You Find This Preschooler Making Successfully?

a computer by playing different sounds conveying anger, happiness, etc. and then told the computer which emotion was correct for each sound. The computer stored these associations in memory, analyzing which sounds match to which emotion. (The computer was given patterns between particular sounds and the name of an emotional category such as "anger.") Then the teen scientists played new sounds and asked the computer program to tell which emotion was being expressed. The computer had to see how similar the new sound was to those the teenagers had already coded for emotions. It had to figure out which category contained sounds closest to the new sound it had received. Their program works quite well. It is more reliable at figuring out emotions, albeit a very limited number of them, than other computer programs (Lichtenstein 2011).

If that example does not make complete sense to you, an easier example is how computers recognize handwriting. While people learn the same letters of the alphabet, they write them in a wide variety of ways. So a computer has to be trained that the printed letter "A" can appear as a capital letter or not. And even within those basic categories, the way the letter is written varies tremendously. Take capitals, for instance. Just by varying the font they can appear as A *A* 𝒜 **A** or 𝒜. What does the computer look at to determine these are all the same letter? For the capital letter you can imagine the computer being programmed to find two slanted lines intersecting at the top with a horizontal line slicing between them. But what about the lower case letter? This one is more difficult because there are at least two different types of lower case typefaces including those that look/appear like this *a* (loop on the left side and straight line on the right) versus another group which look/appear like this ɑ (loop on the left side but smaller than the other version and a line on the right that curls at the top toward the lower loop). These variations are just the tip of the iceberg because people write letters with a much wider degree of variation. When the computer encounters a hand-written address on an envelope (such as the letters the Postal Service has to process), then it must be able to process all that variation in a fraction of a second as it scans the address. The computer will make some mistakes, but most of the time it will be right. It doesn't *understand* the writing, it just analyzes it statistically, categorically. That is, it must first separate written or typed words into letters and then it must match or categorize each letter based on examples stored in memory. The human brain must decipher writing as well. It may not operate exactly as a computer operates, but the brain does organize observations into categories too (Macrae & Bodenhausen 2000). In this case, our brains would not only have to figure out the letters and words we observe, but process their meaning as well. That is, we typically have a great deal of related information to calculate at any given time. And this is a major reason why conserving mental energy by storing experiences is so important. If every time we walked down a sidewalk while conversing and our brains calculated anew all the mental processes it takes to do that, we'd feel the strain of all that computing.

The fact that we can do so many things at the same time—and yet, compared to most other animals, depend less on inborn behavioral tendencies (instincts)—reflects the fact that we somehow store experiences in our brains. The more we draw on those experiences and those neural circuits, the stronger they get and the less we have to work to accomplish what we need to do. This is how we go from feeling nervous or uncomfortable when trying a new experience for the first time to feeling completely at ease after we have performed that action a number of times. The same is true with figuring out people; when we first meet someone we have to do extra work (although probably subconsciously) to calculate who this person is—including basics like gender, race, and age—but also more difficult information to find out, such as the person's motivations and trustworthiness. If the person conforms to our unstated expectations, we usually feel comfortable with the person. Feeling comfortable does not in this case mean we like the person; it means we know this person well enough that we no longer have to calculate everything about him or her. Essentially, what we do is categorize the person without really thinking consciously about it and then stick with our categorization (Macrae & Bodenhausen 2000). Recall the phrase, "First impressions are hard to change"? Now you know why.

It is time to start explaining my second answer to why the brain matters to cultural comforts. This answer involves a bit more information about our brain's structure. When we compare humans (and our closest genetic relatives, the apes) against other species, we find that the big distinction we higher primates have is in our neocortex. As illustrated in Figure 3.2, the neocortex is a thin (only a few millimeters thick) wrinkled sheet of tissue forming the surface of the cerebrum which, in turn, sits atop the cerebellum (Seung 2012). The newest addition to the brain, it is the squiggly, gray material that most diagrams of the brain show, the folded part of the brain that is divided into two hemispheres (left and right). Each hemisphere has four different areas called "lobes." The lobes include the frontal (forehead to top of head), the temporal (lower side area over the ears), the occipital (back), and the parietal (area behind the frontal lobe, over the temporal lobe, and in front of the occipital lobe).

I'll return to the neocortex in a moment, for this part of the brain is the most plastic; it is continually being shaped and reshaped during childhood and well into the third decade of life. Think about babies you have known. Their heads grow incredibly fast during the first few months of life. So there is a lot of growth going on, much of which has to do with the neocortex. Why?

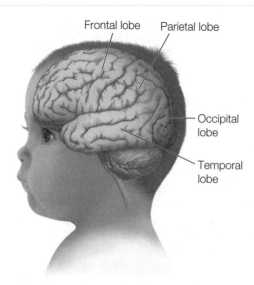

Frontal lobe   Parietal lobe

Occipital lobe

Temporal lobe

FIGURE 3.2   One Hemisphere of a Human Brain's Cortex Showing Its Four Lobes; also Shown is the Cerebellum atop the Spinal Chord.

As mentioned in Chapter 2, it turns out that human babies come into the world a bit too early gestationally. We could use some more time in the womb, especially for our organs like the brain to continue their development. If newborns' heads grew any larger, however, they would not fit through the birth canal (Dunbar 2010). As illustrated in Figure 3.3, the average baby's head is larger than its mother's birth canal, which is why giving birth is so painful for humans. That's not true for our closest genetic cousins. Chimpanzees, gorillas, and bonobos have less difficult births. Their birth canals are larger relative to their newborns' heads. Why? It has to do with the fact that they use all four limbs to move while we walk upright. To walk upright requires shifts in the bones of the hip girdle, and this compresses the birth canal. Evolutionarily, our ancestors started walking upright millions of years before our brains expanded. This fact is well documented, ever since the discoveries in East Africa of human ancestors' fossilized footsteps and of the skeleton of "Lucy," an ancient ancestor whose musculature showed that small-brained humans walked upright (Johanson & Edey 1981). Well, what was good for walking became a problem for giving birth. Human infants' brains continue to grow so

Inlet   Midplane   Outlet

Chimp

Human

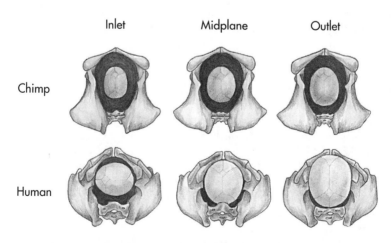

FIGURE 3.3   Chimpanzees are our Closest Primate Relatives yet their Births are Much Less Painful. Here You Can Easily See Why. The Human Baby's Head Barley Fits through the Birth Canal. If We Were Born with Heads Even a Little Bit Larger, Most Newborns and their Mothers Might Not Survive.

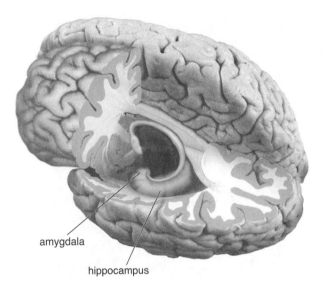

amygdala

hippocampus

The Brain's Emotional & Memory Headquarters: the Amygdala and Hippocampus.

rapidly after they're born because, in effect, they are continuing processes that should happen in the womb but cannot (Dunbar 2010).

So, babies are born with their brains still rapidly growing and developing; they can accommodate huge amounts of new information and there is a lot to learn. Even the cerebellum, a segment of the lower brain that is involved with body movement, is not completely formed. Consequently, newborn humans, unlike many other newborn mammals such as elephants, horses, and chimpanzees, have to work harder to coordinate their motor activities. In other words, and as mentioned earlier in the chapter, babies have to learn hand–eye coordination; they have to learn how to lift and balance their heads; and they have to learn to sit up and then to walk. All of these take a toll on babies' brains, requiring time and huge amounts of energy to process this information. Given that we learn motor skills at the same time we learn culture, even our body language becomes culturally inflected. We all learn to talk and walk, but we learn to do these as those around us do. They are part of our cultural competence learning. Just how babies learn these competencies is not fully known yet but research in this area is taking off.

Our brains are not only designed for cultural learning, but they also link—unavoidably— what is often referred to as "rational" learning (such as decision making, prioritizing, and analyzing) with emotions. This has everything to do with culture being *felt* as comfort and discomfort. Culture is emotional in part because some of our nerves have to pass from the neocortex through several parts of the limbic system (the hippocampus and amygdala in particular) to the rest of the body. The almond-shaped amygdala and the ribbed hippocampus are located inside the cerebrum, between the neocortex and the brain stem, the part of the brain that connects to the spinal cord and thus to the body. This means that many neural pathways, the communication highways between body and brain, literally pass through the limbic system en route to the neocortex and back (Ramachandran 2011).

Although the relationship between culture and feeling is obviously quite complicated, the simple version of the story is that our deep-seated emotions and emotional memories processed by the limbic system affect the "rational" parts of our brain, and vice versa. These emotions not only affect how we behave, but also how we view others (Fiske 2004). In other words, rational and emotional are not biological opposites; rather, the neuron circuits connect the different regions of the brain associated with higher-order functions controlled by the frontal cortex to those associated with the emotions.

I like to think of it this way. No matter how rational we are, our emotions affect us. And no matter how well our senses work, the information they communicate to our brains

Sarah and Toddler Sophie Making a Comfort Food Together. What Foods Most Comfort You?

is typically affected by our emotions too. If you think about it in the context of your own life, you'll come up with examples. For instance, you smell something that evokes a powerful but mysterious memory in you. For me, this occurs with certain cleaning products such as Lysol and Mr. Clean. I have strong, deep memories of a babysitter's home where these products were used. I cannot separate the two. And since I did not like being at the babysitter's, I also do not like to smell either of these cleaning products. On the other hand, often when we smell our comfort foods, we actually feel comforted just by the aroma. What are *your* comfort foods? (I love freshly baked chocolate chip cookies.) Can you link these to your childhood to help you understand what caused them to be your comfort foods? Looking at them now, are they healthy foods or some type of sweet, salty, or fatty treat? Take a moment to reflect upon your comfort foods, why you have come to associate them with comfort, and whether or not you'd choose them for your own children and why.

Learning to relate culture to feeling comfort is not that easy because culture is largely invisible to us until we encounter something different, something foreign. That wakes up our brains. Therefore, we tend to be more consciously aware of our cultural discomforts than our cultural comforts. Thus, it is really important to reflect now on how certain foods (as well as other products and customs) came to be comforting to you. Indeed, we should not underestimate the importance of emotion to culture. One of the reasons why we think we *have* culture is because we feel like culture is located deep down inside of us. Experiences frequently, if not always, become memories in association with emotion. Sometimes emotions can interfere with our thinking processes—particularly when they are the really strong emotions like fear, or hate. The military knows this well. It's the primary reason behind training and chain of command. In perilous situations like warfare, soldiers' emotions could overpower their ability to execute their orders and that could mean disaster for the mission. Among Navy SEALs, an elite U.S. military unit, there is a test that trainees must pass—although most fail—in order to become a SEAL. It involves submerging them in a pool with their ankles tied together and requiring them to keep their hands behind their backs. They have to do a variety of tasks this way, including grabbing an object at the bottom of the pool with their teeth. The challenge is that they have to do these things while facing the very real possibility of drowning. The brain's fear reaction systems thrust into high gear when we feel we are about to drown; it drowns out (note how appropriate this metaphor is!) the decision-making part of the brain, which "knows" how to solve the situation but loses function because it is overwhelmed by fear. SEALs have to go through rigorous training to ensure that their fear does not overpower their ability to handle their circumstances. Most never make it and have to join another part of the Navy.

For the military, memory is serious business; the neural circuits have to function accurately even if we do not think about them consciously. Military training is a good analogy to culture in general. We do culturally appropriate things so routinely that we never think about them, at least not deliberately. It's as if we have no awareness of them at all. We certainly don't actively think about getting dressed as *doing* culture, but we *do* pay attention to what clothing we put on. This makes sense when applying what I have been trying to communicate in this chapter:

- The human brain has more to do in comparison to other species because we rely least on genetically determined behavioral predispositions. This is our evolutionary trade-off: species that learn more depend less on "hard-wired" behaviors, and vice versa.
- Learning means we have to take in a lot of information and rapidly calculate what is going on in order to respond appropriately. Some estimate that at any given second, our brains are processing as many as 11 million pieces of information (Wilson 2004). Early life is particularly taxing on the brain because babies have to learn motor skills at the same time as they learn spoken and body language (Gardner 1983). Psychologists, following the work of Jean Piaget, often refer to this as the sensorimotor stage of childhood. Piaget was among the first researchers to appreciate the importance of routines, repeated behaviors, to learning in young children.
- No wonder the brain is a huge energy sinkhole, consuming twice as much energy in childhood as in adulthood (Meltzoff et al. 2009; Ratey 2002: 35).
- To save energy, our brains literally take shortcuts or, as we often refer to them when referencing people—stereotypes (Macrae, Miline, & Bodenhausen 1994). When we experience something for the first time, the brain records it physiologically in the form of synapse connections between neurons. The next time we encounter something similar, the brain recognizes the pattern and jumps to the shortcut (what psychologists refer to as a "schema" and Piaget originally called a "schemata"). These shortcuts, stereotypes, biases or whatever we call them are powerful. Our brains jump to conclusions even *before* we recognize that we are observing something or someone (e.g., Greenwald & Krieger 2006). When we build these connections our brains make instant subconscious inferences from what we are experiencing to this bank of past experiences. When there is consistency, no problem. We are on autopilot and just involuntarily assume that these are the same. When there is inconsistency, however— what we experience does *not* fit the models we have built in our heads, then we pay attention. At least we pay more attention and sometimes the differences bring all this to our consciousness (Wilson 2004).

Brains, synapses, shortcuts, (sub)conscious—it's quite a lot of abstraction, so here is a concrete example. A researcher had lunch at an Italian restaurant with her preschool-age son, his father, and another man. The 4-year-old noticed that he, his father, and the other man ate pizza whereas his mother ordered lasagna. On his way home in the car he announced that he had figured it out: "Men eat pizza and women don't!" (Bjorklund 2000: 361). The boy took one experience and inferred from that to make a conclusion about gender overall. In his case, he came to the wrong general conclusion from his single observation. He stereotyped, but he was doing what children his age do—figuring out the patterns in people's behaviors and applying them. After all, children learning culture are, in the words of one researcher, "irrepressible taxonomizers" (Bloom 2009: 11–12).

CUTTING PATHWAYS THROUGH THE (BRAIN'S) FOREST OF EXPERIENCE

It is easy to see from this example how people come to stereotype subconsciously given that our experiences, exposure, and information is acquired in early childhood before we can really be aware of, let alone control, these processes. I point this out not to condone stereotyping but, rather, to highlight how important the content of children's early exposure is. However unfortunate the outcome may occasionally be, taking such neural shortcuts helps us to survive because it conserves brain energy. To calculate and recalculate the same information each time we encounter something similar is just not efficient. So we have evolved the ability to cut away quite a bit of the complexity by packaging it into routines, the rituals of everyday life, and these become physiologically registered in our brains as neural circuits. This is what research shows. What I argue additionally is that these same processes produce in us cultural comfort.

This is precisely how as young children we move quickly from the infinite cultural flexibility we are born with to the much more limited—but never completely inflexible—set of cultural abilities we learn and use—our culture. And we use that more limited set over and over, making it feel more and more comfortable. That is, since what we experience socially connects our brain's neurons and then strengthens those connections with each repeat of the experience, we build our own cultural comfort zones. Because they are comfortable and our brains jump to these shortcuts, we tend to stay close to home culturally, repeating the same activities over and over again until, without ever realizing it, we have dug deep cultural ruts. To really understand what this is about, think of learning culture as bushwhacking your way through a very thick forest with bushes and trees from the forest floor to the sky. Imagine a newborn as having to

Imagine How Tempting Taking the Path Would Be Instead of Cutting Your Own New Way Through This Forest of Experience.

cut through her way through this forest of experience. The first time she goes through it is a very difficult journey. She has to find her way through tall trees, thick underbrush, and a variety of strange creatures. She slashes her way to the best of her ability. (Think of this as the really hard work of analyzing new people and social contexts, looking for patterns while also having to pay close attention to walking so as not to trip.) The next time she attempts to go down the same path, she has less work to do because she's already cut a path. The third and subsequent times she goes through this forest, she is likely to experiment less with possible routes than during her previous journeys. After all, she has worked hard to cut the path; to diverge from it would mean more work. (Think of this as the shortcuts represented by patterns. Even if she doesn't encounter *exactly* the same experience, her brain will categorize it as belonging to a known pattern.) Subsequently, traveling down the same path becomes easier and easier until the path itself becomes worn and grooved. Without realizing it at all, she has not only cut a path through the forest, but the path has cut a rut into the ground that makes it difficult for her to get out, even if she wants or needs to get out. While she is in the rut, perhaps she is threatened by a flash flood (a metaphor for unplanned change), but the rut is too deep for her to escape when the water rushes in. In this case, she has become so culturally comfortable in her ways that she cannot change even when it is critical to her survival.

What about if she stays away from this forest (cultural context) for a long time and when she returns the path has grown thick again? She will have to work hard to cut a path where before she traveled effortlessly. This symbolizes how we can be culturally comfortable in certain contexts or environments during eras in our lives but stop practicing these comforts and gradually lose these competencies. (Recall that the brain prunes connections that are not being used.) Merely think about how well you were able to fit in with your friends in elementary school but by high school you'd changed your behaviors. If you tried to go back to elementary school, you'd feel awkward and when you've been an adult for a while, it may be fun to reminisce about high school but you would likely have a hard time going back to the cultural comforts from that point in your life. That is, we continuously gain and lose cultural comforts but rarely perceive this as part of life—particularly when we think of culture as a possession that we get early in life and keep with us, largely unchanged, for the rest of our lives.

Cultural comfort, then, is analogous to cutting paths through the forest that, once cut, make us less likely to stray from them because it would take a lot more effort. Additionally, we tend not to leave comforts—though we can—because when we do we feel uncomfortable, or even anxious or afraid. The more time we spend in our cultural comforts, the more we dig them deeper, making it more and more difficult to break out of them—even if we want to. I hope this and the material in this chapter explains more broadly why we think and do what we think and do. However, I do not want to imply that just because we grow up with our cultural comforts they are desirable or ethical. Conversely, this book is about explaining culture as comfort so that you *also* embrace discomfort, so you also push yourself and others you care about to expand your cultural comforts to include experiences that you have not had before. That is our evolutionary gift, yet we do not enjoy it as much as we could because we tend to prefer our comforts.

Cultural comfort is a predicament of being a cultural species. We cannot avoid cutting pathways though the thicket of cultural experience since we must cut them to survive during childhood. As children, we are not able to see what we have done (we are not conscious of learning culture) until the paths are so well worn that we follow them unthinkingly. Actually, the analogy between learning culture and cutting paths through a forest should include

FIGURE 3.4   Can You Break Out of Your Cultural Ruts?

another factor. Imagine now that you were dropped into a forest where the underbrush is very thick but where there are deeply grooved paths that your relatives had cut long before you arrived. Would you follow the paths or strike out on your own by cutting a new path? We have a name for such paths: *traditions*. We could try not to follow the traditional paths that our relatives have followed. However, this is very unlikely because when we arrive, we are led through the forest and along these well-worn paths by our caregivers who know the paths well and often obligate us to follow them. Completely without knowing it, we have traded the cultural flexibility we are born with for predictable, comfortable, yet more finite paths through life.

I view culture this way. While instincts are, to my way of thinking, the deeply rutted paths that we are given by Mother Nature, culture is about how people dig our own ruts in addition to those few we inherit. To repeat the phrase I use in Chapter 2, we build our own social order. As you have seen, there are perfectly good reasons for this. Our huge capacity for learning means we are highly adaptable to different climates and conditions. We arrive into the world with nearly infinite adaptability, but we also arrive nearly completely helpless. This obliges us to learn what others around us do and think, whether intentionally or not. As we learn, we participate actively in finding comfort and predictability in a world that otherwise would be enormously unpredictable, frightening, and difficult to understand. As we experience, we build neural pathways in our brains that make travel along these circuits easier with each additional trip. This human dilemma is helpful and limiting at the same time. It is helpful because the next time we come to the same crossroads, we do not have to do the really hard work of breaking open a new pathway. For example, when we meet a new person again, we draw on our previous encounters with that person and other similar people who enable us to shortcut the huge cognitive load on our brains involved in assessing that person. The third and subsequent times we meet that person, the cognitive shortcut (synapse connection) gets even faster. This is why first impressions are so deep and so hard to dislodge. Our brains categorize the new into the familiar, the new to normal to norm.

So, it's time to take a Planned Pause for you to think about your deepest cultural ruts, and write them down. Try to think beyond the obvious ones—the "bad habits" you have accumulated in life. They are important, but you are aware of them and many are personal habits not cultural comforts. Most of our cultural ruts escape our conscious attention, so that's why I'd like you to think about what you normally ignore.

PLANNED PAUSE 3-2

MY CULTURAL RUTS—AND HOW TO BREAK OUT OF THEM

Instructions: *Think about the cultural ruts you have but avoid your personal bad habits. (Cultural ruts are shared.) Then answer the questions below.*

Part 1: List at least two of your cultural ruts here. Explain each briefly.

Part 2: Select **one** *of your cultural ruts. Plan a strategy for pulling yourself out of this cultural rut. Make sure that you apply the concepts from the book to your response.*

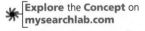 Explore the Concept on mysearchlab.com

FROM LIFE'S ROUTINES TO NORMS TO NORMAL: CULTURE, TRADITION, AND INSTITUTIONALIZATION

One of my favorite phrases about culture as comfort is to say, "It's so cultural, it's natural. It's second nature." Our language confuses us. In some ways, it prevents us from seeing that we internalize patterns and then conform to them as what is normal. Most of what we do day in and day out conforms to unwritten norms for how we should behave and think. What feels normal thus becomes normative, which, in many cases, is also viewed as moral. That is, it's not just the way things usually are; it's the way things *should* be. As we learn culture, we not only learn to take the peculiar practices of our people as normative (patterned), we also learn them as normal and correct. As we acquire culture we become, by necessity not by choice, ethnocentric. That is, we learn to see ourselves (ethnos) as if we were in the center (centric) of the world and everyone *else* were different. In many if not most cases, seeing others as different and ourselves as in the center of our world produces judgments about others as not only different but strange and inferior (more on that in later chapters).

Our own ethnocentrism is thus very hard to see until we step beyond our cultural comforts. Take this example: On what side of the road do people drive in your country? If I ask this in many countries, people will respond by saying "the right side of the road." What about people in England, the Bahamas, or Japan? If you have ever been there you know that they drive on the left side of the road, but it feels like it's the *wrong* side if you are accustomed to living where people drive (and walk) on the right side. The reverse is true for those who grew up driving (and walking) on the left. Try to switch and your head will end up very confused. So many people get confused in London that in the central city each pedestrian crosswalk is labeled to remind visitors from right-side-driving countries to look to their right before crossing—the opposite of what their "instincts" tell them to do. This is a quick example of how norms are understood as normal. When we stay in our comfort zones, we rarely recognize this isomorphism; when we leave our comfort zones we find that what's normal to us is very strange to another, hence this book's subtitle: "Many Things You Know About Culture (But Might Not Realize)."

One of the great things that happens to us when we leave our comfort zones is that our awareness gets stimulated. Daily life is full of new things to witness, of differences. We suddenly observe the sounds, smells, and sights that in our own context we would ignore because they have been filed away as normative. If you've ever traveled somewhere that is very unlike your normal social contexts, you probably can relate to what I am saying. Remember, our brains are designed to pay attention to newness; when we encounter newness, our mind gets busy figuring out what's going on. Some people thrive in new settings whereas others shy away from them; still others, like cultural anthropologists, are professional outsiders. We expose ourselves regularly to discomfort zones; we learn by observing all that is new—because we perceive it as different—when we leave the tried and true for the

Crossing a Street in London: Visitors from Abroad Tend to Look Left and Easily Get Hit by Drivers Coming from the Right. Changing Deeply Ingrained Patterns is Hard Even When We Are Consciously Aware of Them.

untried and new. It's a great technique because our data, almost literally, jumps out at us. The newness strikes us; we are aware of it because it does not fit the patterns we have internalized unconsciously. As we have seen before, this is how our brains work. We pay attention to newness, work hard to identify new patterns around us, and then store these away as cultural knowledge. When we encounter newness it is often a difficult task to understand what's going on. For adults, this is often "discomforting" because we feel inadequate and often anxious, perhaps even stupid. Anthropologists studying different societies are often perceived by people we study as if we were children; we are treated as such because we do not know how to properly talk, act, and think in the unfamiliar culture. As I have discussed throughout this book, when individuals go against the cultural grain, it causes disruption and unease among members of that society. So a common way for cultural insiders to handle foreign anthropologists is to treat us as if we were children, people culturally accepted as those who are still learning the correct ways to think, talk, and behave.

Anthropologists are, of course, not the only people who confront cultural discomfort on a regular basis. You do too. No matter how tightly you stick to your comfort zones, you actually travel across cultural spaces all the time and do so nearly effortlessly. You *are* multicultural already; you start your day in the cultural comfort of your home and then you leave it for work, school, or some other activity. Each of these places involves practicing at least some different cultural norms than those you practice elsewhere. At home you have the privacy to do things that you probably would not dare do in public, so what's normal for you at home is going to differ from what's normal for you outside home. And at work or school you are likely to be subject to a series of rules and regulations that you are thankful you don't have to abide by at home. There are also the peculiar traditions of different groups you might belong to. For example, if you are a man who never wears makeup in everyday life, you might feel completely normal painting your face the colors of a favorite sports team on game night.

Different contexts have different norms, and you don't necessarily see them as strange or contradictory in the least. They are still normal—normal for you, that is, and for those with whom you share these contexts and their customs. I know of children of immigrants who daily cross and re-cross cultural comfort zone borders. As I discuss more thoroughly in Chapter 6, they leave home where they practice one language, eat certain comfort foods, and negotiate correctly their body language with everyone else. And they go to school, where they practice flawlessly another language, eat different comfort foods, and negotiate a completely different yet also correct body language with their peers. Studies on such bilingual, bicultural individuals indicate that they are more culturally flexible than others who learn one language and don't cross such significant cultural borders (Burns et al. 2003; Fennel et al. 2007). They may be *more* flexible, but we all flex. We alter our thinking and behavior based on the context in which we find ourselves. We can learn new tricks, but we need to put ourselves where we are exposed to them. That's the hard part. We have this incredible cultural ability, but it comes with that need, that desire for comfort. Think of this cultural ability in terms of muscles. The more you flex your cultural muscles, the easier it becomes, but when you do not use the muscles, they atrophy.

Routines, norms, and comfort all coalesce in what we call our traditions. What are traditions? They are culturally specific ways of behaving and believing that are shared by people. The more people share traditions, the more people perpetuate them and the more likely they will live on across generations. Traditions can also be specific to families and are really important to a family's sense of identity, of people belonging together. This is one reason why people are frequently emotional about traditions and treat them as possessions.

They are like family secrets that, if shared, would no longer be special. Traditions not only are protected by families; they are among the most basic of building blocks for larger groupings of people: neighborhoods and cities, ethnic associations and religious groups, nations and countries all claim and protect their traditions. An interesting thing about traditions is that they both foster a strong sense of belonging among those who practice them and they distinguish practitioners from people who do not share the tradition. They simultaneously create feelings of "us" and "them." Because we do our traditions differently from yours, we know that you are different even more than we know that we are similar. If you start adopting our traditions, we could welcome you into our tent—but this does not always happen. Often, when "others" become more like us, we feel we may "lose" our culture; we don't feel as unique as we did before. Traditions are "things," right? If they are things, then we can lose them, and as we lose them we lose our culture. Thinking this way is common but problematic because, once again, it treats culture as a *thing* (a possession) when we actually *do* culture (actions).

Since we give these rituals the label of traditions, we also think that they have deep roots. Such reasoning gives us the feeling of continuity over time even if the roots are truly shallow. You've probably heard people say something like, "We've been doing it this way since before anyone can remember" or "Their way of life has not changed in thousands of years." Yet this is often more feeling than truth. For quite a few years now, social scientists have been documenting the fact that a really large percentage of seemingly old, deep traditions are actually quite shallow (e.g., Anderson 1991; Barth 1975; Hobsbawm & Ranger 1983). Instead of just citing scholarship here, I think you'll be more familiar with the famous Thanksgiving turkey tradition. According to this classic story, a woman is starting to cook her family's Thanksgiving dinner. In her family the tradition is not to stuff the turkey (as is the case in many other families) but, rather, to cut the uncooked turkey in half and roast one half. She knows this is her family's tradition, but why this odd tradition? So she asks her mother, who tells her, "I don't know why. This is just the way my mother did it." So the woman asks her grandmother and her grandmother tells her, "I don't know why. That is just the way my mother did it." Now the woman is lucky since her great-grandmother is still alive, so she asks her about the tradition. Her great-grandmother says, "I did that because my oven was too small to fit a whole turkey inside at one time." The turkey tradition story illustrates in a fun way that traditions are invented and that many "deep" traditions are really shallow, yet we hold on to them fiercely. Why? It's culture as comfort again. Traditions help us to reproduce the very cultural connections to others that make us *feel* connected. The key is not how deep or shallow these traditions are but, rather, how they help people feel community. Eating particular foods during these traditions is important since, as we have seen, we acquire some of our comfort foods this way.

We are born capable of adopting any tradition; we learn the traditions of those people around us who practice them and we then reproduce them ourselves. Why? It's tradition! Now that you can contextualize traditions as the paths others have cut for us, hopefully you can see, too, that traditions, while comforting, may not always be useful to keep practicing. Sometimes it is important to exercise more our cultural flexibility than our cultural comforts. A case in point is traditions that, while useful to build cultural comforts, are harmful to at least some individuals. Most every society has such traditions; in the United States fraternity hazing has been banned on many campuses owing to the occasional death or other physical/mental torment inflicted on initiates. Classic examples outside the United States are female genital mutilation and foot binding. Such traditions often persist despite efforts to stop them not because they cannot be halted quickly (foot binding in China is a good example of an old tradition that ended rapidly), but because, among other reasons, so many people reproduce traditions day in and day out that we are invested in them and their cultural comforts.

Conclusion

Childhood is the period in life when we most learn culture. We learn how to behave and think in ways that align with, and thus are intelligible to, those with whom we interact. We learn through interactions, which we store as patterns in our brains; the more we follow these patterns, the more comfortable we are but the less flexible we become; we also become "us" and others become "them." Because children are born dependent upon caregivers for their survival, they cannot stray too far from the caregivers' customs, from relatives' well-worn paths. Children are often thought of as rule-breakers, people whose "natural" tendency is to do what they want and thus have to be corralled into doing what their parents and society want. Quite the reverse is overwhelmingly true. Children look for, detect, and enforce rules more than they break them. It makes their lives more comfortable than when rules are unambiguous because in early life there are so many rules and so many people to learn about. Comfort arises through repeated sensory experiences that quickly become wired in our brains. These enable us to interpret what others do and also predict what they are likely to do. When we are able to predict what a person we interact with will do, albeit completely subconsciously, we develop foundational trust. This type of trust is not the same as trusting that the person will be good to us. Rather, it's the type of trust in such phrases as, "I trust that you will get your work done on time." In other words, it's predictability that is a foundation, I argue, for all types of more complex trusting, like trusting that someone will look out for our best interests and not tell our secrets.

When we feel culturally comfortable, we do not consciously link this comfort to predictability, but this association should now be easy to see. Think of the greater degree of comfort (ease) we feel when faced with natural disasters that are predictable—hurricanes, for example—versus those that give no warning, such as earthquakes and tornados. Another way to look at comfort and predictability is by thinking about things that make us nervous, such as public speaking. When we practice our speech over and over, particularly if we do so in front of a friendly audience, we typically grow less frightened. Why? Because we have increased the predictability of the event. We cannot control *all* the circumstances of the event, but we can control at least some and this means we can feel more at ease.

A great irony of the human condition, however, is that as we learn the cultural patterns around us, we quickly lose a lot of the very flexibility to adapt to different and changing circumstances that culture affords us, the flexibility that is our greatest evolutionary gift. For example, newborns, though they already prefer the language of those they have listened to while in the womb, still pay attention to *all* sounds they hear. But by the end of their first year, they pay attention overwhelmingly to the sounds of what will become their native language(s) (Begley 2007; Eliot 1999; Gopnik 2009; Werker et al. 1981). We begin life with enormous flexibility and adaptability but as we adapt, we ineluctably lose this infinite possibility (but great uncertainty) for the comforts of culture. And these comforts vary from people to people. That is, although the human condition requires that we learn culture and that we learn culture in similar ways, *what* we learn varies tremendously, both within any given society and between societies. And this makes all the difference—at least, if we believe that cultural learning ends with childhood. I do *not* see it that way, but I do recognize that the cultural pathways we walk as children make it more difficult and certainly more uncomfortable to walk new pathways later on. Well-worn paths become rutted so they take more effort to abandon. That said, it is not good to only emphasize the *loss* to our flexibility that typically occurs as we learn cultural competencies. We are still incredibly inventive; we create things we have never seen or heard all the time. We can and should continue to flex our cultural muscles. This, too, is our evolutionary heritage in culture.

Much as young children do not merely memorize language, but use words and grammatical rules to create sentences they've never heard before, we take the building blocks of culture and build new cultural environments all the time. So culture is no straitjacket we put on early in life; however, culture *is* about comfort. The more comfort we need, the fewer risks we are likely to take.

Yes, culture is about comfort and about comfortable ruts, but this does *not* mean we are condemned to repeat the past. If culture remains a mystery to us or we treat it largely as something we acquire and have to defend, then we will ignore the most incredible aspect of culture—that we continue to experience and acquire new cultural competencies throughout life. We are all multicultural and we can improve upon our multicultural abilities. However, most of us have come to see ourselves as monocultural not multicultural. *Others* are multicultural (which means they don't know who they really are) while we are monocultural, right? Before reading this book, didn't you think of yourself as having *one* culture? The more we embrace our cultural flexibility, our continued capacity to learn new cultural practices, the more we empower ourselves culturally. To do so, we have to see culture as our learned, shared understanding of interrelationships. Even at very advanced ages, we can still build synapses when we expose ourselves to new ideas and new contexts or reconnect synapses that have been pruned (Begley 2007; Seung 2012). Even late in life, the brain still is doing the same games of scrutinizing what we encounter: Is it the same as before? Travel down the well-worn path. Different? Build a new path. What keeps the brain churning is newness. That means that throughout life we can continue to grow culturally. We just have to be willing to take a few risks beyond our comfort zones.

It is the end of the chapters in which I have laid out the thesis of the whole book—that culture is about comfort—so it is a good place to pause to check in with your understanding. Please stop reading and take a few moments to consider these questions: What does "culture as comfort" mean to you now? Does viewing culture from the perspective of comfort differ from how you thought about culture before? If so, how? What questions do you have that you'd like answered?

One question I anticipate that many of you might have is, "What about individual personalities? Aren't they important to how we think and behave?" That *is* an important question, and I have not tried to be sneaky by avoiding the issue of personality. Obviously people do vary a lot by what we refer to as personality, although that term, much like culture, is shorthand for a complex concept (Holmes 2011; Sroufe et al. 2005). Personality certainly adds an additional layer of intricacy to understanding and predicting human behavior. However, whereas culture is the term we use to talk about what people *share*, personality is a term we use more to talk about how we *differ* as individuals despite sharing culture. People can have very different personalities and yet, when speaking with one another, share the same expectation about how far apart their faces should be from each other (an expectation that varies considerably around the world). So while it makes sense to talk about one person having a personality, it does not make sense to talk about only one person having a culture. Culture is definitely learned and shared. Personality, on the other hand, is both inherited genetically and affected by experience, but leans more toward the inherited side than does culture (e.g., Eysenck 2006; Holmes 2011). Both culture and personality are affected by interacting with the environment—nature *and* nurture.

Why, then, do we sometimes have trouble distinguishing between cultural similarities and personality similarities? There have been several attempts to understand groups of people as if they had personality types. For instance, years ago some anthropologists, referred to as the Culture and Personality School (e.g., Benedict 1959), tried to categorize peoples (they used the term "cultures") according to personality types. They labeled some peoples as more restrained or more fun loving, for example. Decades later psychologist Geert Hofstede (1980) began somewhat similar work. Using large surveys conducted in many countries, he sought to identify certain widely distributed value orientations within populations (for instance, risk taking versus risk aversion and individual independence versus interdependence). Hofstede and others (e.g., Hofstede and McCrae 2004) who have pursued this type of research generalize their findings into what they call "national cultures."

While I understand these researchers' objectives, I also see how their work can muddy the work of truly understanding culture—and that is the primary objective of this book.

If you are now at a point where you are beginning to feel like you understand culture better, then I am really pleased. I do not expect that any readers will immediately change their perspective because the "culture as thing" view is one that you've lived with all your life. Transformations often take time. They usually take a lot of effort as well. Think of this book as taking you through a process that will, I hope, transform your thinking about culture. It is then a type of rite of passage, kind of like the rituals used to celebrate children's entry into adulthood. Rites of passage are a cultural tool to help people transform their customary ways of doing things and their social statuses. You're in the middle stage. By the end of the book, I hope that you'll have gone through this transformation and permanently leave behind your old view of culture.

To Be Human Is to Integrate Socially

We have made Italy; now we have to make Italians.

—Speech made by Italian leader Massimo d'Azeglio to Parliament
following the unification of Italy as a country (quoted in
Hobsbawm & Kertzer 1992: 4)

The previous chapter introduced the research on young infants that is rapidly uncovering the processes babies use to learn what we have come to call culture. For me, understanding culture through the lens of learning "it" has important consequences for our lives and for improving our human relations broadly as well as individually. We evolved these complex abilities to learn to handle a huge challenge our ancestors faced—rapid environmental change—and since then this cultural flexibility has enabled our species to populate every environment on Earth and to create an abundance of different ways of life. So the advantages of being a cultural species should now be clear—we are not locked into behaviors encoded in our genes. The disadvantages should also be coming clear. We are born highly flexible but very, very quickly we acquire and repeat patterns we observe so that we adapt to our particular society's culturally constructed ways of life. As we do, we feel comfort but we become less plastic, less inclined to change, and we also become more like the people around us but different from people we don't know.

Becoming culturally competent in a narrower set of cultural abilities than we could have learned at birth, however, does not mean we cannot continue to learn in life. New things are good for our brains no matter our age. When we attempt novel activities—even in our senior years—the brain continues to build new neural pathways. Researchers call this "neuroplasticity" (Pascual-Leone et al. 2005). The more stimulation we encounter, the more we can alter our brains. When we abandon activities, the neurons may be pruned or redirected. Even when regions of the brain have been damaged, other areas of the brain can be reorganized to take over the damaged area's functions (Begley 2007; Eliot 1999; Ramachandran 2011). The brain is a constant work in progress; it is a constant *cultural* work in progress since the brain's architecture is constructed through experience. How much our brains change, however, reflects how much we experience novel things and have to adapt to them. If circumstances don't change, then we become very set in our ways and, like species dependent upon instincts, we will suffer when our environments, social as well as natural, change. The more we use our brains to do similar things, the stronger the neural highways become; and the more that happens, the less likely we are to divert onto side roads. Think of a child practicing an instrument and the old adage "practice makes perfect." Practicing reinforces the brain's circuits. Stopping an activity lets those connections atrophy. Now we can better understand why this is true.

So this is the thesis of this book. The rest of the book provides examples of how useful this perspective on culture is for solving the real-world problems and issues we face. In other words, the rest of the book answers the biggest question of all: This perspective is nice, but what does it matter? In this chapter I develop the first of a series of different responses to this question, and in each subsequent chapter I discuss others, but this is just a partial list of applications. I am sure that you will find many more applications as you get used to the concept of "culture as comfort" over "culture as a thing."

LEARNING CULTURE IS ABOUT SOCIALLY INTEGRATING NEW PEOPLE INTO GROUPS

As people learn culture, they become integrated socially into their society (and they also adapt to the physical environments around them). Through this adaptive process, they develop a sense of belonging with the people of their society; when away from these people, they feel as if they're among strangers. We do not recall the processes of integrating we experienced as a young child, but if we can now see them for what they are, we can be more mindful of how we, as adults, participate in the social integration of newcomers—and not just babies. We integrate newcomers into our schools, workplaces, clubs, places of worship, communities, nations, and even virtual communities. Although the ways in which we integrate people are remarkably similar, for most of us they remain mysterious. In the next pages, I show how we gain feelings of belonging by examining various cases of how we integrate newcomers. At the end, you will have tools to be more conscientious in your efforts to integrate people into your environments, regardless of what they are. You will be more empowered to integrate yourself as well as to integrate others. This is what we do as people so I hope it will be helpful.

As social integration is a process (or processes) that transforms a person's status from newcomer/outsider to native/insider, it is to my mind most helpful to think of the process as analogous to a rite of passage. The typical application of this concept, rite of passage, in anthropology and other social sciences is to understand specific rituals in life that are involved with status changes. I think rites of passage are excellent for understanding the broadest idea of social integration more generally. In studying many rituals across different cultural groups, anthropologists Arnold van Gennep (1960) and Victor Turner (1967, 1977) identified commonalities in the structure of these rituals. People who are being inducted into a group are first separated out from the broader population, after which they undergo some type of experience while they are separated. This experience transforms them, and then they are allowed to re-enter society equipped with their status change; they are now members of a new status group. So there are three stages: separation, transition, and reentry. At the beginning a person has one particular social status; that status is altered in the transition period and then the person emerges from transition with a new status. This new status is recognized by the society or sector of society into which the person is integrating and typically this new status is accompanied by one or more symbols so that everyone knows

Young Men Going Through a Rite of Passage into Adulthood. Note How Dress Separates Them into a Group. Where Might this Ritual Take Place? What Cues Do You Use to Decide?

the new status has been achieved. It's a very simple recipe, but it is applied in such a wide array of ways that we often do not see the recipe, only the finished meal.

Integrating People into Families

From the previous two chapters, you should have a strong idea about the enormous amount of cultural knowledge that babies learn extraordinarily quickly to adapt to their social environments. So they do their part to integrate. However, the people around them must do their part as well. They do this through interaction, as already explained, but one of the most important ways they do this is much less known: social birth. Social birth is an anthropological concept that is the outcome of studies involving the search for patterns or regularities in what peoples do cross-culturally (Montgomery 2009). It turns out that peoples everywhere practice a rite of passage to integrate infants into their social group(s), called social birth (Lancy 2010). I can almost hear you saying to yourself, "What? Integrate a baby? A baby is born into a family." True, but being born biologically is different from being born socially. This is best seen through examples.

Common examples of social birth can be found in religious rituals. Among many Christians, for example, this is accomplished through infant baptism. As you may have seen, baptism follows the classic rite of passage stages: The infant is cradled by his or her parents, but they separate from their friends and family by heading to the front of the sanctuary to initialize the ritual. The dress of the baby (typically in all white, a symbol of purity) also identifies separation from ordinary clothes. When the parents hand the baby to the pastor or priest, the transition phase begins. It continues when the pastor anoints the baby with water while saying a blessing, and it ends when the pastor presents the baby to the congregation as a new member. This last step marks the baby's integration into the Christian community, the public acknowledgment of the baby's social birth. Most social births are marked by not only a ritual, but also some type of party or feast to which members of the larger social group are invited. Note that the baptism occurs some time *after* biological birth. Another case among Jews is the brit or bris, the removal of a baby boy's penile foreskin eight days following birth. Traditionally, this social birth, like baptism, involved the transition phase being done at home by a religious specialist (the Mohel); now, the transition is often performed by a doctor in a hospital, and is celebrated later with a party at the infant's home. Although the act itself is somewhat de-ritualized within the hospital, the infant's social birth is still acknowledged by a gathering of the social group into which the child has now been integrated. In each of these cases, appropriate gifts for the infant would be anything symbolic of his new status, such as jewelry or clothing with a cross or Star of David or religious storybooks.

According to anthropologist Alma Gottlieb (2004), most African Muslim peoples confer social birth by naming their children about a week after their biological birth. In her own research among the Beng peoples of the Ivory Coast in West Africa, Gottlieb learned of their belief that babies carry the reincarnated soul of an ancestor. It takes a long time for babies to achieve complete membership in Beng society since these reincarnated souls are always tempted to leave the physical world for the *wrugbe*, the afterlife (literally, the "village of souls"), which is a sweeter place to dwell than on Earth. The Beng feel that the pull of *wrugbe* is so powerful that they must entice babies to remain among the living by elaborately bathing and decorating them (as mentioned earlier), co-sleeping with them, and making life on Earth as inviting as possible. Gottlieb (2004: 93) writes that babies are thought of as living "betwixt and between" two worlds; as such, they are seen as only weakly attached to each world while they slowly make the transition from one to the other. Not surprisingly, Beng social birth takes a lot of effort and time. It begins, but certainly does not end, when the baby's umbilical cord falls off. On that day (and among other rituals), the baby is washed four times by its maternal grandmother and is given its first necklace made of savannah grass to encourage its health and growth. Baby girls also have their ears pierced.

Although these illustrations of social birth vary enormously in terms of the particulars of rites of passage and the symbols of the newfound status for infants, they all follow the rite of passage recipe. Additionally, they all are examples of social birth that *follows* biological birth. There is a gap of hours to months between being born physically and being born socially. Research trying to understand why there is always a gap suggests that it helps to protect the social group, and particularly the mother, from greater emotional trauma should the child die shortly after birth (Lancy 2010; Kaufman and Morgan 2005). Until very recently in most societies, infant mortality was so high—especially in the first weeks and months following birth—that investing a lot of emotional work into socially integrating a new member could easily result in huge emotional duress with every loss of an infant. Separating social birth from biological birth, then, protects caregivers from too much attachment and thus the heartache that can accompany the loss of a child (Lancy 2010; Scheper-Hughes 1992). Social birth, thus, provides a ritual to mark the commencement of greater emotional investment, a public acknowledgment that the child is now likely to survive.

In recent decades, however, the science of childbearing has opened up much greater knowledge of fetal development in the womb. And since the appearance of ultrasound technology, expectant parents can view their baby and hear its heartbeat before birth itself. Scholars studying obstetric technology acknowledge that among many people now, social birth *precedes* biological birth (Kaufman & Morgan 2005; Mitchell & Georges 1998; Montgomery 2009; Taylor 2008). Infants are being incorporated into their social groups, particularly into families, earlier and earlier and thus social birth is accomplished through the ritual of the first ultrasound itself. Before the invention of ultrasound and other technologies used to view the womb, a woman was typically viewed as pregnant, but the social status of her fetus was ambiguous. Was it a human being, a human being in the making, or a pre–human being? Peoples around the world take various perspectives on the social status of a baby in utero (e.g., Huber & Breedlove 2007). For example, the Qur'an states that the soul enters the fetus at 120 days at which time Muslims begin to refer to its personhood (Montgomery 2009: 83). However, new technologies can shift this perspective, particularly among peoples who view pregnancy as that of an unborn *child*. When we refer to a child, there is a subtle understanding that this being is a *person* and when we refer to "our" child, we acknowledge him or her as a *member* of our family. How do you feel? At what point does social birth take place in your understanding: at conception, in the womb, at birth, or after a ritual is performed after birth? These are hugely important questions for many people and we often argue and debate over them without being aware of the larger cultural phenomenon that all people face—socially integrating new members. In the United States, battles over the legality of abortion have shifted to hinge on social birth—when a fetus is officially accorded personhood status. Whenever personhood status (social birth in this case as a citizen of the country) begins, so, too, begin the rights accorded to that person.

With the help of technology, expectant families also typically learn the sex of the baby. Armed with this information, the family incorporates the baby into his or her new setting by buying the symbols of that new status: often pink for a daughter or blue for a son. The extended family and coworkers are told about the pregnancy, the child's sex, and the names being considered (naming is itself an acknowledgment of social birth). All of this emotional investment indicates that social birth has occurred. Therefore, should anything happen except a normal biological birth, the emotional toll is huge, much larger than in societies where social birth follows biological. The debates are basically about social birth—when is a fetus a member of society with full social rights? When is a fetus a full member of a family? Understanding that people respond differently to these questions helps explain the very emotional debates in many parts of the world over abortion.

Of course, birth is but one of the events marked by rites of passage in the course of human life. Among the most important other rites that are extremely common if not universal to all societies are weddings and funerals. Think about these rituals for a moment and see if you can now trace the separation, transition, and reincorporation stages in marriages and funerals. Stop for a moment and identify the stages for a funeral. After you finish, continue reading as I will analyze marriages.

Weddings vary a great deal in specifics, but they have a lot of commonalities in terms of their basic elements as rites of passage. First of all, they are all about incorporating new people into established groups. People who have little to no social belonging now become attached. Weddings knit together different families who thereafter have obligations that they did not have before. These new bonds are acknowledged by giving the newly integrated members a particular term—"in-laws" (or, as in my family, people often refer to themselves jokingly as the "out-laws"). Again, see if you can identify the separation, transition, and reintegration phases of marriage that result in not only the joining of the spouses, but also of their families. Do you see how the special clothing of both the groom and, especially, the bride symbolize that they are the ones undergoing the ritual? And, of course, you can see the transition in the ceremony itself, particularly the vows, and the fact that, in many traditions at least, the couple faces away from the society bearing witness. That symbolizes their separation from the group (even though they are in the same room).

On occasion, a covering over the couple during the transition part of the ritual symbolizes their separation from everyone else. How about the reintegration with their new

The Wedding as Rite of Passage: Note How the Bride and Groom Walk Up to the Ceremony Along Their Relatives' Side and Walk Down Along Their New In-Laws' Side. As the Two Become Family Officially, Their Families Change Too.

change of status? Just think about when the person officiating pronounces the couple as newly married, mentions their new names, if any, and permits them to kiss. The couple then turns toward their social group and literally reintegrates themselves by walking right through the audience. Something that reinforces this is the way the bride is facing; as she walks down the aisle to be married, she is seen best by her own relatives on her left side and she is accompanied by her maid of honor on that side. After she is married, she turns around and immediately is next to the groom's best man. Then she walks back up the aisle and in so doing literally passes all her new in-laws sitting on the opposite side of the aisle. Then there is the reception party where everyone participates. What are the symbols of the couple's new status? Rings worn on the fourth finger are a common symbol, as are new forms of addressing the newly married couple and their newly acquired family members (e.g., *Mrs.* versus *Ms.* or *Miss*; in-laws). Additionally, there is a wide variety of markers of married status, especially for women. For example, a common practice among married Hindu women is to wear the *bindi*, a dark red dot on the forehead. What do these symbols represent? That someone is married, of course, but also that this person is now supposed to be off limits to sexual attention from anyone other than the spouse. They also represent the person's successful transition into a new, acknowledged social status. I believe that this is where the rub comes with gay marriage. Whether or not you favor gay marriage, you should be able to see that prohibiting gays to marry leaves them in an unsettled social-integration position. They are neither single nor married. Civil unions do not settle the issue because they do not involve full reintegration, which is the *sine qua non* of rites of passage. Unions provide some rights and status differences, but the most important socially speaking is acceptance into the broader family, or society. As many religions as well as governments prohibit gay marriage, that broader acceptance is not granted to gay couples.

Now, it's important to recall that these examples of rites of passage are only part of the overall objective of this chapter: to show how learning and doing culture is about socially integrating people into their groups. There are many things to learn, many cultural competencies to acquire around important rituals, especially marriage. No wonder they typically are planned far in advance. Traditions are passed down during weddings, perhaps more than at any other time in life, and traditions take a lot of effort to learn so they can be reproduced later. Marriages do not happen each and every day, so the traditions associated with them must be learned well in order for them to be reproduced properly. No wonder, then, that many weddings involve young boys and girls in the rituals so that they can begin to learn all that is involved. No wonder also that even though marriages involve rites of passage that are now easily recognizable, people accustomed to certain traditions will feel very much like "fish out of water" in someone else's traditions. Next time you attend a wedding, apply the rite of passage lens to it. You should see and appreciate it differently. Perhaps, if you're not yet married, you will plan your own wedding (or your children's weddings) with a new awareness of its rite of passage elements.

INTEGRATING PEOPLE INTO (FACE-TO-FACE) INSTITUTIONAL GROUPS

Arguably, the most important group all people need to integrate into, and feel we belong in, is our families. Yet during the course of our lives, we also integrate into a wide variety of additional groups. Some of these groups consist of people we know, while others are so big that we cannot know everyone in them, and yet we still somehow feel a part of them. Large companies and clubs, as well as nations, are examples of these latter groups. Despite wide variations in types and sizes, however, the basic process for integration remains similar. We go through a transition from outsider or uninitiated member to insider or full member; therefore, integration processes can be viewed as rites of passage. In the following examples, I highlight the rites of passage of integration, but it is important to recognize that groups are more than just clusters of individuals; when I refer to a "group," I really mean a "cultural context shared by people." When you join the military, for example, you do not just remain the same as when you were a civilian. You must learn the *cultural practices* of the military, as these differ quite significantly from civilian life. When you enlist, you do not know this cultural context (unless you grew up in a military family), so you must be *trained*. "Training" is another word for learning the particular ways of a new cultural context. So, when we integrate into new groups, we must learn new cultural ideas and practices. We are therefore learning culture even as adults.

Becoming Soldiers in Real Life and Online

Since I have already mentioned joining the military and its rites of passage are very marked, let's begin by talking about them. In this transition a person begins as a civilian. Civilians enlist voluntarily, are recruited, or are drafted into the military. At this point, they are separated from the broader society as uninitiated members, but they must go through a transition during which they are transformed into soldiers. What is that transition called? If you guessed boot camp, you are right. But think a bit more about what boot camp involves. When people are going through a transition, this phase in their rite of passage has them separated from both the cultural context of their original status (civilian) and from the cultural context they will assume (solider). This separation is physical but also symbolic. What do you know about how boot camp separates newcomers physically and symbolically? If you are not sure, *imagine* what happens. The key is to think about how people going through transformations pass through certain stages in their rituals—separation from the broader group or society, a collective experience, and then reemergence into that society with a new status.

Now compare your responses against what those who have studied this transition have found. Recruits undergo physical separation by going to the camp itself and staying there, away from civilian society, for weeks. They undergo a variety of symbolic separations that not only communicate that they are now in the military, but also work toward getting them to lose their individuality in order to enforce that they are now part of a larger organization that is more important than any individual. As part of this deindividualization process, they are issued "uniforms." You may not think about the significance of that word, but it means to make everyone similar. When we wear uniforms, we symbolize the larger organization of which we are a part. We wear them to show our social integration into this organization; when other people see our uniform, they typically see us as representatives (symbols) of that organization. So, issuing new recruits military uniforms and forbidding them to wear civilian clothes during boot camp communicates who they are expected to become. Additionally, the military uniform is decorated by a multitude of symbols that communicate rank and thus the hierarchy of the new cultural context. A soldier is expected to respond to the rank, rather than to the individual behind the rank.

Another ritual that forms part of the initiation into military life is the haircut. Hairstyles help people symbolize membership in groups (e.g., wearing "pig tails" symbolizes being a little girl, whereas older girls often wear a "pony tail"; wearing dread locks is highly associated with Rastafarians; Sikhs and many Afghani men wrap their hair in turbans; "punks" dye their hair in bright colors). Hair is often used to communicate individuality, personal style (e.g., shaving a name or image into the haircut; coloring one shock of hair or decorating hair with beads or bows). For the military, individuality is out while uniformity is in. By making short hair the standard—crew cuts for men and above shoulder-length hair for women—the military greatly reduces visible individuality. For the same reasons, adornments are prohibited, such as nose rings, men's earrings, and visible or offensive tattoos. Similarly, even a new recruit's personal effects must be standardized; beds and belongings must be kept in exactly the same order. When all is said and done, the separation from civilian life leaves little of the individual. The only markers of it are the recruits' last names stitched onto their uniforms.

My Step-Grandson Anthony Before and After Military Boot Camp.

The first step in the rite of passage is thus complete—separation. Now it is time for the transitional stage to begin. At this stage, rites of passage of all different varieties have initiates undergo an ordeal while sequestered from the rest of society. *The more intense the ordeal, the more initiates feel bonded both to each other and to their new group when they emerge.* The ordeal is the transition phase, but it also produces camaraderie. For this reason, military recruits in boot camp are challenged physically (with exhausting workouts, marches, predawn exercises, etc.) as well as psychologically and emotionally (e.g., being humiliated by superiors who shout at them and chastise them publicly). For weeks, recruits are at the complete mercy and domination of their superiors. During boot camp they are, quite literally, torn into pieces as individuals and then melded back together as a group. In an interesting book detailing the boot camp experiences of a platoon of Marine recruits, Thomas Ricks (1997) begins by telling how the 36 young men he observed for ten weeks were transported many hours by bus to Parris Island, South Carolina, where Marine Basic Training occurs. They arrived after midnight to see the gate symbolized by a huge sign "PARRIS ISLAND: WHERE THE DIFFERENCE BEGINS." Instead of being led to bed, however, they were lined up by their drill sergeant, told to memorize their new unit number, stripped of their clothes and jewelry, and issued uniforms and bedding. Finally, they were given the famously short buzz haircuts as well as a predawn lesson on how to march as a group. The whole next day continued with their "disorientation" and "cultural indoctrination" because, as Ricks comments, "Before they can learn to fight, they must learn to be Marines" (1997: 37).

Boot camp strips the men of their individuality and makes them into complete team players; anyone who cannot put the team ahead of himself is not a good Marine because he cannot be fully trusted. Military boot camp, then, can and should be seen as a classic rite of passage; it is very intentional about transforming recruits who come from a society valuing the individual and individual freedoms into inseparable "buddies." Such separation from "normal" life and the intensity of their *common* experience produce strong feelings of *communitas* (bonding) toward other initiates and a strong appreciation of hierarchy toward their superiors. (However, you do not have to go to boot camp or a police academy to have similar experiences. The formula is largely the same: intense emotions during activities done in the company of others that produce group solidarity [Collins 2004; Dunbar 2010; Kitayama & Uskul 2011; Siegel 1999].)

Two of the most important characteristics soldiers must have are solidarity with peers and deference to authority. When this is accomplished, when civilians have transformed into fledgling soldiers, then the recruits pass into the third and final stage of the rite of passage: reincorporation. Those who have survived without quitting go through a public ceremony that their families may attend, and for which the new soldiers are given special "dress" uniforms. They have emerged from confinement and are now integrated into military life. They have transformed and, arguably most important, they have strong feelings of *belonging* to the military. The solidarity they feel with each other and with the greater institution of the military will be critical to their survival as soldiers deployed in combat. The emotions of living with a small cohort of buddies who, despite continual threat of attack, continue to depend upon one another for survival (trust), take this feeling of belonging to a new intensity. It is no wonder that reentry into civilian life for soldiers can feel so lonely (e.g., Shaw & Hector 2010), particularly when that reentry is not accompanied by rites of passage similar to their transition into military life.

People want to feel they belong; we are social creatures, after all. Bonds cemented during warfare are among the most intense we feel as human beings, perhaps second only to family bonds, so it is no wonder to me that many of the virtual ways we create community involve simulations of warfare. If you are an online gamer (and chances are pretty high that many readers are), then perhaps you can identify how you become a "gamer." Think about the games you most play. How did you become integrated into the games? How did you go from outsider to "gamer"? Almost certainly you went through some type of rite of passage, even if you skipped over the intense learning phase (the "ordeal"), by doing some research online about the game so that you could raise your level quickly. Let's take, for example, World of Warcraft, a war-simulation game and one of the most popular online games of all time. In order to play, you must pick the groups in which you want to integrate; in this game that means picking your "faction," or side, and "race," or allied group to the faction. You don't just do this mentally; you have to symbolize these choices through selecting and decorating your avatar, which is your online figure. If you are part of the Alliance faction, you could choose to be a human, a dwarf, or a gnome, for example; and if you desire to be part of the Horde faction, you would choose

Preparing an Avatar to Enter into World of Warcraft. When You Create an Avatar You Pay Attention to What You Want Your Avatar to Symbolize. Do You Pay as Much Attention to How *You* Symbolize Your Social Statuses? Why or Why Not?

to be a troll, goblin, or orc. You also have to choose a gender; so even this fictive world is divided up not only by sides in the conflict but also by gender. Then you get to customize your avatar based on the options available to your faction and race. You might choose a particular type of hair or tusk, for example. And then you must pick your name, which has to be unique. Much like with becoming a soldier, then, you take on a uniform with very limited variation but you are permitted a unique name. How do other players know your rank? In the military, this is symbolized via stripes, badges, and medals on the uniform. In World of Warcraft and other similar games, you wear your level of achievement next to your name. Level one is the lowest, and the highest level depends on the particular game; as players achieve the highest level, programmers are preparing the next levels of the game so that the best players stay interested.

Let's suppose that you have not learned via watching other players or by consulting online forums to find out more about the rules of the game (i.e., the way of life in this online cultural context). In that case, upon selecting and robing your avatar, you would then enter a beginner's space, a place to practice that is separate from the actual space where experienced players interact. Here, you can practice moving your avatar with computer controls and learn to interact with other players—only players who are from your side of the war, however. The computer program will help you learn the ropes and context by giving you tips. Of course, this is not an ordeal like boot camp, so the effect on your feelings of belonging will not be that strong, but you will begin to feel that you belong and that you know how this cultural context operates. That is the purpose of separation, to have you feel that you are now entering a new phase, a new reality, a new cultural context in which you cannot expect that you will behave as you did before entering it. In other words, you are preparing yourself psychologically as well as learning the special skills you'll need to integrate. In World of Warcraft and other similar games such as Call of Duty and Black Ops, the transition phase is the playing phase and it is full of emotion like any transition phase—fear, excitement, bonding, rage, and so on. Unlike boot camp, however, online games do not serve as ritual preparation for a transitional ordeal and reentry into society as a person socially integrated into a new group. Rather, a great appeal of online games is that what is typically transitional in other rituals of social integration can be infinitely extended in the gaming environment. You transition into the game but do not have to leave it for reentry into the greater society. This is probably one reason why, among many people, games become addicting. We all need belonging, and online games provide that feeling while simultaneously allowing us to be individuals as well as members of larger institutions.

Integrating into Schools, Universities and Jobs as Cultural Contexts

The first day of my daughter Sophie's school year always began with exactly the same ritual of integration. She'd put on the school uniform that she had ignored all summer, grab her backpack (which she had also ignored all summer), stuff in some school utensils (pens, lined paper [which she never used except for schoolwork], pencils, erasers, etc.) and head off to the campus with the postcard she'd received in the mail indicating which homeroom she had been assigned to for the year. In most cases, she'd have found out who else among her friends was assigned to the same homeroom in the week or so before classes began and would meet up with them on the first day. The bell would ring, symbolizing the end of non-school time and the beginning of the school day; this was followed by the teacher entreating students to be quiet and to find their seats. Once the room was quiet, the teacher would ritualistically welcome them back to school. Next, the teacher would turn on the closed-circuit television and the principal of the school would appear, also welcome the students, and begin the morning rituals of the Pledge of Allegiance, the national anthem,

Pledging Allegiance to the Nation...But Do They Understand?

and the school's alma mater. After all those steps were complete, the principal would give the announcements and perhaps introduce some other people to the students. Then the teacher would turn off the TV, turn to the students, and hand out a sheet outlining the rules of homeroom. The homeroom rules are just what I'm sure you have experienced or can imagine—a set of regulations laying out proper behavior and punishments for improper behavior. Students were not invited to participate in creating or modifying these rules but, nevertheless, had to sign off on them, as did their parents. After the class had finished going over the rules, Sophie and the others would march off to their first class of the day where this same ritual was performed. By the end of the day, she had visited some six classes and accumulated about six contracts that she and I would have to sign that evening. In addition, the school sent home another abundance of paperwork including emergency contact forms, applications for free or reduced-price lunch programs, and so on.

One of the nice things about this yearly ritual, at least to an anthropologist, was the fact that the rules were explicit. Most cultural contexts come with *implicit* rules that you are not taught outright; you have to learn them by observing others and by sometimes making mistakes, just as newborns do. But many of the norms governing school life—at least before you go on to college—are taught in black-and-white terms. Young children really need clear lines and have a hard time with ambiguity. The example of Hans wearing a tutu at Sophie's daycare mentioned earlier illustrated kids' discomfort with "in-betweenness." Given this discomfort, making many of the rules of conduct explicit seems appropriate for kids. Of course, there are a lot of other unstated expectations for behavior that children have to learn as well, so the ones they stuffed into their backpacks were just the beginning. For example, it's one thing to know to raise your hand when you want to respond to a question from the teacher (instead of jumping up and down or shouting, for instance); it's another thing to learn that raising your hand often might get you labeled as a "teacher's pet" and chastised by your fellow classmates. So, while I really did not like the yearly distribution of the "laws," I could also appreciate that this ritual, repeated each year in almost exactly the same way, did help young children integrate and reintegrate into school each year.

Schools are society's most deliberate educational institutions. As many social scientists have observed, however (e.g., Connolly 1998; Lopez 2003; Thorne 1993; Van Ausdale & Feagin 2001), they are not only about teaching reading, writing, and arithmetic. They socialize children into institutional life with its rules, roles (myriad social hierarchies), and regulations for time (class periods versus lunch and recess). Students come to identify with their schools over the years by their rituals and the sheer number of waking hours they spend there during the week. However, given that most elementary, middle, and high schools are publicly funded, they don't need to expend so much effort on marketing and branding themselves as do private schools. Private schools at the K–12 level and beyond, by contrast, typically invest a lot more energy into the social integration of students for very particular reasons: they market their brand and they also want alumni to financially support the schools. If students do not come out of schools identifying strongly with them, they are less likely to sponsor them later.

The more that privately funded schools market themselves based on their reputation, the more intense their integration rituals tend to be. The purpose is to create a community through exclusivity, one marked by symbols that nonmembers recognize but cannot access. All universities, much like schools in general, have their rites of passage. Think, for instance, of all the steps students (at least American ones) must take in order to gain entry into a university: taking the SAT exam, meeting with the school counselor, filling out applications, writing the personal essay, and visiting potential schools, among others. And universities

Florida International University Students and Fans Sporting the School's Brand (Symbols). How Did They Become Bonded?

celebrate similar rituals to mark the end of the student's transformation—commencement with all its pomp and circumstance. The really important phase for promoting student loyalty, however—not just to each other but to the university as an institution—is student life *during* the college years. This is the classic phase of transformation in the rite of passage, the "test," so to speak. The more intense colleges can make this phase, the more likely they are to have loyal alumni for life. So what do schools do? One thing is to create a brand for themselves. This involves selecting the school colors, mascot (symbol), alma mater, name and so on. They order and sell all these symbols of belonging, requiring everyone who represents the school officially (such as the president and higher administration, sports teams, etc.) to wear these symbols wherever they go. Universities and colleges also either reproduce traditions that have worked in the past, or they have to invent new ones that will work today and into the future. If you understand how schools generate feelings of belonging and loyalty ("spirit" or esprit d corps), you will have the tools you need to build belonging among the people in your life as well. The basic building blocks are emotionally charged time spent together during ritual activities and symbols that continuously remind members that they belong—and that they should continue practicing the rituals of belonging.

BEYOND FACE-TO-FACE: INTEGRATING INTO IMAGINED COMMUNITIES

For almost all of human life on Earth, people lived in very small communities, which anthropologists call bands. A typical band would consist of 20–40 people related to one another by birth or marriage. These were the classic face-to-face groups that our food foraging ancestors would live within during the whole course of their lives. Occasionally bands would meet up to hold ceremonies, share resources, and so on, but day-to-day life revolved around a small set of very close ties to a limited number of people (Allen 2008; Lee 1979). In these small social settings you should be able to see that it would not take much intentional effort to integrate babies into the band and for them, indeed for all band members, to have strong feelings of belonging. Constant day-to-day interaction would guarantee this and would also easily transmit the band's cultural knowledge from generation to generation. Individual members would still vary somewhat from each other, owing to their personalities, gender, and age, but culturally everyone would be very similar.

Starting about 10,000 years ago, a few peoples began cultivating the first crops and consequently settling in geographic areas for longer and longer periods of time; beforehand, bands were highly mobile, moving during the course of the year to find food resources. When people settled, and when other related changes in behavior took place (that we are still trying to understand), populations begin to grow above the small size of the typical band and even beyond the groupings of 100-150 people when bands periodically would meet up with each other. It is critical to understand that for the overwhelming majority of human existence on Earth, we lived as food foragers in very small bands within which we felt an incredibly strong social belonging (cultural comfort). However, just a few thousand years ago—a drop in the bucket of human time—our populations grew beyond the point where everyone in a society could know each other extremely well. Scholars studying this critical issue, most famously Robin Dunbar (1993, 2003, 2008), estimate that a profound change occurs when groups reach about 150 members. When our brains cannot keep track of all the members of our society, there is a decrease in the social pressures that operate informally to keep people in cultural alignment (as opposed to formal rules or government). This situation provokes a need to culturally innovate how to feel we belong to people with whom we will not have intense social contact (Barnard 2008; Dunbar & Barrett 2007; Dunbar 2010). What happens?

When everyone knows each other well, belonging is not a problem the society typically faces. People who grow up together with the same language, customs, expectations, and rituals become culturally comfortable with each other for reasons already explained here. Social solidarity is so tight that there is rarely room for breaking out of the society's particular mold. Among food foragers in band societies, people who did not conform either left to found their own new band, or they were expelled and had to find another band with which to live (Lee 1979). As the size of a society increases, however, individuals' belonging and conformity to social norms become increasingly difficult and take more effort. A very common "solution" to this problem across human history is to create what many social scientists refer to as "imagined" communities, a term that was coined quite a few years ago by a political scientist studying nations (Anderson 1991).

Benedict Anderson (1991) did not mean to imply that "imagined" communities were imaginary. Quite the contrary, they are very real groups. However, as Anderson explained, the ways in which people come to feel that we are members of very large groups—countries, in his case—differ from the feeling of belonging that arises when we interact directly with the people around us. We are not born knowing our nationality; just like so many other culturally specific aspects of our lives, we have to learn to feel that belonging. Anderson (and many others after him) argue that because we are never going to meet everyone who shares this feeling of membership, then the community is not a face-to-face community but one that exists in our mind—in our imaginations. We have *real* feelings of belonging but how is it we feel something truly in common with thousands or millions of other people whom we'll never actually meet? This is a terrific and important question that social scientists have been working hard to explain. Understanding how we learn culture in general, I believe, offers new insights into this curious phenomenon.

Let's begin by taking the exact same case that Anderson and others have worked so hard to explain: How do people who will never meet each other face-to-face, or even online, still learn to feel and assert that they are members of a country? We may be granted citizenship by being born in or to parents from a particular country, but that does not mean that we *feel* loyalty to that country and to other members of that country. There are rites of passage for people who change their citizenship; these are called naturalization ceremonies and involve people collectively affirming their allegiance to their new nation. What else produces *loyal* citizens, in this case among those who are native born? You probably have never thought about how you came to see yourself as a member of your country, but it is time to think about it now. It is not simple, nor is this feeling learned quickly. There are scholars studying how and when children begin to feel a sense of nationality (e.g., Scourfield et al. 2006). The research is ongoing and not yet conclusive but indicates that kids learn obvious, visual "embodied" identities earliest, such as gender (e.g., Bussey & Bandura 1999; Durkin 2005; Jahoda & Lewis 1988; Lancy 2010; LeVine & New 2008; Maccoby 2002; Martin et al. 2002; Paley 1984; Rogoff 2003; Warin 2000; Whiting & Edwards 1988; Wenger 2008) and race (Aboud 1988; Barrett 2007; Hirschfeld 2005; Van Ausdale & Feagin 2001). More subtle social status differences such as kinship, class, rank, and nationality that are not necessarily apparent visually take a while longer to learn (e.g., Toren 1988). That makes sense because in order to understand the concept of nationality, for example, children need to understand geography as well as the fact that there are different peoples in the world; that is, they need to be able to perceive beyond their own experiences. Nationality and nationalism take quite a long time and quite a bit of effort to understand and to feel, but nationalism-promoting techniques used around the world are pretty similar.

Before thinking about how *you* have gained feelings of belonging to your nation, let's take the case of what leaders did in the past to cultivate allegiance among people who had just been unified into a country. Italy is a good case in point. Italy became a nation-state in 1861 after long battles pitting different regions against each other. Almost no "Italians" at that time spoke Italian; they spoke a wide variety of regional dialects. People felt loyalties to their towns and the regions those towns belong to. No wonder, then, that after Italy was unified and its new government established, the famous Italian leader Massimo d'Azeglio remarked to Parliament: "We have made Italy; now we have to make Italians" (Hobsbawm & Kertzer 1992: 4).

Babies may be conferred national citizenship upon birth in most countries (other countries confer it based on ethnic background or "blood" ties), but this does not mean they understand what a nation is, nor does it make them feel they belong. Think now about how *you* were encouraged to feel nationalism toward your country. Where and how was your national identity cultivated? Think about those school rituals of saying the Pledge of Allegiance to the national flag, singing the national anthem, and dressing up in your country's colors on national holidays. Perhaps you took a field trip to visit statues of heroes or other monuments, and what about all those years you studied national history? Outside of school you probably went to sports events that often began with the playing of the national anthem too. Did you ever wonder why? What do local sporting events have to do with national patriotism? And, if ever you attended a parade on Independence Day, watching wave after wave of marching band and military group go by carrying national (and state and local) flags, did you ever see them as symbols of belonging? Thinking back now, you should be able to recognize these as intended to build your sense of belonging to your country— though you probably did not see them as anything but normal growing up. And there are much more subtle ways we become members of our national imagined communities as well, for example, weather maps often just provide our own country and ignore the surrounding countries and world maps in our history books tend to place our country in the center even if that means the continents have to be split.

By now, you are hopefully beginning to appreciate the fact that generating emotional ties to imagined communities like nations takes a lot of work; it does not just happen but has to be cultivated. With effort, children do learn effectively from all these symbols and rituals and feel connected to people they will never meet (Barrett 2007; Jahoda 1963). I remember when my daughter was in about second grade and I asked her what "pledge" and "allegiance" were. She had no idea what they meant, but she could certainly say the Pledge of Allegiance and she knew full well that the "Star-Spangled Banner" was the name of the national anthem and referred to the flag of the United States. When she had just started fourth grade, the World Trade Towers and Pentagon were attacked on September 11, 2001. Immediately thereafter, the elementary school she attended, as well as schools all around Miami where we lived, began displaying flags ever more prominently. The children held parades in which they waved American flags; parents hung flags from their homes and cars. It was a time of enormous national emotion, grief, and affirmation. In Miami, the patriotic sentiments were even clearer because only a year before there had been a huge competition for Miamians' loyalties. A young Cuban boy, Elián González, was involved in a custody battle between his father, who wanted to return him to Cuba, and his mother's family, who wanted him to stay (his mother had died while bringing Elián by boat to the United States). During the months of the custody battle the two sides used national symbols—the Cuban flag (ironically, to symbolize that the boy should stay in the United States) and the American flag (also ironically, symbolizing he should return)—to communicate their positions. That year, cars in Miami bore symbols of people's passionate divide, one half flying Cuban flags and the other half flying U.S. flags.

National flags, pledges, anthems, history museums, monuments, parades, myths, heroes, and even national trees and flowers are all important symbols and rituals that foster our feelings of belonging to large "imagined" communities. We might even translate those feelings into actual behaviors by fighting for our country or, when abroad, assisting fellow citizens who need help even though we don't know them. We might help them merely because they share the same nationality, not because we are obligated to assist them. These symbols and rituals, however, are still only the most obvious ways that nationalism is taught and promoted. There are many others that we probably never think about. For example, the fact that most countries declare a particular language (or languages) as official, and insist that it be taught in the nation's schools, helps to literally bring about common communication. This is what Italy did after its unification in 1861. Countries typically also develop a national educational curriculum so that all children have common lessons in history, language, civics, and so on. When people around us use the same language we do not feel shut out; when we are around people using a different language, however, we typically feel we do not belong, that we are outsiders. There are other common ways of thinking and behaving that typically mark people who come from the same country. It is very hard to "see" them unless you travel outside your country and then try to identify who is from your country and who is not. You'll recognize people by language and accent as well as by their clothing styles, foods they eat, books or phones they carry, body language, etc. What other cues tell you that you are among your own? The next time you have the opportunity, pay attention. How close do people from your country stand when they are talking to one another? How close do people from other countries stand? What gestures are common and what would be strange or even obscene? What television programs, films, and websites do people speak about and why? Who do people call to the "founding fathers" or "mothers" of their nation? All of these and much more contribute to people's *feelings* of cultural commonality that a country—in which most members will never meet each other—needs people to feel, or else the nation could fracture. And these also contribute to our sense that we have only *one* culture. What we truly have are some cultural comforts that extend widely across cultural contexts (such as spoken and body language, values, unstated assumptions that affect our behavior, etc.) and others that are more regional and local (dialects, foods, manners, etc.). Politicians work hard to promote national identities in us and to encourage us to place our national identification above our regional, local, and even family loyalties, but in our lives we socially integrate into many, many cultural spaces and groups. They wish us to think we have "one" culture when in fact we move seamlessly from cultural context to cultural context.

Another factor that confuses our ideas about culture and nation is that we often claim one national culture yet most countries have diverse populations (of course, to varying degrees and of varying types—ethnic, religious, linguistic, etc.). Such diversity can make it more difficult to cultivate national sentiments, since these identities often compete against other forms of belonging. Countries created by colonial powers who erected national borders across long-standing ethnic or religious lines often have difficulty getting people to cherish the nation over their own group. Iraq and Afghanistan are good contemporary examples. Countries that receive large influxes of immigrants and/or refugees, particularly when those influxes arrive very rapidly, also find that their national identity can feel threatened; these countries often react by expelling the newcomers, limiting their access to resources, or responding to them with outright xenophobia and attacks, both verbal and physical. The rise in anti-immigrant sentiment within the United States and many European countries reflects some of the strains of building and maintaining huge imagined communities, full of cultural diversity, under the banner of commonality and community. It is odd but understandable that the phenomenon of people seeking entry into your country can stir up both feelings of pride (the feeling that my country must be great because people want to come in) and fear (that the newcomers might change my way of life).

Ever since our ancestors started living in groups exceeding about 150 members, we have been finding cultural techniques to feel commonality with those whom we will never meet or know well, yet who we consider part of our imagined communities. No matter how many imagined communities we belong to, we still usually feel closest to those with whom we have real, sustained contact. Face-to-face contact still seems to be best, but electronic or virtual contact arguably generates some strong attachments as well. Intensity of interaction is important to belonging. Think about this point by reflecting a moment on your experiences with Facebook, Twitter, or another social networking medium. How many people do you really keep up with or interact with every week? Yes, you may have tweeted or friended a lot of people and be able to access their information, but how many of them do you truly check in with weekly? Would you be surprised to learn that, on average, people only interact regularly with about seven of their friends, even though they have around 120? That is what a researcher at Facebook found. One hundred and twenty is close to the number that social scientists argue has been the upper limit on face-to-face communities since we were food foragers (Miller 2012). Once populations exceed 150, we begin to create institutions to organize them; it is just too hard to keep everyone feeling they belong (and to keep everyone within the rules) when our groups get bigger.

Conclusion

This chapter has explored how throughout their lives people continue to be integrated into many social groups or communities, even as adults. We are truly fortunate that we can still forge new relationships despite getting older, that we can find and feel belonging with other people, even people with whom we do not think we share much in common. Because of our neuroplasticity we are able to continue learning throughout our lives, and therefore we can integrate into new cultural contexts. However, given that culture is about comfort we have to be willing and able to go through some discomforts that often accompany the processes of integration. That takes work, both cognitive work to build new neural pathways in our brains and emotional work to overcome the inertia of comfort. The less we challenge our established ways of doing things, and the less we break out of our established groups, the more difficult it becomes for us to accommodate newness. We know this is true from our own experiences, and now it is affirmed by scientists' understanding of our brains' architecture. Once routines build neural superhighways in our brains, it's pretty hard to divert us onto side roads.

Diverting onto the mind's side roads is exactly the experience that many, if not most, immigrants and refugees have when they arrive in a new land. Recall that the brain goes through two major periods of building huge numbers of new connections during early childhood and adolescence. That means that after this second period, in particular, it becomes more and more difficult—but never impossible—to retrain the brain. Yet most people migrate as adults, and they migrate during their prime working and family-raising years. No matter how much they might want to learn new languages, customs, and gestures, their brains are just not as plastic as they were during their adolescence and infancy. It takes much more effort to reconfigure their brains' architecture and, unfortunately, they often do not have the luxury of time to devote to those integration processes. Some countries such as Canada are quite understanding of these huge challenges for newcomers and offer them time and resources to adapt. Other countries such as the United States basically expect immigrants and refugees to adapt with minimal, if any, assistance

(Bloemraad 2006). It should not be surprising, then, that new immigrants tend to gravitate to neighborhoods where their compatriots live, and where they will not have to learn the new cultural knowledge immediately. Where I have lived in Miami, it is possible to arrive from a Spanish-speaking country and never learn English, since so much of daily life is conducted in Spanish. Latin Americans integrate more easily this way since there is much less for them to *have* to learn upon arrival. They also reinvigorate Miami's Latin American and Caribbean cultural comforts by speaking in Spanish, making their comfort foods, practicing their home country rituals of belonging, and so on. They reinforce their own cultural comforts, which, however inadvertently, often discomfort outsiders. Such are cultural borderlands—places where those used to live in the majority may suddenly find themselves marginalized. The next time you have a chance to spend time in one of these borderlands where you are an outsider, put on your *culture as comfort* lenses to see it with different eyes. Embrace your discomforts. And the next time you encounter a recent immigrant, put yourself in that person's shoes by imagining that you are the newcomer rather than he. Imagine that you feel awkward or even stupid because you don't understand what people are saying and you have to have your child translate for you at the bank or grocery store, for example. Remember that children's minds are much more plastic, so they learn quickly and usually will adapt fine; but it can be, and often is, very shameful for parents to have to depend on them, since it reverses the normal parent–child role in the new cultural context (Warner & Srole 1976). I return to issues regarding immigrants, particularly as they relate to generations and integration, in Chapter 6.

You do not need to live among immigrants to use the knowledge you have gained in this chapter. The key thing to recall is that people desire to belong socially. We want to feel comfortable and accepted in our social settings and groups. We are a social species; until very recently it would have been highly unusual, if not bizarre, for someone to spend significant time alone. Being human, though, means that we acclimate into groups at an early age and thus are not typically aware of the adaptation processes. Often, we don't even realize that we are a part of these communities; that is, until we step beyond our cultural comfort zones. Now *you* know this much more consciously and that could make a huge difference since you also know that belonging is not that difficult to create. The critical ingredient is rituals, most importantly rites of passage. Rites of passage help people bond with the communities they belong to, or wish to belong to. They facilitate changes in people's statuses; people start out with one status (such as outsider) and by the end of the ritual they have attained a new, socially recognized status (such as insider or member). To be most effective, such rituals need to have a very powerful, meaningful transition phase, and afterward the neophytes need to be acknowledged as having achieved a new, improved status. The best rites of passage produce bonds that last a lifetime. Fraternity and sorority rituals for inducting new members (often referred to as hazing, although this word has humiliating and dangerous connotations that are not necessary to bonding) typically fall into this category. Initiates start out as candidates and end up lifelong fraternity brothers or sorority sisters. In many societies, rites of passage used to transform children into adults also generate tight bonds, especially when initiates go through the rituals together (Turner 1967, 1977).

Unfortunately, in many contemporary societies such as the United States, there are no really clear rites of passage into adulthood. There are many rituals and symbols for achieving adulthood (such as obtaining a driver's license, graduating from high school or college, and getting a first job or buying a first home), but none of these is sufficient for clearly marking the transition into adulthood. Perhaps this explains why adolescence is so extended and also often fraught with anxiety. Statuses that are unclear tend to provoke discomfort. And that brings me back to immigrants. When does an immigrant transition into a full-fledged member of the new society, an "American" in the U.S. case? Does that happen after attending the naturalization ceremony? I don't think so, in most cases. That ritual confers a right of citizenship, but not necessarily the sentiment of belonging. Can immigrants or refugees belong completely to the new context? How much effort must they put forth to be awarded acceptance? What about their children? Certainly children born and raised completely in the new country are full-fledged members of that society—aren't they? Now that we have discovered how important it is for people to feel they belong and for rituals to promote those feelings—both among initiates and among those who receive them—it

Initiating New Sorority Sisters: Those Humiliated Today Will Bond Together and Delight in Hazing Next Year's Initiates.

Does Taking the Oath of Citizenship Make an Immigrant a Full Member of Society? If Not, What Criteria Qualify? Does Legal Status Confer Social Acceptance?

is truly time for all of us to examine how we aid and also prevent people from joining us.

Who are the people you know who have not been welcomed into the communities you inhabit? What have you done and/or what do you do to keep them out, intentionally or not? What do others do? Why not think about rituals that will include them? Are there fractures in your family? What kinds of experience (i.e., common rituals) might pull you together? Is there stress and/or dissention where you work? Do your coworkers divide into factions more than they collaborate as colleagues? If so, is there any effort at your job to bring people together?

Is there any effort to integrate people into the team, into new social statuses that everyone recognizes? If not, what might you do to promote cohesion and thereby improve your work life? These are all applications of understanding culture as belonging and comfort. To reiterate a theme running through this book, we *do* culture. Nevertheless, we think that we *have* culture, and that misperception debilitates us when we most need to emphasize our creative, innovative, problem-solving abilities. Now is a good time for you to demonstrate your abilities to heal wounds dividing the groups that are important in your life.

PLANNED PAUSE 4-1

HELPING BRIDGE CULTURAL DISCOMFORTS

Instructions: *In this Planned Pause you will describe a situation familiar to you in which some people feel culturally discomforted. This could be at your workplace, in your school, within your family or community. After writing a paragraph describing this situation and explaining how it causes cultural discomforts to some people involved, write a second paragraph discussing **two** ideas you have for helping those discomforted feel culturally included. Make sure to utilize the material discussed in the book to this point, particularly that in this chapter on the building blocks of belonging.*

Explore the **Concept** on
mysearchlab.com

Encountering "Others"

You've got to be taught to hate and fear,
You've got to be taught from year to year,
It's got to be drummed in your dear little ear.
You've got to be carefully taught!

You've got to be taught to be afraid
Of people whose eyes are oddly made,
And people whose skin is a different shade,
You've got to be carefully taught.

You've got to be taught before it's too late,
Before you are six or seven or eight,
To hate all the people your relatives hate,
You've got to be carefully taught!
You've got to be carefully taught!

—By Richard Rodgers and Oscar
Hammerstein II, "You've Got To Be Carefully Taught"

Up to this point in the book you've been learning about how we acquire culture, how this produces in us feelings of belonging and comfort with those people who *do* culture similarly to ourselves. Yet from the tiny worlds in which we live as babies—interacting with a relatively small number of people on a regular basis—we somehow have to learn to navigate the really populated and problematic social spaces of the wider world. In particular, we have to deal with people who are dissimilar from ourselves and our social groups. That is, we encounter "others." What are the consequences of encountering others for our senses of belonging and comfort? Answering that question is the primary task of this chapter. Additionally, the chapter addresses the seemingly contradictory fact that as we learn culture we become *both* insiders and outsiders; that is, as we become increasingly similar to our people and our way of life, we also, and necessarily, grow at least somewhat dissimilar from others. This is one of the greatest paradoxes of being a cultural species, an important paradox, yet one that few think about day to day. Now you are going to face it straight on. How well you understand this great paradox will likely have enormous consequences for you, given that you are more likely than any generation before yours to interact with people who are different from you. How you encounter "others" matters.

From Chapter 2 you learned that when babies are learning culture their brains package prior experiences into shortcuts, what many psychologists refer to as "schemas." Schemas are bundles of information that pass along the brain's web of neurons. The microrituals of everyday life for infants are full of schemas, from bathing and diaper-changing to smiling and sitting up. As babies interact with their caregivers, they have to learn how to coordinate their muscles at the same time that they are learning to interpret the caregivers' facial and body gestures, spoken language, and movements—just to name a few of the many things we have to learn. It's a *lot* to have to calculate at the same time, so, as explained earlier in the book, the brain takes shortcuts to preserve its calculating power for the most pressing needs. Whenever a new encounter appears similar to an encounter already experienced, the baby's brain automatically jumps to the schema stored in memory and applies it subconsciously. This saves a lot of energy, and energy is what the brain eats up in huge quantities, so saving energy is very important to the baby's survival.

If energy were infinite in people, then a baby's brain would work much more like computers do. Artificial intelligence has come a long way in recent decades, but computers still "learn" by running massive calculations over and over. Sound odd? Well, let's return to the case of Watson, the IBM computer that beat the top-ranked players on *Jeopardy!* The computer won, but it won because it had huge amounts of computing power to apply to one task at a time—that of figuring out the answer. It wasn't concerned about maxing its capacity. The human brain, by contrast, had to evolve when energy resources were scarce. So when Watson was faced with a question such as identifying the title of a song from a string of lyrics, it searched and searched billions of documents in its memory to find associations between the lyrical phrase and song titles; massive computing power enabled it to do these calculations in a fraction of a second so it could answer correctly. But when faced with a question that requires creativity, such as a play-on-words, Watson's "brain" was challenged not only to comb its databases for information related to this topic but also to associate this information with culture-specific knowledge. The computer failed at that second task miserably. For instance, in response to the clue, "From the Latin for 'end,' this is where trains can also originate," Watson responded, "finis" (a correct response because "finis" means "end" in Latin) but missed the play on words embedded in the winning response, "terminus."

Well, humans do something similar with our minds and we, like Watson, also make mistakes. Sometimes our brains jump to the wrong conclusions; we make bad associations between pieces of information. Babies' brains do that too. People, both young and old, however, are most likely to make these mistakes when encountering people who do not fit neatly into our cultural expectations. We subconsciously expect them to do "normal" things that people we share culture with do—and when they don't, we get confused. Only when people *appear* different to us (as in wearing clothing, jewelry, or other decorations we do not use), then our brains say, "Oh, this person is different so I cannot expect her to act like everyone I know." This is one of the reasons why marking our identities very distinctively, as in the way we dress or model our hair, is so important to other people's ability to read us correctly. As you become more mindful about how you *do* culture day in and day out, then you have more power over the messages you send to others through your appearance.

As you now know, culture is a word that refers to the ways we order our reality, of creating and imposing categories and rules onto our evolutionary flexibility. Since people participate in these processes of creating, reproducing, and even changing our cultural order, we not only are vested in it, but we understand our way to be normal. This is why we

This Photo Depicts Highland Peruvians Wearing the Characteristic Dress of Their Communities. It Demonstrates Vividly How People Use Dress to Mark Themselves as Members of a Group ("Us") and as Different from Others ("Them"). Imagine, However, if People Did *Not* Dress Differently. What Other Ways Do People Distinguish their Group from Another?

all become ethnocentric as we learn culture; it's inevitable—at least until we are exposed to "others." However, the cultural categorization processes that identify "others" outside of our comfort zones are the very same ones that mark social distinctions *within* our cultural comfort zones. That is because there are social distinctions *within* as well as *across* different cultural groups. Therefore, as babies, we learn the skills of both identifying with and versus other people. In other words, to know who *we* are, we need to know who we are *not*.

HOW SOCIAL DISTINCTIONS ARISE

There are so many ways that people differ from one another today that it can be very hard to get a grasp on which distinctions have been most important to human existence unless we take a very long look at human life. If today we differentiate ourselves from others around the world through our "identities" such as nationality, religion, race, sexual orientation, occupation, club membership, or level of education, which of these, if any, have been used from time immemorial? Can understanding how the earliest peoples of the world distinguished themselves from one another help us to understand what we do now and why we do it? I am a firm believer that this type of comparison is very helpful but, as I mention later, it is important to be a bit skeptical of making comparisons when the information is not perfect.

For many, many generations until some 10,000 years ago, all members of our species and all previous human species living on Earth were food foragers. What is a food forager? You may be more familiar with the term "hunter-gatherers," which is frequently used as a synonym for food foragers. So, although this will not be a Planned Pause, take a moment and

Don't Be Fooled By Your First Impressions of this Photo. What Does the Coke Bottle Truly Represent? It is Very Easy to Misinterpret.

think about what you know, or at least think you know, about food foragers and where you recall getting this information.

Chances are unless you are a History Channel, National Geographic, or NOVA enthusiast, or a student of anthropology, you have had little to no exposure to food foraging as the way of life followed by all of our ancestors—except that which the film industry has used to entertain us with in such movies as *Clan of the Cave Bear*, *10,000 B.C.*, or *The Gods Must Be Crazy*. If you've seen those movies or others like them, you've been watching fiction. They are important examples of how easy it is to make ethnocentric conclusions about our ancestors and about human nature in general. We do this by applying to food foragers our unstated assumptions about human nature taken from how we live today. A perfect example of this is the Coke bottle in *The Gods Must Be Crazy*. It is about the so-called Bushmen of the Kalahari Desert in southern Africa (they do not use that name traditionally to identify themselves) who, as is true for food foragers, gather foods and hunt prey to sustain themselves while moving from location to location depending on resources. Even living in the desert, these people find the resources they need until one day, a Coke bottle is inexplicably tossed out from a plane overhead and lands where men are hunting. The Coke bottle represents a very contemporary assumption (and the foundational idea behind the field of economics) that *all* resources are scarce. Since people have infinite wants but resources are scarce, we have to compete against each other to satisfy all human needs. In this film, the bottle arrives and unlike all the Bushmen's other resources, it is unique. Watch the film and see what happens, but watch it realizing that the film uses the "primitive" Bushmen to make statements about human nature. These assumptions need to be questioned, not readily accepted. Anthropologists studying a variety of food-foraging peoples systematically—including the Bushmen—have been better at figuring out what they can teach us about our ancestors more generally. The rub is that people living as food foragers in the 20th century largely survived by moving to very remote climates like deserts and jungles where other peoples left them alone. Those difficult environments would not be the same as where food foragers lived before. Up until only a few thousand years ago, all people were food foragers and lived in almost every corner of the Earth.

What do we know about food foragers, and how does this help us understand learning to see "us" versus "them"? I will talk a bit about the first part of this question and then spend much more time on the more difficult second half. What we know about food foragers in general is often referred to as the early human model (Allen et al. 2008). Throughout almost all of human existence—dating back to our ancestors even before modern humans evolved a few hundred thousand years ago—people lived daily life in the company of a few dozen people. As mentioned before, anthropologists refer to these small groups as bands (not to be confused with tribes, which are much larger groups and appear only after people start producing food). Band members would be related by birth or by marriage. A typical band would be a couple of siblings, their children, and their grandchildren, for example. People lived in small groups because they moved to find resources. Once they found them, they would stay there until the resources became harder to find, and then they would move again. They would move with the food seasons, shifting from one food resource (such as nuts, fruits, and game) as it became available and then on to another resource. It wasn't that food itself was scarce; it was plentiful but bands could not stay in one location forever or they would exhaust the resources.

A Hazda Child with Her Mother in the Company of Other Band Members. The Hazda, Living in Tanzania, are One of Only a Few Peoples Worldwide Who Still Food Forage. Imagine this Child's Ways of Learning Culture. Similar to Children Whom You Know or Not?

So what would life be like in a band of a couple dozen people? When you think about this question, focus on the fact that in bands *everyone would know everyone else extremely well*. Relationships would be, literally, face-to-face. In fact, people could grow up, live, and die with the same individuals. As you think about this type of life it may or may not appeal to you (probably depending on how well you get along with members of your own family!). Try not to let your mind go in that direction. Instead, keep it focused on what living in this type of group would mean for *feeling a sense of belonging*, for feeling comfortable with the people. If you think as I do, then you probably will come to the conclusion that for food foragers belonging is not an issue because all babies would be born into the group and quickly absorb its cultural patterns. In fact, studies of food foragers today show that babies are frequently cared for by other band members, not just their mothers, although they usually are nursed on demand by their mothers (Hewlett & Lamb 2005a: 15; Hrdy 2009; LeVine & New 2008). That means that babies would learn to read other band members' faces and intentions (introduced earlier in the book as theory of mind) very early on in their childhoods. In a band with only a few dozen people to get to know and, presumably, people whose behaviors and beliefs are not only patterned but highly uniform, infants would encounter a great environment in which to learn culture quickly. Some of you who are familiar with educational theories of how children learn might make the connection between what I am describing and Vygotsky's "zone of proximal development" (1978). Vygotsky, a

An Elder From the Acjachemen (A-ha-che-men) Nation, a Native American Group From Southern California, Captivates His Audience with a Story. Imagine How the Children Are Learning Theory of Mind This Way.

famous Russian psychologist, argued that children learn by being close to people who are more skilled at doing something; the children watch them perform this activity and then try it out with the teacher right there to guide them. In food-foraging bands, the teachers could be adults, but they are just as likely to be other children since in small bands children would have played across different ages and helped care for one another.

Without television, telephones, the Internet, and other non-face-to-face forms of communication, our food-foraging ancestors perfected face-to-face communication and cultural learning by telling stories around a fire, working together in gathering, hunting, and cooking activities, and engaging in play (Allen et al. 2008; Hewlett & Lamb 2005b). Some argue that beyond entertainment and the passing on of cultural beliefs and knowledge, storytelling emphasizes learning about and understanding characters' intentions and orientations (Dunbar 2008) and that this understanding, in turn, would help young children develop their own theory of mind (their ability to understand others' points of view) quickly. Reading storybooks and telling stories today probably serves the same purpose, but watching videos and thumbing through books is arguably different than sitting with everyone you know and hearing people take turns spinning long, complex tales day after day.

At this point I hope you agree with me that among food foragers, belonging and the cultural comforts that come with it would have been very intense. This does not mean there wouldn't be some individuals who would not fit well within their bands; people have personalities as well as cultural comforts, and there will always be some basis for personality conflicts as well as cultural misfits—but when this would occur among bands the individual would split off and join another band (Kelly 2000; Hrdy 2009). For the overwhelming majority of band members, however, belonging was assured.

The question to ask now, and which will consume the rest of the chapter, is, What does learning to feel "us" ultimately teach us about differentiating between "us" and "them"? The song from the famous musical *South Pacific* about prejudice quoted at the beginning of this chapter speaks to this issue. As we create "we," we simultaneously create "they." How does this work among food foragers? Examining these simultaneous processes of group cohesion *and* distinctiveness among food foragers is very helpful for explaining cultural diversity. Food foragers might have all hunted and gathered their food, but that does not mean they shared the same language, traditions, dress, rites of passage, and so on. In fact, living with just a small group of people would facilitate cultural diversification of bands from one another. Yet bands would not be completely isolated either; studies of bands show that occasionally they would gather together during the year for rituals, to find marriage partners, and so on. During these times their numbers would increase to 100 or 200 people (Allen et al. 2008; Dunbar 1993). Imagine what this would be like. You would be excited to see people whom you had not seen for quite some time, but you might also be a bit nervous when encountering people you didn't know very well. Young children who were unfamiliar with new faces would be particularly anxious in this situation.

Now it is really hard to know for sure how these gatherings generated in people sentiments of "us" versus "them," but it is very easy to imagine the emotions of such encounters. One thing is certain—you would definitely know who were members of your band and who were not. Your mind, always drawn to newness, to what is unfamiliar, would be attentive to how the others *differed from your people.* You would think, how are they different? What do they say, do, or think that differs from us? Our categorical minds work this way, so you cannot really help but think in categories—especially since, as a food forager, you would not encounter a lot of differences to study within your band. When the bands would gather, however, your mind would be kept busy comparing and contrasting—your way versus their way; your speech versus their speech—the ones you don't understand. Your people's jewelry, clothing, and body decorations versus the ways they decorate themselves. Your mind would translate this subconsciously into "we are 'normal' and they are 'different'."

The lesson to take away from this scenario is that such gatherings of bands would stimulate thinking about *differences between groups (bands)*, even if it occurred subconsciously. Young children would be exceptionally attuned to figuring all of this out. With multiple band gatherings producing 100–200 people, however, it would still be possible to get to know everyone or almost everyone. These are still face-to-face situations, but they represent the human numerical upper limit. As described before, this "Dunbar number" of 150 social relationships is about as many as any human being can manage. Should it be surprising to find that the same number is, roughly, the population of these multiband get-togethers? And is it surprising that during these events people, for many millennia, would be learning the basics of distinguishing between "us" and "them"? Scholars who study these very processes of what we now typically call group "identity" suggest that distinctiveness would surely have been felt in subtle, dialect-like differences in people's language (Boyd & Richerson 2006; Dunbar 2004, 2008, 2010). That is, the different bands would be able to understand each other but they would notice differences. Given that bands would spend most of the year apart, there would be a lot of opportunity for them to invent their own new words, terms, and expressions. For similar reasons, there probably would also have been differences in the ways that bands would perform rituals, tell stories, clothe and decorate themselves, and so on. In short, people at these multiband gatherings would be similar enough to feel highly comfortable with each other, but just dissimilar enough to feel that there were differences as well. All this comparing and contrasting would produce shades of distinctiveness or "otherness." Bands that would meet up periodically would be the closest outsiders to each other's band, while bands with members no one in those bands knew would be more distant "outsiders," especially if their language (or dialect), dress, and customs were very different. And those differences could, occasionally, spark conflicts as they do among all peoples. However, there is great debate over whether or not conflicts would escalate into wars among food-foraging bands (Bowles 2009; Kelly 2000, 2005) or whether conflicts resulted more in people just picking up with certain band members and leaving (Layton 2008).

It is critical to note here that what I have been describing—and what reflects our understanding of the topic to date—is how for many, many thousands of years people used the same technology to meet their dietary needs (food foraging) but still developed different languages, diets, rituals, beliefs, and so on. Yet, and this is just as important, *differences did not become the basis for some bands dominating others*. There were differences, and people would favor their group because learning culture inevitably causes us all to become ethnocentric (see our group as normal), but this did not produce ranking among bands. As far as we know, not only was there no hierarchy among bands in which, for example, a band would control resources other bands could access, there were also minimal status differences among members within bands (such as leaders or wealthier individuals). Rather, food foraging is a highly egalitarian lifestyle in which status differences are minimized. That is, there is evidence from anthropological studies among food foragers to show that when there were occasions for *individuals* to try to shine above other members of the band, they were put back in their equal place alongside others through joking, ridicule, avoidance, or similar techniques (e.g., Lee 1972; Marshall 1961). The group, the band, was much more important than any one person. Any individual who threatened the group by trying to cheat or get ahead had to be checked.

Today, differences between groups are often (if not almost always) used to rank groups against each other. For example, we speak about "developed" countries versus "less developed" or "developing" countries and these are clearly ranked. By showing how *for most of human existence people made group distinctions without turning those into rankings*, I hope you can see that inequality is *not* human nature. Human nature, if there is such a thing, is much more about cooperation than conflict (Boyd & Richerson 2006; Bowles & Gintis 2011; de Waal 2009). When we compare ourselves using the appropriate measuring

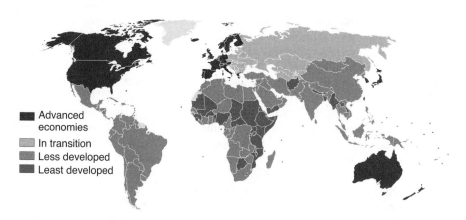

FIGURE 5.1 Typical Map Highlighting "Advanced" Versus "Less Developed" Countries. Note How It Visually Communicates a Global Hierarchy among Nations and, Thus, of Peoples Competing over Collaborating.

stick we see this. When we compare appropriately how we live today against food foragers, we find out that how we live today is the *exception*, not the rule, in human life on Earth. When we compare humans against other similar primate mammals, we find out that we are *more* cooperative than they are (Layton 2008). When we look at human societies today and see wars and conflicts aplenty, or when we read about Darwin's "law" of evolution as the survival of the fittest, we just assume that human nature is to compete and that the most aggressive people win (survival of the fittest). Yet this is a very slanted perspective. Yes, we humans are very different from one another, but for most of our existence differences did not produce hierarchies. Recently, however, we have been conditioned to believe people are more competitive than cooperative. Today there is certainly a lot of evidence for conflict—just watch the news. (Remember, however, that the news focuses on exceptional events over normative ones.)

THE INTERNAL LINES THAT DIVIDE ALL HUMAN GROUPS

So among food foragers we see the building blocks of all distinctions, of all feelings of "us" and "them." Band members would feel a very strong "us" among themselves. When bands meet up, they could compare themselves against the other bands (i.e., band–band differentiation). What about *inside* a band? People today not only distinguish ourselves by our group versus your group, but we differentiate within groups (such as by gender, race, age, religion, etc.). Going back in human history, did food-foraging bands also have internal differences like these? In other words, we can imagine that food foragers experience many "ties that bind," but do they also have "lines that divide"? Well, answering that question is a key to understanding how food foragers differ from most people living today. There are two very important parts of my response, which I ask you to pay close attention to because they are likely to be outside your experience and comfort zone.

First, food foragers—*like all peoples everywhere*—make distinctions within their groups based on kin (family/non-family), gender and generation (the latter refers to age or, more accurately, level of maturity, as in child versus adult). Even though all peoples make these distinctions, exactly *how* these distinctions are manifested varies among food foragers just like they do cross-culturally among societies today. That is, all societies differentiate between males and females; but in some societies, for example, men cover their heads whereas in others women cover their heads. The *way* people distinguish between male and female varies, but not the fact that gender is an important social category that all peoples recognize. Thus, regardless of being a food forager or a suburbanite today, young children learn to distinguish between males and females and learn this around the same time developmentally. Another key distinction all human societies make is generation. In a book of this length, I do not have enough space to explain in great detail how different food foraging peoples differentiate between kin and non-kin nor between different generations (that is, people living in the same group but located at different stages in the life cycle). Suffice it to say that all peoples recognize that children have different abilities and responsibilities than adults do, but exactly when children transition into adulthood varies enormously, as do the rites of passage associated with this transition. In most societies, if you have not gone through a rite of passage into adulthood then you cannot marry and are also denied other social rights afforded only to adults. And in terms of seniority in adulthood, you might think that it would lead to leadership positions, but among food foragers there are no people recognized as leaders. To the contrary, although there *are* differences (as with any group of people) in individuals' intelligence, personalities, and ability to tell stories and to hunt or gather, these do not become the basis for determining leadership. Rather, any individuals' tendencies to stand out from the rest of the band are discouraged because bands emphasize equality among members—not sameness, but status equality.

This leads me to the second major part of my response to the question about whether or not food foragers have lines that divide them. The lines of gender, kin and generation exist but they do not affect members very much aside from ordering work (e.g., women's work versus men's and children's activities versus adults'). Referred to as egalitarian societies because the social status for all members is very close to equal, food-forager bands are made up of members who enjoy the same basic rights and obligations. There are no leaders or chiefs, someone who has more power or resources than anyone else. That is, these internal differences between females and males or children and adults do not become the foundations for stratification. That is to say, as far as we know, foragers did not rank each other within or across bands as being superior or inferior.

When I was young, I wondered if the social status differences I observed in the world had always existed: Have men always dominated women? Have there always been poor and rich? Are people "naturally" competitive and are wars inevitable, or are people "naturally" peaceful and warfare comes into existence at some point in human history? These questions gnawed at me and I wanted answers, but answers were really hard to find—at least in part because I didn't get to study social sciences in high school (we did have "social studies" but these were limited to some history and civics). When I got to college only anthropology courses offered a window into the lives of people living beyond urban, industrial environments. Those courses exposed me not only to the huge variation in human societies both today and yesterday, but also to ways I could analyze these peoples for similarities and differences. The most important tool for analysis I learned was comparison—comparing what contemporary peoples do against what anthropologists found out about our ancestors. This is a great technique because our species lived far longer as food foragers than the ways we live today, but by the time researchers started studying food foragers, most had either been decimated through disease or war, or had been pushed into the Earth's most difficult environments by food-producing peoples who wanted the food foragers' land and resources. Therefore, it is always important to be cautious in drawing conclusions from data gathered on the few food-foraging groups who survived to be studied. Nonetheless, those who do careful studies have helped us gain a perspective on human life that is impossible to achieve without doing comparisons.

To summarize what I hope you have learned from this short foray into the lives of food foragers is, first, they did not all look, act, or think the same; rather, the fact that small bands lived in different locations throughout the globe helped them develop cultural differences from one another. They had different languages, customs, ideas, beliefs, myths, clothing styles, and so on. Second, this cultural *distinctiveness* did *not* mean that they used their differences to create social hierarchies among bands. Because we learn culture as comfort, as belonging, we favor our own people over others, but that ethnocentrism, I argue, does not necessarily mean we privilege our group by hording resources from other groups or devising other ways to benefit ourselves over others. So culturally distinctive bands could coexist without being socially ranked and the same is largely true of band members. Additionally, within their bands food foragers emphasized *equal social status* among members. Although band members varied by personality and they also recognized gender, kin and generation differences, each person would have similar access to the resources of the band. The food-foraging/band lifestyle of our ancestors would have depended on a small group of related people all sharing resources with each other and cooperating in activities from foraging to parenting. Just as in today's close-knit families, there would have been some lines that divide individuals, but they would not have overwhelmed the feeling of "family first," or family solidarity. That's why we will sacrifice more for our family members than for pretty much anyone else.

Only when people start supplementing foraging with growing their own food do we begin to see groups socially stratify (such as by nation, ethnic group, race, religion, etc.). At this point cultural distinctiveness becomes translated into social hierarchies among groups. Before tackling this really important yet complex issue that social scientists have pondered for a long time, I want to focus in closely at the age-old distinctions that people have always made because these hold clues as to how we learn distinctiveness and also how we can translate difference into ranking. If even food foragers distinguished between male and female, child and adult, then we should expect that these are learned very early and probably at a similar stage of child development across all peoples in the world. And the evidence suggests that babies get really busy learning gender but toddlers become gender fanatics . . .

FROM SOCIAL CATEGORY TO CATEGORICALLY UNEQUAL

Gender

Gender is a universal human category; all peoples distinguish between males and females, yet they do so in almost infinite ways. That is why gender should not be confused with sex—although many, if not most, people do. Why differentiate them? Social scientists care because while genetics determine whether we are male or female (or, in rare cases, people born with both sets of genitalia), the *cultural meaning* people give to that distinction varies hugely. The social meaning we give to biological differences is gender. We *give* meaning to male/female to make them even more different than what nature alone provides. We *do* gender, just as we *do* culture. So think for a moment about how you and people you associate with distinguish male from female (in terms of what we do, where we can go, what types of work we can do, what we wear, etc.). What are the gender rules (although typically unspoken and unlegislated) in your society? What expectations are there for how males and females should behave differently? Write your response in the Planned Pause 5-1 on the next page.

There are few, if any, genetic reasons why girls and boys, women and men dress differently and otherwise adorn themselves differently, speak differently, and even behave differently. Gender differences, then, are overwhelmingly cultural; we know this because they vary so much from society to society. Even though they are cultural (and thus not innate) people mostly learn to make these distinctions unconsciously and therefore uncritically. In fact, as we will see in a moment, doing gender is one of the first if not *the* first social category that young children master, and they become experts at doing the "boundary work" (Gieryn 1983; Lamont & Molnár 2002) between girls and boys. What is meant by "boundary work"? Well, once people invent a socially distinctive category such as gender everyone has to learn the boundaries between groups within a category—in this case how to distinguish between being female and male. Categories will not stick unless they are applied to everyday life. We can be born male or female but unless we dress differently, fix our hair differently, do different types of work, etc. there are actually very few naturally occurring distinctions between the biological categories of male and female (such as in pitch of voice, body size, etc.). Not enough distinctiveness probably for babies to learn the gender category, so we accentuate

PLANNED PAUSE 5-1

DOING GENDER IN MY SOCIETY

Instructions: *Write down the ways in your society that males and females distinguish themselves (e.g., in dress, hairstyles, places they go, work they do, how much their activities are regulated versus free, etc.). Now analyze whether or not these differences in gender that people do are just differences or are there status differences (hierarchies) involved as well? Do these status differences, if any, vary from cultural context to cultural context (e.g., when a woman or man is at home versus in a club, in a company versus in a religious organization)? Why or why not?*

Part 1: How do people do gender in your society? Provide several examples.

Part 2: Discuss if gender differences are hierarchical. Give an example.

Part 3: Compare and contrast how gender differences and social statuses shift between **two** *different cultural contexts. Explain these contexts and how context affects gender.*

Explore the Concept on
mysearchlab.com

these naturally occurring differences. Another case in point is race; there are debates about when variation in skin color, hair type, etc. began to matter among peoples. Those physical differences existed long before they became the basis for racially categorizing people. As I will explain in greater detail soon, race becomes a social category only during European colonization, long after variations in skin color, etc. had evolved (Smedley 2007). In short, when I refer to doing boundary work I mean the ways that people do the cultural work of maintaining (and sometimes breaking or shifting) these categorical boundaries. A great deal of doing culture is boundary work because the clearer we make boundaries the clearer and unambiguous our categories. As we have seen before, when people cannot categorize easily, when some things are in-between categories, we often feel anxious. It can be very taxing mentally and emotionally. You've probably felt this but didn't know why. Now you should not only understand better when you feel this way, but you should also be able to apply this understanding to life around you. Work in a large organization? If so, it's full of categories and maybe the boundaries between them are not clear or perhaps they are shifting and employees are nervous about the changes. You should be able to intervene more usefully now that you know more about what causes this type of stress.

In sum, we all do culture; we do "it" to ourselves *and to others* but we rarely see ourselves doing "it." However, we can see it in toddlers. Recall from Chapter 2 the story of Hans, the little boy in my daughter's daycare. Hans was the one who donned a tutu and was ridiculed for doing so by the girls. "Boys do not wear dresses!" they'd insist. Hans didn't care what they said—a good example that there are always some people who don't conform to the cultural rules—but the fact that he refused to obey helped all the children learn very profoundly that there *are* cultural rules about gender. And that is the critical point. We have to learn these rules; we are not born with them.

We all learn gender and the scholarship in this area points to learning gender right from birth; very quickly we gain a deep understanding of how the world is divided up along gender lines and of how each of us fits into that world. As with any academic endeavor there are debates and disputes over exactly how toddlers learn gender and when they know that they're a boy or a girl (e.g., Bussey & Bandura 1999; Durkin 2005; Martin et al. 2002). If you look at these debates through a microscope as a specialist, then, you are unlikely to see a consensus, but if you look at them with a wide-angle lens, as I do, there is quite a bit of agreement. The evidence shows quite convincingly and, increasingly, cross-culturally that children learn gender distinctions and then perform these during the same early months and years of life. They learn the specific ways gender is encoded in their cultural contexts (Jahoda & Lewis 1988; Lancy 2010; LeVine & New 2008; Rogoff 2003; Wenger 2008; Whiting & Edwards 1988). This gender coding is complex. There are different symbols that infants must learn and they also have to realize that the different symbols all point to the same gender distinction.

Imagine that you are a young infant. As you listen to people talking, you notice that some of their voices are higher and others are lower. You also notice that some people have long hair and others have short hair. Like tiny statisticians, babies observe everything and sort it out into life's regularities (categories or patterns). As you read in a previous chapter, they are irrepressible taxonomizers. Under experimental conditions (i.e., as observed by scientists in research settings that are not necessarily like what children normally encounter at home), infants as young as a few months old are able to differentiate male from female voices and pay attention to how men and women do gender by varying their hair length and clothing type. By 9–12 months old, babies are very good at distinguishing male and female faces. Now the next step is combining these traits into a composite of what is male versus what is female. That's more complicated, but by the end of their first year, babies seem to be able to associate male and female faces with gender-specific objects such as a hammer or a silk scarf (Levy & Haaf 1994; Martin et al. 2002). This is the beginning of being able to label gender associations to not only people (male or female) but objects as well (a truck is for boys and a doll is for girls). Of course, associating objects with males or females varies from society to society. Where there are no hammers there might be bows to indicate men's objects, and where there are no scarves there might be skirts. What matters is not the objects themselves, but their association with the really important gender lines that children are learning.

In their second year, children's ability to distinguish between male and female gets more and more intense and they impose gender order intensively too—again the case of Hans and the tutu is a great example. Toddlers begin to not only understand that the world is segregated by gender, but they also know which side they are on. They then self-segregate into girls' and boys' groups, into girls' and boys' activities, and this segregation becomes more and more defined through middle childhood. Between ages 5 and 8, kids pass through the most sexist period of life, largely because they do not see gender as flexible. Rather, they see it in almost biological terms, as an essential, not changeable, aspect of life (Bloom 2011). And they attach morality to proper gender behavior. A boy wearing a dress is not only making a mistake, he is doing something *wrong* (Maccoby 2002). Once they learn about boys and know that they are boys, boys want to stick with boys and do boy things while girls want to be with girls. They feel really strong in-group preferences (think gendered ethnocentrism) (Bloom 2010; Martin et al. 2002; Massey 2007; Sherif et al. 2010). One researcher (Warin 2000) tested the strength of these emotions among a large group of 4- to 6-year-olds. The children were asked to change their clothes into the ones stereotyped for the opposite sex— frilly dresses for boys and army fatigues for girls. Many kids responded with grimaces and nearly half of them flat out refused (see also Bussey & Bandura 1999). They were doing gendered boundary work—keeping themselves and others within the culturally defined borders of gender appropriateness. We all do boundary work but we are rarely aware that we participate in enforcing cultural boundaries.

As they learn gender rules and boundaries as well as where they fit, young children discipline each other to stay within gender boundaries. Now I do not look at this as worrisome or extreme. For me, it all makes sense when we understand what childhood is all

Doing Masculinity with Dad. It Does Not Come Naturally; It Takes Practice.

about in terms of learning culture. Childhood is the period of life when we are learning our people's cultural *order*. We are looking for rules and when we find them they provide us with cultural comfort. So children are comforted when they learn rules like gender; it's only when they become really fluent in the rules that they can begin to feel OK with the fact that in real life cultural rules are guides more than they are laws. People's behavior tends to follow these, but there are exceptions to rules and there are people who break the rules. When you are *learning* the rules, however, it is hard to see the world in anything less than black and white. Children love knowing and enforcing rules. If you say, "But I know so many toddlers who impishly break the rules. What about them?" you are right. But rule-breaking is a way of learning the limits or boundaries of rules. If you don't test the boundaries of the rules, how do you really know what they are? Just watch a toddler some day. She will stare at her parent in the eye just as she implies she's going to break a rule, watching carefully to see how mom or dad will react. It's an important testing of boundaries. In my experience, young children break the rules primarily with those whom they trust—the very people with whom they can most test those boundaries without being shunned or expelled from their group or family.

We learn gender as young children and, importantly, we learn it (like so many other cultural categories) when we are too young to be aware of what we are doing. Yet we continue to do gender all our lives; as some scholars say, gender is "a lifelong work in progress" (Ferree & Hess 1987: xviii). Do we ever grow more conscious of how we do gender? I definitely believe that we do, but in part this is because *gender is not just a category of distinction; it is also a category used to rank people.* Gender distinctions are not value-neutral like, for example, categorizing people by their blood type. We differ by blood type but that does not mean we are more valued socially because we have one blood type versus another. This *could* happen but it does not. Gender, however, involves status differences. That is, gender has become an extremely important basis for social stratification among food-producing peoples. If being male or female were considered separate but equal, then there would be some pressure to distinguish the two, but there is more pressure given the fact that they are almost never considered equal. There are all sorts of explanations for why across societies today and going back throughout recorded history, being male has overwhelmingly been a higher social status than being female. Some people argue that it is God's design, while others believe it is due to the fact that, on average, men are larger and stronger than women and thus can control them physically. Alternatively, some anthropologists argue that women's status varies from society to society according to how much they contribute economically to their families and households (Friedl 1975; Rosaldo & Lamphere 1974). There is also a very promising new social-psychological approach that argues that gender operates differently from other social categories, like race, ethnicity, and class, all of which also create unequal social statuses. This approach holds that while those in power can exclude less powerful groups, even legally, such as what occurred in the United States during the Jim Crow era of racial segregation and South Africa under Apartheid, this kind of exclusion cannot occur with women. Men, though powerful, cannot separate themselves permanently from women since they are tied to them in family bonds of marriage and descent. So females can be accorded low social status by males but they cannot be completely socially excluded like other low-status groups (Glick & Fiske 1996; Massey 2007).

My point here is not to enter into these debates because it would take up more than an entire book. Rather, in this chapter and particularly in this section, I am explaining how people can at once belong to a society and yet also belong to smaller groups within that society, groups that are also hierarchically ordered. In other words, *we simultaneously can belong to multiple social groups: gender, nation, citizenship, ethnicity, race, class, religion, etc.* When we talk about these multiple belongings we typically refer to them as our "identities." Take a look at the photo to the right and try to figure out the person's multiple social groups (see list in sentence above). The same person can be, just to give an example, a citizen of the United States, a woman of Lebanese ethnicity who is white and middle class, and also a Muslim. I really dislike the term "identities" since this term, like "culture," makes relationships seem like personal possessions. We *do* culture but we typically say we *have* culture. We *act* Lebanese but we typically say we *are* Lebanese. We also typically say that we *have* identities when from a culture as comfort perspective, we actually *do* these distinctions. Some people who share this perspective have begun to talk about "identifications" instead of identities because at least with that variation of the word there is some process implied (to identify oneself) (Brubaker & Cooper 2000; Nederveen Pieterse 2007) but most people continue just talking about having identities.

This Person is *Doing* Many Social Distinctions. How Many Can You Detect? What Clues Do You Use?

Some social categories that people use to differentiate ourselves become the building blocks of social status differences. Among the most well known of these "categorical inequalities" (Massey 2007; Tilly 2001) are gender and race. The history behind how these two categories become categorical inequalities is not the same. As I summarized above, the reasons for gender inequality are debated; but, as I explain below, the history giving rise to racial categories (based on biologically visible features) is extremely well documented. Before I tell that history, however, I think it's important to take a few moments to discuss in greater detail the general steps involved in making social status hierarchies out of social categories. I turn to that now.

People have been one species for many thousands of years. We are far more similar than we are different, but, as you know, our brains are organized to look for differences. This talent was extremely useful for learning about and adapting to differences in ecological environments. However, that talent also means that we pay attention to the ways in which people differ. Differences observed became categories used to differentiate types of people and peoples. Over generations we have developed many social categories to distinguish ourselves, but only a subset of those are the ones we use to stratify ourselves and not all of the ones we use are used around the world. Recall that for almost all of human existence we lived as food foragers who were highly egalitarian. So stratification is a quite new human phenomenon, even if many people think that we have always ranked each other. Stratification begins as a consequence of settled life; that is, as an outcome of people starting to produce their own food by farming and herding. People settle and populations begin to grow and also to stratify. People begin to differentiate in terms of occupations (such as soldiers and religious specialists and artisans) and we also begin to see leaders with more power than others in the society. As you might guess, there are different theories about why these huge changes come about and I cannot go into them here, but there are really good sources you can consult (e.g., Chase 1980; Diamond 2005; McElreath, Boyd, & Richerson 2003; Nettle & Dunbar 1997; Price & Bar-Yosef 2011). I need to skip those debates because what really matters is that stratification begins in human societies at that point.

Once social categories become the basis for ranking, we see the appearance of many different social stratifications. Ranking is enormously important yet accomplished simply. According to sociologist Douglas S. Massey (2007: 5–6) in his book *Categorically Unequal*, "All stratification processes boil down to a combination of two simple but powerful mechanisms: the allocation of people to social categories, and the institutionalization of practices that allocate resources unequally across these categories." This is a very simple, elegant formula. People are classified into categories but it is only when these categories are used to stratify that separate becomes separate *and* unequal. Who gets to decide which group(s) get more resources? That's what social scientists study all the time. The shorthand term for that is "power." There are many ways to gain power over others, too many to go into here. What I think is equally as important but much less understood, however, is how easily people invent stratification systems once we are categorized (put into groups). Let's look at a couple of famous examples.

In the early 1950s, long before there were strict controls on doing experiments with people, a couple of psychologists showed how simple it is to create powerful new feelings of solidarity within groups and prejudice between them. In the famous Robbers Cave experiment (Sherif et al. 2010), preteen boys from white, middle-class families were brought to a summer camp and intentionally separated into two different groups. Half the boys were brought by one bus and the other half came in another bus so that they did not know about each other. The experimenters wanted to see if these seemingly similar boys might, with some help, differentiate themselves and they did. One group named itself the "Rattlers" and the other the "Eagles." In a few days' time each developed its own symbols and rituals of group belonging. At that point, the researchers put the two groups into contact for the first time and the groups immediately competed against each other and became very hostile. In other words, each group saw itself as not only different, but also superior to the other and tried to enforce that superiority. The hostility became so strong—for example, the groups raided each other's cabin and burned each other's flags—that the researchers had to stop that contact phase early and move the boys into the final stage of the experiment. During that stage the warring groups were put together to see if they could put aside their group "identities" and reconcile. The boys were asked to fix the camp's water supply and to pool their funds so they could watch a movie together. Almost as quickly as they had formed groups, in-group preferences, and dislike for the other group, the boys bonded again but now as one large group all cooperating together. By the time they went home at the end of the experiment, they had forgotten about the Rattlers and the Eagles.

Does the Robbers Cave experiment remind you of anything you have encountered in the book before? My mind immediately jumps back to the experiences of boot camp. Intense rites of passage build really strong bonds.

Race

Lest you think that only boys and men bond, watch the classic 1970 documentary film *The Eye of the Storm*, a segment of which shows elementary school teacher Jane Elliott doing her famous "blue-eyed, brown-eyed" experiment with her third-grade class in small-town Iowa. All her students are white and she wants them to understand racial prejudice in the days immediately after Martin Luther King Jr.'s assassination. They can't understand why he was killed, so she decides to help these students understand racial prejudice despite living in a racially homogeneous town. She begins her lesson by asking them if they understand what it is like to be treated differently just because of the color of their skin, and they all agree that they can't imagine that. So she then asks them if they think they would want to try categorizing by eye color and they agree that this would be a good idea. But she does not only categorize them, she tells them that having one color (first blue because that is her own eye color, but the next day she switches to brown) is better than the other group. She stratifies them and then she treats each group differently. "Blue-eyed people are the better people in this classroom," Elliott tells her third graders, and the children at first disagree. But she continues, "Oh yes, they are. Blue-eyed people are smarter than brown-eyed people. They are cleaner than brown-eyed people." ("Oooh" can be heard from the children as she says this.) "They are more civilized than brown-eyed people," she insists. And then she tells the children that blue-eyed kids get five extra minutes of recess than the others. She adds that the brown-eyed kids cannot use the water fountain and that the kids can only play with members of their own group. She gives the brown-eyed kids collars to wear so that they can be identified as inferior even from far away. Some of you are familiar with the history of the Holocaust when Jews in many cities in Europe were required to wear yellow stars on their clothing to identify them. Given that physiologically they usually did not look that different from the non-Jewish population where they lived, mere physical appearance was not sufficient to differentiate them. Therefore, the yellow star symbol was added. The children in Elliott's classroom were so used to seeing each other as similar and as friends, the collars served the symbolic purpose of distinguishing them.

At first the kids protest against their categorization and its hierarchy; but very quickly they begin not only to agree with it, but also to enforce it. The blue-eyed kids feel superior and become the main enforcers while the brown-eyed kids feel upset and left out. During recess, one blue-eyed boy calls another boy "brown-eyes" and the boy hits him. Elliott starts a conversation about the incident and other children report that they are all calling each other by their eye colors and the brown-eyed kids feel upset. One boy says, "It's like they're calling us stupid or something." In the elapse of just a few minutes, Elliott later observed, "What I had thought to be wonderful, thoughtful, cooperative children turned into nasty, vicious, discriminating little third graders." The next day she reverses the prejudice by saying to the children, "Yesterday I lied to you. The truth is that brown-eyed people are better than blue-eyed people." And she tells the brown-eyed children that they can put their collars onto a child with blue eyes; they also get all the privileges the other kids had the previous day. Not surprisingly, the brown-eyed children seize their superior status, feeling much better about themselves than the day before. But Elliott tells the children she doesn't feel good because she has blue eyes and blue-eyed people are not as good as brown-eyed people. This allows her to be part of the experiment and she turns her own feelings of discrimination into a conversation about prejudice with the students. The day ends with them taking off their collars and throwing them away, joining together in a circle and affirming that no one should be singled out because of the color of their eyes or skin.

Hopefully, the Robbers Cave and Class Divided experiments convince you how easily children learn not only the social categories we use to differentiate ourselves, but also how to make them into hierarchies. An even more famous study called the Prison

Experiment, conducted by Philip Zimbardo with students at Stanford University in 1971, illustrates just how easily people can be divided up arbitrarily into an in-group and an out-group where the in-group dehumanizes the out-group. Zimbardo created a mock prison in the basement of a campus building and randomly assigned some students to be prisoners and others to be their guards. Within hours the guards applied strict control over the prisoners and even began torturing them. Some student prisoners complained early on and the experiment was stopped. It has remained controversial and, most recently, its findings were used to analyze U.S. military abuses at the Abu Ghraib prison in Iraq. Zimbardo even wrote a book called *The Lucifer Effect: Understanding How Good People Turn Evil* (2007) about these comparisons.

These experiments dramatically document how human, yet inhumane, it is to divide into groups and then prefer one's own group over someone else's. As written in the famous song quoted at the beginning of this chapter,

> You've got to be taught before it's too late,
>
> Before you are six or seven or eight,
>
> To hate all the people your relatives hate,
>
> You've got to be carefully taught!

We all learn to have strong preferences for our family, our group, our people, and our nation (Richter & Kruglanski 2004; Todorov et al. 2011). Yet we rarely consider the consequences of these preferences when we use them to justify treating others poorly, even torturing or annihilating them. Stratifications are very real and have very real consequences. Take a moment now and reflect on your position within some stratification system. Where are you located? Are you more on the privileged side or the discriminated-against side? Why? How did you get to this position and have you been able to change your position during your lifetime? Why or why not? What have been the consequences of your social location within this stratification system?

We often have a strong subconscious understanding of where we fit into social hierarchies around us. Sometimes we know why we are positioned where we are; more frequently we don't. Sometimes our positions shift over the course of our lives because of things we do (such as getting an education to elevate our socioeconomic status) and, probably more often than that, factors outside of our own control affect our positioning. For example, suppose you were in a comfortable family as a child but suddenly your parent loses her job and your family then loses its home and you have to move into an apartment in a new neighborhood that is quite a bit poorer than the one you lived in before. That would affect your social status in many ways. Alternatively, imagine that you live in a country where your group is powerful, but then your country is invaded by another country and your people are suddenly plunged from being powerful to being discriminated against. You might find that the very people you once looked down upon now look down upon you, and you could become very resentful. This happens frequently, not just between countries but between groups. I recall clearly a microcosm of this type of experience when I was in elementary school. My grade had only about 40 students in it as I lived in a tiny dairy farm town in the Catskill Mountain region of upstate New York. My best friend for several years suddenly became aligned with my worst enemy when my friend's mother married my enemy's father. It was devastating and I could do nothing about it. But it taught me a huge lesson about social stratification. You see, my worst enemy was the queen bee of our grade, the prettiest girl who made it her objective to rank all the other kids in the class. If she liked you, then your rank went up and if she disliked you, your rank went down. I was a nerd so my rank was always low, but the queen bee really disliked me. When her dad married my friend's mother, my friend had absolutely no choice—out of social pressure by the bee as well as from her family loyalties—but to betray our relationship for her new sister.

Betrayal, it turns out, is a really powerful way to turn those you love into those you despise. Next is a really emotional example that many children have experienced and continue to experience. These are children raised to a large degree by caregivers whose social status is inferior to the children's (and the children's family more generally). An excellent analysis of this dilemma appears in Rebecca Ginsburg's "The View from the Back Step" (2008), in which she describes what it was like for people she interviewed, now adults, to grow up white but with black nannies during Apartheid in Johannesburg, South Africa. She discovered that most of these white South Africans had very strong emotional memories of their nannies. They remembered that the nannies lived in small huts built behind the children's comfortable suburban homes. As very young children (up until they went to school), they spent their days in these huts where they would be in close physical contact with the nannies, even napping in the same bed. They remembered the huts in categorical contrast to their own middle-class homes. The huts were dark—no electricity, no windows. Mildew and cobwebs lined the ceilings; all the nannies' clothes were hand-me-downs. Both the nannies and their homes had special smells, like paraffin (wax) used to heat up the cornmeal mush the nannies ate.

During their childhoods, these were welcome sensations since the children were cared for by the nannies. But as the children grew older, they gained greater self-awareness and realized that the nannies' homes were not only different from the children's homes, they were inferior. Categorical differences became categorically unequal distinctions and the children began to dislike not only the huts, but their nannies too. By age 7 or 8, they not only stopped going into their nannies' homes, but they also began the boundary work of enforcing their racial superiority against the nannies through verbal insults, such as calling the women *kafir* (similar to "nigger" in American slang), and shunning them altogether. Of course not all children would grow to despise their caregivers, but they would nonetheless learn that these caregivers were socially inferior and they would distance themselves accordingly. Ginsburg did not interview nannies, but one can only imagine how emotionally difficult this type of experience could be. Imagine mothering other people's small children—especially if circumstances denied you the chance to mother your own children—only to have them grow up to ridicule and ostracize you. This is exactly the paradox featured in the blockbuster novel and film *The Help*, about African American maids serving white families in the U.S. South during the 1950s.

Today such bonds between non-family caregivers and children are still regularly broken. Today many black women in South Africa are often still called *kafir* and still raise children in white families, but there are also legions of immigrant nannies caring for the children of the more privileged around the world—in the Middle East, Europe, the United States, Canada, and elsewhere. Much as slave women before them, these immigrant women and the children they care for grow deeply attached in the early years, only in many cases to have those same bonds twisted and turned against them. Imagine how strong the pressures are on these children to reject the very source of so much comfort, to trump gender with race or nationality or citizenship status. But as many people know who have had a relationship fail, love is readily transformable into hate. How do we address it?

LEARNING SOCIAL STATUSES

These examples of children learning to discriminate "us" from "them" and to favor their own groups raise the fundamental question of when they begin this boundary work. When, for example, does race appear as a meaningful social category for children? Does it appear at the same age as gender does—in the early toddler years? And how does learning race relate to learning other categories—such as in the example of how it intertwines with gender in white middle-class South African children's lives under (and post-) Apartheid? The research on learning race is newer than that for gender and, not surprisingly, there is no consensus yet. However, there is general agreement that acquiring race awareness begins, as with gender (Bussey & Bandura 1999; Durkin 2005; Maccoby 1998; Martin et al. 2002; Rogoff 2003), with children identifying differences in people's physical appearances and seeing these as valid and essential, unchanging differences in people overall (*inter alia* Aboud 1988; Barrett & Buchanan-Barrow 2005; Connolly 1998; Hirschfeld 2005; Holmes 1995).

Young children notice all sorts of visible physical differences that do not become racial social statuses; if you've ever had young children sit on your lap and touch your face, especially if they point to an "imperfection" such as a mole or wart, you know what I mean. They are inquisitive and look for what is new, what is *unusual*. They are applying their pattern-seeking skills, dedicating more attention to those things that they have not already figured out. At some point—roughly during the late preschool or early elementary school years (ages 3–7), and depending on how much racial diversity they have around them and how much importance people around them give to racial distinctions—children begin to understand, employ, and manipulate society's racial preferences. If this sounds very similar to acquiring gender, it should. Children quickly begin to see that there are racial differences, identify these differences as the basis for different categories of people, apply these categories, and figure out which category they, themselves, fit into.

Of course, children learn only the race categories that are important to the contexts they experience, which makes sense. If they are located in a society that does not make racial distinctions, their inquisitive work to figure out how people vary physically will not produce recognition of racial social categories. I recall that when my daughter Sophie was 3 or 4 she noticed, but could not really articulate, the fact that she was different physically from other kids in her preschool. The kids were overwhelmingly blonde and blue-eyed. Such was Vermont, where we lived at that time. As she began to express some concern about her darker skin and hair, I talked to her about how she got her "cinnamon skin" from her Dominican father. When we moved to Miami, her new kindergarten class was almost all Latinos and her questions about skin color lessened but her questions about nationality began (since most of her friends were not Dominican but Cuban, Colombian, Venezuelan, etc.).

Has race always been a category people have used to distinguish each other? This question has been researched quite extensively and the answer is resoundingly *no*. People do vary by skin color, hair type and so on, but the translation of these differences in our appearance did not become the basis for racial hierarchies—ranked racial categories—until around five hundred years ago under European colonization (Alleyne 2002; Massey 2007; Smedley 2007). Why? The very short version of this complex history is that in the Americas there was a labor shortage. The colonists needed more labor than could be acquired locally among the native populations. The next source of inexpensive labor was supplied by indentured servants of European origin—people who worked off their debts for a set period of years after which they were free to leave. Indentured servants were also not sufficient to meet the labor demands so the colonists imported slaves from Africa. This proved critical because slaves could be readily distinguished from the indentured servants and the native peoples by skin color. The "pigmentocracy" which emerged placed darker people on the bottom of the new racially based social hierarchy and the lighter skinned people at the top. And this racial hierarchy was enforced through racial prejudice as well as legal systems systematically favoring white colonists over all others. Additionally, of course, children began to learn race because it had become an important social category. And children have been learning and applying race ever since; they will continue to do this so long as race endures as having social significance . . .

Ethnographies of Learning Race

Much of what we now know about how children acquire culture is learned by doing research on infants in laboratory settings. This makes sense since these settings are specifically designed to test children's abilities at detecting and producing patterns in behavior. However, laboratories typically do not imitate real life; they cannot do that, since in order to test something they need to control most other things going on. To observe children learning about and negotiating their social categories/statuses more naturally, then, some researchers have turned to ethnographic research. Primarily, this means that they observe young children's activities in typical settings for kids and carefully record and analyze what they observe. These studies occur in preschools and homes so that what is observed may not be generalizable to all children—particularly when we think about how different the lives of children around the world can be—but they do provide rich illustrations of how gender, age/maturity, sexuality, race, and language are typically experienced together as opposed to separately. The ethnography by Paul Connolly, *Racism, Gender Identities and Young Children* (1998) provides many such illustrations. By observing children in multi-ethnic kindergartens in the United Kingdom, he found that race, gender, nationality/ethnicity, and sexuality are ever present in those young children's lives and that children perform them together by segregating themselves into gendered, racialized, and even sexualized spheres of friendships. Gender lines were the brightest, but they were rarely the only boundaries being negotiated. For example, Connolly saw white girls playing imaginary games together like "Mommies and Daddies," "Mommies and Babies," and "Shops" in which they tested out heterosexual relationships and roles. South Asian girls were excluded from these games by the culturally and numerically dominant white girls, so the South Asians played by themselves. Most black girls were also excluded so they tried to enhance their status by competing in the boys' arena of athletics. The boys did not appreciate this, as it meant that girls encroached on their territory—where they dominated.

   Boys and girls rarely played together; when they did, it typically involved a boy-dominated heterosexual game called "Kiss Chase" in which the boys chased the girls and, when they caught them, kissed them. The boys competed with each other; those who were better at catching and kissing the girls earned higher status. But black girls were not chased because the boys viewed them as too masculine. So the black girls were excluded from feminine activities by the other groups and were excluded by the boys as not being feminine enough to merit their own sexualized interests. The black boys were the most sexualized; a group of them dominated Kiss Chase. Called the "bad boys" by the other children and teachers alike, this group constantly used sexual references and slang to compete among each other for the girls. Each *kindergartner* staked out his social territory by selecting and protecting girlfriends.

The bad boys denigrated other boys in order to reign supreme in the male world, and white boys would fight them in order to affirm their masculinity. Meanwhile, Pakistani boys were stereotyped by all the other groups as teacher's pets for doing well in school and for being eager to please. Teachers made it worse for these boys by praising them and favoring them over the others. In this social hierarchy, Pakistanis were definitely at the bottom. Connolly describes how Pakistanis' low status and the tendency of other kids to stereotype them (e.g., by calling all Asian kids "Pakis") led some Pakistanis to look for innovative ways to improve their social status. One Pakistani girl turned to sexuality and femininity to enhance her status: she started bringing lipstick and hair ornaments to kindergarten, which she traded for access to higher-status friends. Another girl whose background was both English and Turkish, but who found herself being marginalized at the social bottom as a "Paki," defended her status by insisting that Turkish was not Pakistani.

As we are beginning to see in this chapter, one of the most profound and enduring ways to denigrate is through shame. One of the most common ways to shame people is to associate them with dirty, smelly, unclean activities and things—things not befitting a really "cultured" human being. This is a tactic you often hear on playgrounds among young children, and it was certainly true in the kindergarten class Connolly observed (and elsewhere, as I will elaborate on in a moment). Recall that disgust is one of the few universal emotions people are born being able to express and interpret. However, people are not born knowing what is disgusting. I know it may be counterintuitive, but research shows that we *learn* what's disgusting. Even our own basic bodily functions are fascinating, not disgusting to young children. They have to be taught to find them disgusting and usually disgust of one's own feces is one of the earliest applications learned (Rozin et al. 2008). It makes sense, then, that children would draw on this emotion early in life as they jockey with each other for their position in the local social status hierarchy.

This brief summary of what Connolly found in kindergarten probably sounds pretty horrifying, more akin to the famous novel *Lord of the Flies* than to youngsters learning their ABCs. But it is certainly not unique. Debra Van Ausdale and Joe E. Feagin (2001) spent a year in a multicultural preschool in the United States and observed very similar relationships among *preschoolers*. One 4-year-old white boy taunted a mixed-race (black/white) 4-year-old girl by telling her that she couldn't celebrate Kwanzaa, the week-long holiday following Christmas invented in the 1960s to celebrate African heritage and also to provide a less materialistic and more spiritual antidote to the excesses of Christmas. He viewed Kwanzaa as a distinctly African American holiday and taunted the girl because, to him, she was not really African American enough to qualify for Kwanzaa. The girl responded back that she was black enough, that her father and his parents were from Africa. This same girl also stereotyped others. One day the researchers found her calling out to the Asian preschoolers when an Asian parent would show up at the end of the day. The girl did not correctly match the children with their parents; she saw an Asian parent and called out to the wrong Asian child that his or her parent had arrived. In another incident witnessed, a mixed-race (Asian/white) 3-year-old boy refused to sleep in a cot next to a 4-year-old black girl because "I can't sleep next to a nigger. Niggers are stinky." (Note how the boy also chose to demean her on the basis of bodily disgust—in this case a claim to a bad smell.) And a 4-year-old white girl refused to believe that a 4-year-old black boy could have a white rabbit because "blacks can't have whites." This last example is really important because it shows how children learn the racial categories of black and white and extend them to non-human creatures and things, even though society does not do so. In other words, if black and white divide the human world, that pattern must also be true for the rest of the world. One day the researcher had a

3½-year-old black girl on her lap and a 3-year-old white girl wanted the lap for herself. She managed to slip onto the lap when the black girl went to get something. When the black girl returned and tried to reclaim her spot, the white girl refused to give up her seat and screamed, "Get off me, you're dirty!" Another day, the same black girl was told by another white girl that she was the same color as rabbit feces. Note the use of disgust in negotiating social status again. The white girl found a pellet of rabbit food in the sand box and held it up against the black girl's arm, saying, "See? Your skin is shitty! You have to leave. We don't allow shit in the sandbox."

These incidents occurred "naturally" when the children were just interacting with each other and their negotiation of social status around race was observed by the researchers. Not surprisingly, such incidents caused the teachers and researchers alike to ask where the children were getting these ideas. When asked, parents insisted that their kids were not learning these attitudes at home. So where were they getting them? From other kids, from the media, from where? There are clues in the research that the very curriculum used by the preschool, which was deliberately designed to help children become aware and tolerant of race differences, was at least partially to blame. For example, children were asked many times to engage in activities that drew attention to their racial differences, particularly artistic activities such as collages and drawings. The intent of these activities was to help the children identify positively about their "obvious" racial identities. But the teachers were probably not schooled themselves in how children think in categorical terms, so their efforts often produced the opposite results from those they intended. In one case witnessed by the researchers, for example, a teacher showed the children a book with photographs of children from around the world. She then asked each child to select a photo that looked most like him- or herself. One white boy chose a photo of a dark-skinned girl wearing a red robe and exclaimed, "That's me!" But the teacher admonished him, "No honey, that's a little black girl. Which people look like you?" After the exercise, one of the researchers realized that the boy selected that particular photo because, just like the girl in the photo, he was wearing a red shirt. Red clothing was what he categorized as common between them, not gender or race. He was redirected, however, to privilege categorizing around skin, not clothing, color. In another instance, children were making prints of their hands. They were asked to choose the paint color that most resembled that of their own hands. One black girl chose pink; another chose to have dark brown paint for one hand and light brown paint for the other. As they observed, the researchers realized the children were selecting paint that matched the color of their palms as well as the backs of their hands. Most children, however, ignored paints in hues of skin color, preferring instead reds and yellows. The lesson? Children, at least in this preschool, were indeed making racial categorical distinctions, but they were not making the ones their teachers were expecting. Perhaps by following the curriculum, the teachers were unwittingly encouraging children to acquire society's preexisting racial categories. A possible remedy might have been to *encourage* children whose handprints did not match their "true" skin color and to celebrate all the beautiful hues of the prints the kids did create.

Conclusion

This chapter has only begun to explain the complex learning processes children go through en route to knowing how they are socially located in their worlds. Only gender, race, and, to a lesser extent, age have been discussed but we learn so many more "identities" such as ethnicity, religion, social class, and so on. Additionally, these social statuses are not independent but interrelate, as we saw in several examples. Researchers are learning how children acquire these social categories and in what order we acquire them. Gender and race are most studied but there are important insights into others (e.g., for nationality, see Barrett [2005, 2007]; for social status via kinship, see Toren [1988]). This research is important and would be a great career for any readers who wish to make big contributions to the ideas I am posing here. Why is all this research so important? It is my firm conviction that knowing much more about children's tendency to seek out and apply the cultural categories around them helps us understand why so many instances of racism are acted out on the playground. In the 1940s, the famous black doll/white doll experiments performed by psychologists Kenneth and Mamie Clark documented that prejudice is learned very early in life. Their experiments showed clearly how the broader society's prejudice against being nonwhite affected children's choice of a toy; overwhelmingly, children preferred the white doll. These experiments became the research foundation to fighting school segregation in the United States, ultimately resulting in legally enforced desegregation through the famous Supreme Court ruling *Brown v. the Board of Education*. Despite those findings (and many since), the stereotype of blacks' inferiority persists.

I recall beginning to teach about racial stratification at the University of Vermont when the book *The Bell Curve* was published collaboratively by a psychologist and a political scientist in 1994. This book became a controversial bestseller overnight in large part because the authors, both scholars, used a mountain of studies to make their case that intelligence is highly (if not dominantly) inherited genetically and thus, if blacks have lower IQs they must be inferior to other racial groups. The resulting uproar in the 1990s was huge and additional scholars criticized the *Bell Curve*'s authors of selective reporting of the research and questionable data analysis methods, particularly on the relationship between race and intelligence. That is, other scholars most accused the book's authors of favoring research that supported their hypotheses while overlooking studies that argued the opposite. Despite this criticism, there were many people who still clung to the book as if it were the Bible. I had a personal experience with this. A number of years ago, I was asked to accompany a high-profile European visitor to my current campus, Florida International University (FIU), for a meeting with the then president. The visitor was interested in knowing how FIU was able to graduate so many minority students. FIU does graduate more Hispanics than any other campus in the country, and it is one of the top institutions granting degrees to black students as well. In fact, FIU could not be more different in demography (and many other characteristics!) than my previous school, the University of Vermont. But this now past president of FIU proceeded to tell his visitor—with several faculty including myself present at the meeting—that Hispanics did well but that black students were

Why Might Black Children Play with Dolls of a Different Race?

inferior. I recall cringing when I heard him say this (though he was known for not being careful with other statements), and I glanced away, embarrassed. My glance fell upon the bookcase in his office where we were meeting. Then I saw it right there: prominently featured on a shelf holding few other volumes was *The Bell Curve*. Up to that point I had been willing to give the university leader the benefit of the doubt that he had just misspoken, but when I saw the book I realized that he had expressed his actual view. Unfortunately, the social context of the meeting (as well as my own status, which was not high enough to permit me to criticize him directly) mitigated against my desire to protest then and there. I did not, nor did anyone else. After the meeting was over, however, another colleague and I did our best to give the visitor additional viewpoints.

The story I just told hopefully illustrates how individuals *do* categorical inequality and, in so doing, help to reproduce the importance of race as a socially stratifying form of difference. What we do, conscious or not, to maintain and reinforce these stratifying categories in our everyday life matters. What people in greater positions of power and authority do matters even more, but we all can participate (wittingly or not) in keeping alive the very markers of inferiority by race, gender, class, sexual orientation, religion, and so on, that make so many children—and adults— miserable. We want to belong to groups; group-making, though, typically involves not only distinguishing between "us" and "them" but also *favoring* us over them.

So what can we do with this knowledge? If you were a teacher in the preschools studied by Paul Connolly or Debra Van Ausdale and Joe Feagin, knowing what you know now, would you try to *avoid* references to racial categories and let the children discover them elsewhere? Or would you continue the curriculum, but perhaps adjust it so as not to obligate children to identify by race when they chose to identify by t-shirt color or some other nonracial category? If you were a parent, what would you want your children to learn about race and gender as well as other social distinctions we typically use to rank one another? In my opinion, we need to ask these questions in order to become more conscious of how we raise our children. There is nothing we can do about the fact that all children are born looking for the patterns in the social life around

them because they need these patterns to belong culturally. Thank goodness children are able to find, learn, and apply patterns en route to gaining cultural comforts. During this journey we need to recognize, however, that they (we all) also become ethnocentric, favoring their group's cultural understandings and definitions over others.

Even more important than researching how children learn social categories and their related hierarchies, however, is applying what we already know *mindfully* to raising children. What do I mean by "mindfully"? In this book you are learning that most of what we do in life we do without consciously thinking about it. This is to preserve energy since the brain puts a heavy drain on our calorie intake. (Given the obesity epidemic today, this might seem trivial, but during most of human existence calories were not to be wasted.) Categorical thinking results in a lot of automatic, habitual behavior that is not necessarily what we would choose to do if we were really, truly aware of what we are doing. To get to a state of awareness, we need to become more mindful; we should pay attention to what we *know* implicitly yet rarely think about. I wrote this in large part to show that we take brain shortcuts; we cannot pay attention to everything we observe in our lives, so we passively ignore most of what we see, hear, smell, and feel. And even if we do not ignore something, our brains from an early age have learned to quickly process information by linking what we do observe to previous knowledge. Instead of *truly* looking at someone, we read her cues through her clothing, hairstyle, voice, and so on, and make categorical judgments about her. Now that you are more aware of these judgments, i.e. stereotypes, and why and how we do them, you have the ability to be a more *mindful*, attentive person as you go around both doing culture and observing others doing culture. What do you—yes, *you*—do to *promote* the continued existence of social categories like gender, race or ethnicity, and class as unequal? Don't you *do gender* in the way you dress? Don't you *do class* in the ways you socialize, speak, and purchase your car and clothing? What about how you do other "identities"? Can you look at yourself now—and not just at others—and be more mindfully aware of how you contribute to these social distinctions that young children are learning? So long as you, I, and everyone else continue to mark these differences as socially important, children will continue to learn them and perpetuate them into the next generation. So long as you and I and others continue to not only mark distinctiveness, but also to use these social categories as the building blocks for status differences, for social hierarchies, then children will too. What can we do, then, with this knowledge? In the next and final chapter of this book, I offer some of my own ideas about applying this knowledge. Before you continue on, please take this moment to become your own creative problem solver. *Apply your knowledge from this book* in one or more ways that promote human understanding through more mindfully raising our children.

PLANNED PAUSE 5-2

MY IDEAS FOR RAISING CHILDREN TO CREATE A BETTER FUTURE FOR ALL

Instructions: *If you are a parent, discuss below* **two** *ways that you would change your parenting given what you have learned in this book so far. If you are not a parent you still do culture around children so discuss* **two** *ways that you would more mindfully do culture around children. Be specific and link your ideas/responses to specific points developed in this chapter.* **Explain your ideas. Do not just list them.**

✳ Explore the Concept on
  mysearchlab.com

Doing Culture More Mindfully

*. . . the things which we take fore granted without inquiry or reflection
are just the things which determine our conscious thinking and decide
our conclusions. And these habitudes which lie below the level of reflection are just those which have been formed in the constant give and
take of relationship with others.*

— *John Dewey Democracy and Education (1916: 22)*

The last Planned Pause in Chapter 5 hopefully has you thinking about all the ways to apply
the ideas from *Culture as Comfort*. When I started this project years ago, what I wanted to
do was to find a more useful way to *teach* what culture "is." Much later, as I was finally able
to start working on the book, it became more important to me to help shift how we actually
think about culture because how we understand culture has everything to do with empower-
ing ourselves culturally. In other words, why find a better way to understand culture if you
don't apply that understanding? So this chapter is all about applications. What can you and
I, we and they, do to apply our cultural abilities more mindfully in order to improve our
social relationships, to combat the Culture Wars (note the conflict metaphor), and to build
bridges with family, coworkers, friends, and enemies too? I have some ideas but they are
just the tip of a huge iceberg of ideas to which all of you reading this book can contribute.
The name of this chapter is "*Doing* Culture More Mindfully" and what I mean by that is
being much more aware of what you do, what others do, and how we do it. Through our
interactions, we are constantly doing culture—although most of the time, we do not think
about what we do this way. Recall that the word *culture* started out as a verb in Latin and
only later became fixed as a noun. I would like you to change it back to a verb to emphasize
that we *do* culture. Now it is time to be more consciously aware as you do culture and watch
others doing culture too.

To prepare you to make the most of this chapter, let's go over the points that this book
emphasizes to have them fresh in your mind. Afterward, I will make some suggestions of
ways to apply these ideas in our everyday lives. I will end by asking you to provide your own
ideas. After all, true learning involves applying acquired understanding to new purposes.
We do not just learn to do things the same way others do; that would be fine if life did not
involve change. But life is constantly changing—perhaps more today than ever before in
human existence—so we need to learn skills and ways of understanding that we can take and
apply to new contexts, to solve new problems, to produce new insights. That's the genius of

being a cultural species—our flexibility to be creative. Yes, we like to stay within our known cultural comforts, *but we can and should create new comforts and even new discomforts*, for when we are discomforted we are most likely to learn. In the spirit of promoting this creativity, let me recap what I aim to have you understand so that it's clear and candid. These are the conceptual tools that will empower you to embrace your cultural discomforts en route to coming up with powerful, new, culturally creative solutions to dilemmas we all face.

CULTURE AS COMFORT'S MAIN POINTS

First, *view culture more as relational than material.* People speak about culture as if it were some "thing" we possess and can measure. We talk about being able to lose culture, but strangely, given that we learn culture, we do not talk about gaining culture. Yet culture is not a robe we cloak ourselves in, nor is it a box (or baggage) we carry around with our own particular tricks inside. Rather, culture is how we relate to other people in ways that we understand. We interact and we can interpret those interactions. Once we've learned them, the ways we act are patterned and this enables us to interpret and even predict what others will do, although our brains do this subconsciously. I mean, would you really want to take a chance that the car coming from the other direction won't stay on the opposite side of the road? Do you want your brain to be busy trying to figure that out, or do you want the car's driver to just know the cultural rules of the road so your brain can be thinking about other things?

Given that culture is relational, that it grows out of interactions, then *culture is about being collaborative more than competitive* (de Waal 2005; Nowak 2011). Even during infancy, people spontaneously share; other closely related species like chimpanzees do not do that. Yet, at least since the appearance of Darwin's theory of evolution (and for those of you familiar with philosophers like Thomas Hobbes, this perspective dates well before Darwin), people tend to focus more on how humans compete than on how we cooperate. Survival of the fittest is premised on the idea that individuals compete to get more resources than others. That may be true for most species, but it really is not so accurate for our own species—at least until we started producing food. The food-foraging way of life that characterized our species for almost all of human existence is a way of life emphasizing cooperation over competition. And even today, although the media show many exceptions, people collaborate more than we compete. We don't need laws to collaborate either, though many laws do help. Families are the great example here. We all grow up in some sort of family environment where we, as infants, contribute virtually nothing, yet are cared for by others (who could see us as competitors!) and we respond by collaborating, cooperating, and becoming just like those around us. Think about how often your family or your friends help each other out versus trying to take advantage of one another.

Culture, then, is about learning. We learn culture; we are not born with it. As we have seen in this book, from the womb babies learn cultural preferences and cultural acquisition processes are most intense during early childhood. Babies are "pattern hungry"; they are born with this ability that interfaces with their experiences. They observe others, participate in activities, and often imitate others. Just one experience frequently is enough for them to jump to a pattern, a conclusion about the way the world is ordered. Mom eats lasagna and Dad eats pizza becomes "Girls eat lasagna and boys eat pizza." Yes, that's how it works. Fortunately, when kids make the wrong assumption, that shortcut in their brain does not get reinforced again and again like daily repeated rituals do. The more often we do the same

Children Do Not Learn Only in School; Daily Life is their Most Important Learning Environment. Through Participating in the Cultural Patterns of Those Around Them, They Acquire and *Do* Culture.

cultural practices (and particularly with the same or similar people), the more strongly those networks are built into superhighways in our brains. So *culture is about patterns in people's behavior and thought.* Because most of what we think and do is patterned after those with whom we interact, they can understand us and we can understand them. But this comes at a price. *Patterns create order and predictability but as we become more patterned (culturally comfortable) we lose some cultural flexibility.* Our ancestors made this involuntary trade-off because it helped them adapt to rapidly changing climates and we have been a hugely successful species on Earth because of this trade-off. However, it has huge practical implications for human life. Why? Because we tend to favor the tried and true—what we know—over what we can do and become. The more culturally comfortable in our patterned ways, the more we shy away from innovating. This is as true in business as it is in daily life at home. It is the simple message of the business best-seller *Who Moved My Cheese?* (Johnson 1998). If you have not read this book, it's an allegory about businesses when they stop innovating. In this case, mice are used to symbolize businesses. The mice run through a maze each day and find a piece of cheese. They quickly learn how to get through the maze—until one day the maze is changed. The first mouse runs through, always looking for the same path to the cheese as before, but now cannot find it and ultimately gives up. The other mouse isn't so stuck in its ways; it searches and searches for a new path to the cheese until it finds that path. Lesson: Always retain some flexibility to change when circumstances change.

A great real-world example of this same lesson (the need for cultural comforts but to retain some flexibilities) lies in the story about the NUMMI car production plant. Back when this joint venture between General Motors and Toyota began in 1984, GM had been losing its market share for 50 years, in no small part because the cars they turned out were often poorly made and thus unreliable. Toyota offered to team up with GM and teach them secrets to greater reliability in exchange for permission to build cars in the United States, thereby avoiding import taxes. The NUMMI (New United Motor Manufacturing Incorporated) plant in Fremont, California, was chosen. But could the two car companies' extremely different corporate cultures work together? A key difference in the companies' cultures lay in labor-management relations: GM's relations were antagonistic; at Toyota, labor and management worked together. At GM the production line was untouchable and thereby ran everyone at its pace; the simple rule was "*Never* stop the line" because management feared workers would stop the assembly line just to take a break. The outcome was frequent mistakes that were not fixed (because the assembly line could not be stopped), so when mistakes were made, they had to be fixed after the car rolled off the line, costing GM time, money, and reputation. Conversely, on the Toyota assembly line laborers worked in teams and could freely stop the line when a mistake was made. Additionally, they were *encouraged* to innovate ways to improve both production and the product. When NUMMI started, Toyota sent GM workers to Japan to learn the new production culture and the GM workers were stunned at how different it was. They returned enthusiastic about changing GM culture at the NUMMI plant and they did. But on April 1, 1992, NUMMI stopped production. Why did this venture fail? The simple reason is that GM's larger management culture did not change. They were too culturally comfortable as the big boys who had little to learn from the upstart Toyota. Their resistance to cultural change—to becoming more culturally flexible—went on to cost them dearly as they continued to lose market share and, years later, went bankrupt (Glass 2010).

So avoid the GM mistake; learn what your cultural comforts are but embrace your cultural discomforts too. However, as we become more culturally fluent in the ways we feel comfortable, we tend to have a harder time engaging our cultural discomforts. They are discomforting because not only do we feel strange but we also cannot easily (subconsciously) predict what people who are different will do. That makes us feel anxious, and when this happens we frequently shut off engaging in new experiences. They are just too taxing on our brains when we are overloaded emotionally.

Therefore, *after we acquire our cultural comforts—and these can include feeling comfortable in many, many cultural contexts, not just "one" culture—we tend to avoid continuing to acquire new cultural abilities in favor of sticking within our cultural comforts.* Personally, I think that we are *all* multicultural, but most of us have grown up thinking that we have one culture. This perspective leads to defensiveness, and specifically to the idea that we need to make sure no one takes our culture from us (again, as if it were a possession). If, alternatively, we view ourselves as multicultural—not in the current typical usage of the word but in the broad sense that we can and do navigate many cultural contexts with ease—we will focus more on *gaining* additional cultural abilities than on *losing* culture. I'll explain this idea a bit later, but essentially it means that in our daily lives we have to go from home to work to school, and so on, and each environment is a cultural environment we learn to navigate perfectly. So why not see this as being multicultural? The reason, I think, is because "multicultural" has become a word used in particular ways, and those ways inadvertently exclude most people from belonging.

We know that *culture is about belonging* and that *no human being is born culturally integrated.* We all have to *learn to belong.* We have to learn to relate appropriately to others and they have to allow us to feel comfortable by being included. To me, the most important human feeling is not love, for we can survive without love; the most important feeling without which we cannot survive is belonging. As a social species, we are not born to be alone; we must belong with others no matter how dysfunctional that belonging may be. There will always be some so-called loners who claim they prefer to be by themselves, but they would never have grown to maturity by themselves. We all need others. This is why, I believe, children readily cling to even abusive parents. We need to belong. *The irony of cultural belonging is that as we become culturally fluent as "us," we must by necessity differentiate ourselves from "you."* We all need to belong, but being cultural means we cannot all belong to the same cultural comforts. This is a great, quintessentially human, irony and the cause of so many tragedies in our existence. Yet what can we do?

Culture as Comfort is my attempt to make visible what is often invisible—culture. My hope is that, as you see what you typically feel but do not always understand, you'll be bolder in *embracing cultural discomforts.* Given that we are a cultural species, one of our greatest gifts is to be able to *continue our cultural learning over the full course of our lifetime.* Why shouldn't we do this? Isn't it okay to pursue "higher" education and job "training," which involve learning new cultural contexts? Why not, then, just see ourselves as continually capable of expanding our cultural comfort zones through education, training, travel, meeting new people, and so on? Now we can better understand how people create cultural boundaries that separate social categories—male from female, Islamic from Christian, black from brown, wealthy from poor, and so on. We must acknowledge that exclusion is part of inclusion, unless, as I argue later on, we can come to view cultural difference as something other than discomforting. We create cultural belonging all the time but in so doing we almost always exclude too. This does not have to happen, but to avoid it we need to be more culturally conscious and culturally conscientious. I like to talk about this as flexing our cultural muscles lest they atrophy from complacency. You and I, they and others, we can all cross cultural borders as much as we build them. We can travel into our discomfort zones knowing that by facing discomforts we are opening opportunities to grow and expand our cultural comforts, our spheres of belonging, our collaborative opportunities. At the same time, we weaken competitive tendencies, lessen anxieties, open opportunities, build bridges, and culturally comfort ourselves and others. Much as a baby spontaneously shares her toy with another baby, we can stop being afraid of "losing" our culture and focus, instead, on gaining culture. The result is creativity over conflict.

Toddlers, Like All People, Cooperate More than They Compete. Just Watch Carefully.

REVEALING AND ANALYZING YOUR CULTURAL COMFORTS

By now you have read the phrase "cultural comforts" many times and should understand thoroughly what it means. It is one thing, however, to comprehend the concept and another to apply it, particularly to yourself given that your comforts are largely invisible to you. That is why you are asked several times to analyze yours explicitly. Before you can be a truly creative builder of cultural comforts for others, you need to face and analyze your own sources of cultural comfort and discomfort. So take a moment and come up with two of your own cultural comforts.

PLANNED PAUSE 6-1

ANALYZING MY CULTURAL COMFORTS

Instructions: *In the spaces provided below, respond to the following series of questions.*

Part 1: Describe **two** *cultural contexts in which you interact with other people and in which you feel culturally comfortable. Why are they comforting to you? With whom do you interact and where? What makes each cultural context comfortable to you? One of these contexts can be a cyber or online community, but you cannot use an example that you have already developed in a previous Planned Pause.*

Part 2: *Now select just* **one** *of these comforts. Tell the story, in as much detail as you can, of how you came to feel comfortable in this context.*

Part 3: *What about this context makes you feel comfortable now? (Recall the toolkit for creating cultural comforts from earlier chapters in this book– repeated sequences of interactions as in rituals; symbols used to identify this context and the people who belong in it; the foods eaten in this context and their smells; the ways you learned and were taught about this context, and so on.)*

Part 4: What "rules" (most likely unwritten) create the order in this comforting space? What are people supposed to do and not do, supposed to think and not think, within that context?

Part 5: Now that you have provided a lot of information about how people create belonging in this comforting space, let's return to boundary work. How do you and others who occupy this space maintain it for yourselves? How do you exclude (maybe you do not do this consciously, but the whole point here is to see that as we create "us" we create the boundaries between us and them)?

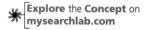

Explore the **Concept** on **mysearchlab.com**

As we have seen in earlier chapters, a lot of boundary work is informal. We learn and apply rules through joking and gossip more than through reading a cultural manual to negotiate what is acceptable and unacceptable in our cultural comforts. We want to feel comfortable so people who don't conform need to change or be excluded. We might bully them a bit; we might call them names. We might even accuse them of being dirty because dirt is symbolic of disorder—and thus being dirty symbolizes being inferior humans (Douglas 1984). Since culture is always about order, but order is never perfect, things get dirty and we clean them as part of boundary work. Sometimes we also negotiate who belongs through the language of purity/impurity. Often those who are considered "pure" are allowed to enter certain cultural spaces whereas those who are dirty, sinful, or impure are excluded. If that sounds familiar, it may be because many if not most religions use pure–impure distinctions to negotiate boundaries of belonging. In the language of purity/impurity, the impure, such as sinners, have to purify themselves by, for example, confessing their sins, sprinkling themselves with holy water, or making an animal sacrifice before they are allowed into most sacred spaces or to participate in important religious rituals.

Among Hindus, the most important purification is performed by ritually bathing in the river Ganges (irrespective of the fact that the waters themselves are now overwhelmingly polluted). The ritual bath is cleansing and liberating; people make pilgrimages to the river to immerse in its waters the ashes of their loved ones so that they can enter heaven and begin their reincarnation journeys. Do not confuse ritual cleansing with physical cleansing (despite perhaps being taught in childhood that "cleanliness is next to godliness" when asked to wash your hands before eating!). They do not always coincide. Another good example of this distinction is how in the Bible (specifically the book of Mark, Chapter 11) Jesus is reported to have thrown moneychangers out of the Temple of the Mount in Jerusalem because they were polluting its sacred ground with their secular activity. The moneychangers, then, were unclean spiritually, not physically, so watch for such metaphors. Translating this story into cultural categories and people's drive to divide our world into them, the moneychangers were mixing what should not be mixed and Jesus reaffirmed the cultural boundaries. He did boundary work.

Would You Feel Clean if, as During this Ritual which Occurs Every Six Years in the Northern City of Allahabad, India, You Would Bathe Yourself Alongside A Million Other People? Ritual Cleansing Holds Different Significance for People than Taking a Typical Bath or Shower. Why?

As you think about the types of boundary work you and others who share your cultural comforts context do, look at the informal ways you shape who belongs. Only in extreme forms of boundary work do we protect our cultural comforts via exclusion—keeping or forcing others out. Sometimes we do this through formal laws such as legislation of the separation of races in South Africa under Apartheid and in the southern United States via slavery and the Jim Crow laws. Today, exclusion at the national level is commonly legislated through immigration regulations, but at the local level shunning works well. Customary among exclusivist religious communities is to banish nonbelievers or those who marry outside the faith. So, what types of boundary work do you do in your cultural comfort space? (Return to the space provided to write your answer.)

How are you doing with getting to know your cultural comforts? If you are having some difficulties, that is to be expected. You are doing something you probably have never done before—making yourself aware of dynamics you have long taken for granted. And, moreover, you're also analyzing yourself, which we rarely do. So, to help you (or to reinforce what you're doing already), let me give you an example from my own storehouse of cultural comforts. The example I'm going to develop is simple and probably most of you can relate to it because it's about eating at your home versus other people's homes.

When I was going into junior high (seventh grade, which for many students is middle school), my family moved to a new town about 30 minutes from the dairy farm town where I grew up. They moved so that my brothers and I could go to a larger school system where, they hoped, we would get a better education than in the little school we had attended for our elementary education. You might think that moving 30 minutes away would not be too difficult. You'd be wrong. It was like moving halfway across the world to me. I went from a really, really culturally comfortable place where I knew everybody (although I was not popular, at least I knew everybody and they knew me) to a place where no one knew me—and if you had not been living in this town your whole life you were a nobody. That's the beginning of this story since it relates to my best friend, Debbie, whom I met in seventh grade; she was one of the few kids who would befriend an outsider like myself. We are still really close today. But Debbie's family was blue-collar working class. Her dad worked as a repairman on the railroad and her mother worked for the post office. They had not gone to college and they lived in a very modest home way outside of town. My parents were both college-educated and had even gone on to get graduate degrees. They were professionals and when we moved, it was to an area known locally as "snob hill." We were therefore "well-to-do" in this town. And, as you know from the last chapter, people *do* their social class. In my case, my family never tried to look different by wearing expensive clothes or buying an extravagant car. Nevertheless, we performed social class at the dining room table each night. We had a separate dining room (while in Debbie's house there was just the kitchen table) and every evening we set the table with candles. We ate by candlelight as if in a restaurant. Additionally, my mother was very fussy about our table manners. She'd insist that we all be served before anyone could start eating, she'd also insist that you put your napkin in your lap as well as other table manners. One of the big rules was "no elbows on the table." So, she'd flick her finger at my elbow if I put it on the table—which I did a lot. This was the etiquette she had learned growing up and that she passed on to my brothers and me as best she could. What is the term I've been using for this type of action? Boundary work. She was instructing us that certain actions were beyond the boundaries of acceptability and to get back inside those boundaries.

At Debbie's house, on the other hand, no one mentioned anything about manners when we ate and there certainly were no candles. The ambience was very informal, while in my house it always felt formal—at least to those visiting, because to us it felt "normal." After all, this was what we did every day and therefore it was a part of our comfort zone. I would feel a bit uncomfortable eating at Debbie's house for dinner because it was "different" (and more like how in my family we ate our breakfasts because we had a breakfast table in the kitchen). But Debbie was really freaked out when she came to eat at our house because it was so different and it felt really awkward. She felt like she was being watched by my parents to see if she could make the grade with her manners! She, of course, never told this to me until many years later. Now we can talk about it and laugh; we also know that what we were really experiencing was one way that our families showed their social-class differences. You don't have to have big differences in social class, however, to feel a bit strange in another person's home. The rituals of eating just need to be slightly different from what you have experienced to make you notice them more. You always notice that which is new, which is different. If you've ever watched the television show *Wife Swap*, you will appreciate how different home cultures can be from one another, even between families who are assumed to share the "same" (national) culture. Now you can do some cultural comparisons more mindfully. Now you know why you sometimes feel uncomfortable when confronted with unfamiliar cultural practices; and because you know why, hopefully, you will not let feeling a little cultural discomfort keep you from venturing out of your comfort zone.

When I visit my parents, they still prefer to eat formally and often by candlelight. I fit right back into this environment because I have lived it for so many years. However, in my home we eat much less formally—about half way between my parents' and my friend Debbie's parents' evening meal culture. I can fit into both easily and do so seamlessly.

So what are the big lessons we derive from discovering and analyzing more than one cultural comfort context? For me, the most important lesson is that we are *all* culturally fluent in many cultural contexts. In this sense, we are *all* multicultural. The problem is that we don't see this cultural flexibility as being multicultural; we are accustomed to thinking of ourselves as having *one* culture, no matter how many different cultural contexts we slide fluidly into and out of during the course of just one day! When you stop and see who occupies these different cultural spaces, and observe that the rituals and symbols vary in addition to how people are incorporated into these spaces and which boundary work rules apply, you will hopefully begin to agree with me that these are different "cultures." If you, I, and virtually all other people on Earth enjoy these cultural fluencies, this multicultural capability, and we exercise them daily, why do we still think of ourselves as having "a" culture and treat that culture as if it were a thing we possess? The problem lies not in what we do, but in how we view what we do.

I assert that we are all multicultural in the sense that we are able to function well in more than one cultural context, but that does not mean that we are all equally culturally fluent. No, some people are more culturally fluent than others because they have had the chance to experience more contexts than others, or because they tend to be more culturally adventuresome than others. As with languages, some people learn cultural comforts more easily than others. Some people also handle change better than others. The more flexible you are as a person, the more likely you will feel at ease in different cultural environments. As mentioned earlier in the book, children who grow up with more than one language tend to acquire additional languages more easily, even as adults. Their brains are wired differently, more flexibly. They typically have more connections among their neurons because languages are complex mental abilities that take up quite a bit of brain "real estate." Given that what we do is wired into our brains, it makes sense that the more we experience early on, the more cultural comforts we will carry forth through life. And the really great part of all this is that we *can* do a lot about our children's cultural comforts. We can also do a lot about our own cultural comforts, since we, too, can continue to learn and adapt—to flex our cultural muscles—even as we get older and our deeply rutted cultural comfort zones make it harder for us to escape than is the case for children.

It is my firm conviction that as people like you and me understand our cultural legacy better, we will *devote more of our efforts to increasing our cultural fluencies* and those we can influence in others. As we learn better how we create, maintain, and change cultural comforts, we can become better at the primary cultural process of our lives: social integration. Think about marriage: it's all about integration. Marriage (and other forms of socially recognized, long-term, interpersonal bonds) is about integrating new members into families. The marriage ceremony is not where that integrative work really takes place; rather, it takes place during the courtship (or, if the marriage is arranged, during the negotiations leading to marriage). There is a great deal of work leading up to the ceremony itself, and integration work continues after marriage by couples and their families as they adapt to new cultural contexts. When you begin to live with someone for the first time as an adult, you realize that even if you share the "same" culture, your cultural comforts vary a lot. Simple patterns and rituals matter—a great deal. Do you brush your teeth in the shower or at the sink? Do you wash dishes before you go to bed or in the morning (or only when they pile up so much that there's no more space!)? Who will handle domestic chores (and does it matter if the chores are inside the house or outside)? All these differences add up to dozens and dozens of "mini" cultural contexts with the potential for discomfort. They have to be harmonized or settled. Yes, you can stick to your ways, your cultural comforts, and then fight over these differences; but you can also see them as classic examples of human adaptability and, in so doing, as great moments for *embracing your cultural discomforts.* And these opportunities do not just arise with new personal relationships; the same is true for adapting to new jobs and new school environments.

Think about heading to a new school, college, or university for the first time; what do you encounter during the first days there? Orientation. How well did those who designed orientation for you manage to cultivate feelings of belonging in you? Did you start to feel a sense of belonging during orientation, or did you feel very discomforted and anxious about the strangeness of the whole scene? Orientation is typically organized to teach you *consciously* the information you need to know about getting an ID, signing up for courses, and so on. But it should also assist you in your emotional and cultural adaptation to your new context. Did the people running your orientation do that? What could they improve? Now you have skills to figure this out and to improve upon their work. You get a new job, and what do you encounter the first days there? Training. Now that you are in the know, how well do you think the trainers integrate you into your new cultural discomfort zones? How quickly do you begin to feel you belong there—not just in terms of doing the job but in a social, cultural sense? Who helps you most and how? How might this period of transition or "in-between-ness" be lessened? For companies, trainings are costly, so anything you can do to improve your successful adaptation and that of other new employees is valuable. Figure out what works and what does not.

What I am now describing is what is typically referred to in social science as "acculturation," "adaptation," "socialization," and even "assimilation." When a baby learns her cultural comforts, it's both similar and different to what happens to adults. It's similar in terms of the fact that both involve social learning. It's different, however, in that a baby is much less aware than an adult of her cultural discomforts because she cannot compare her prior cultural comforts with what she's now experiencing. This dual frame of reference is key; immigrants who arrive into a new context as adults can and do compare what they know already against what they now experience. Once you grow into your cultural comforts you *feel* your discomforts more. You feel the change, although, at least until reading this, you probably could not say exactly what was going on. Still, the basic lesson is that as we go along in life, we are always going to be presented with new cultural contexts—some smaller and some grander—to which we need to adapt. On a small scale, imagine joining a new club or organization. On a larger scale, imagine that you must move to a new country where you do not know the language spoken or the customs, and in which you have few or no friends or family. That is what typically happens with immigrants; and since throughout my career as an anthropologist I have been studying immigrants, I will devote quite a bit of this chapter explaining how culture as comfort helps us understand the immigration experience.

For now, however, I will start with acculturation on a smaller scale. Imagine you belong to a club, organization, or place of worship and you want to increase its membership. What do you need to do first? If I were you, I'd examine how newcomers experience this cultural context. Do they feel comforted or discomforted right at the beginning? Who feels comforted and who feels discomforted? Are those who feel discomforted *least* like the majority of your membership? That would make sense. If you want people who are more diverse to come, then perhaps you have to figure out what they might like. The more you provide them with comfort, the more likely they are to return. What's comforting to some people, however, is discomforting to others. Do you have greeters at the entrance? If so, do they provide a simple "welcome" or do they extend their hands for a handshake or give you a hug? What's culturally comfortable for newcomers? It may be hard to know, but how you *do* that first welcome goes a long way toward determining whether the newcomer will feel comfortable or not. First impressions run deep. We know why—recall that for the brain, things that are new, unexpected, or different from the norm are most attractive to our brains. So we focus on what's new, what's different, and that sticks in our minds. Particularly sticky is newness that feels strange—discomforting. It creates a strong impression that is hard to shake, even if it's inaccurate.

For some years, I have attended different churches and studied their encounters with cultural comforts and discomforts. Places of worship are some of the most important culturally comfortable contexts of our lives, in large part because they typically involve rituals that we become accustomed to very early on in life. We then find comfort in those rituals, and they are often accompanied by strong smells such as incense, or by a particular kind of music that becomes comfortable to us; change something about those rituals and some people always get upset. I recall once serving as a leader in a church that was losing membership, largely because we were not attracting new members and older members were, quite literally, dying. In response, the pastor suggested adopting a more lively format for the service that included using more contemporary songs with upbeat tempos than traditional hymns, updating the sanctuary with modern furniture instead of the old pews, and mixing up the order of the service a bit. Her ideas were met with enthusiasm by some and by passive resistance from most. Later on, she confided in me that she knew the older members would put up with changes in music before architecture and architecture before order of service (liturgy). "So long as I keep the liturgy the same," she told me, "the old timers will go along with a lot of the other changes. But never move the sermon or they'll kill me!" Not long afterward I left that congregation for another one, only to find the same dynamics there. We love our comforts and we have a really hard time seeing them as discomforting to others. That's why it is so, so important to travel beyond our own cultural comforts. This does not mean you have to travel outside your country because every country has diversity within its people. No country is occupied by people whose cultural comforts are exactly the same. Some countries—particularly, but not uniquely, those counties that receive large numbers of immigrants and refugees from very culturally distinctive backgrounds—are more culturally complex than others, but all are culturally diverse.

FOCUSING ON THE IMMIGRANT EXPERIENCE

About 13% of the United States' population is foreign-born; but it's 20% in Canada, 23% in Switzerland, 25% in Australia, and 29% in Saudi Arabia. The countries with the very highest percentages of immigrants are all in the Middle East—87% in the tiny country of Qatar, 70% in the United Arab Emirates (where Dubai is located), 69% in Kuwait, and 46% in Jordan (See Figure 6.1). Around the world more than 200 million people live away from the country where they were born; if they formed their own country it would be the fifth largest in the world. Why so many? Are they just uprooting themselves to find a better life? Not really. Globalization is a major factor; too complicated to get into here, the basic link between globalization and migration is that this process has disturbed traditional ways of life

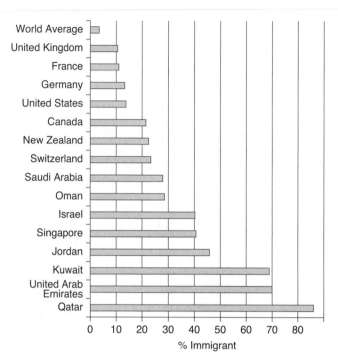

FIGURE 6.1   Percentage of Select Countries' Populations that are Immigrant. Do these Figures Surprise You? If So, Why? Source: MPI Data Hub 2012. http://www.migrationinformation .org/datahub/comparative.cfm.

around the world, thus sending hundreds of millions of people into cities to seek livelihoods when once they were farmers. After people are set into motion by moving from rural to urban areas, they are much more likely to move abroad too. Additionally, disasters such as earthquakes and wars displace huge numbers of people who then have to find new homes. So living as an immigrant or refugee is not at all unusual. When we think back to our heritage as food foragers, we find that moving around geographically is normal; *moving around culturally is what's qualitatively different now.* That is, food foragers shifted where they lived during their lives, but how they lived and with whom they lived changed only negligibly. That is much less true today. Today, we feel the pace of change all the time; we see it on our televisions and computers and we feel it when we swap out our cell phones for the latest model with an awe-inspiring set of applications. Somehow, however, many of us keep our notions of "our culture" frozen as if it did not change too. But if culture is, as I argue here, about how we relate to one another, then despite keeping alive some traditions and customs, our ways of relating are indeed changing rapidly. But that is exactly why we evolved into a cultural species—to be flexible and adaptive to shifting circumstances, rather than stuck in programmed instinctual ruts that doom species to extinction when change is too rapid.

The issue, then, for immigrants as well as for those who do not immigrate, is our *feelings of belonging and comfort*, not our ability to handle cultural change. Even though we are all *able* to feel culturally comfortable in many environments, when we cross into what we feel is a very *different* cultural context, one in which the people we encounter speak and act in ways we cannot immediately understand, we cross into a discomfort zone. The easiest way to understand these discomfort zones is when people we encounter speak a language we do not understand, but this is not the only way. As you have learned in this book, the key characteristic to watch for is *feeling* strange, *feeling* you do not belong. People can speak the same language as you do but with an accent you do not understand, and that can make you feel strange. Actually, you probably feel that *they*—not you—are strange, but the key thing to focus your conscious attention on is that there is a noticeable difference. Remember that our pattern-seeking minds largely ignore similarity but pay close attention to difference because differences have to be compared against existing models, fit into the existing boxes. Now, someone could speak the exact same way that you do, but you could still sense that there are differences. Perhaps this person stands too close or too far away from you when speaking; perhaps his clothing or body decorations (piercings, makeup, tattoos, etc.) seem odd to you. Perhaps you cannot follow his gestures. You sense that something—or many things—are different, and you feel them. Well, this is the immigrant/refugee experience. However, for immigrants and refugees these cultural discomforts are not just isolated experiences, but day-in and day-out feelings of difference, of standing out, and, usually, of feeling that the greater society views you as inferior. Recall that most social distinctions become the basis for making social hierarchies. So, it's not the fact that cultural differences *exist* that makes them so difficult for us to deal with emotionally, it's that differences typically get translated into social statuses. If differences were just differences and not indicative of social statuses, we could just adjust to these distinctions and then grow comfortable with them. When distinctions become status differences, however, they are much more enduring and thus more difficult to deal with. No one wants to be at the bottom of a social hierarchy, so people have to negotiate their groups and the distinctions associated with these groups to try to stay out of the bottom and also to compete for higher status. No group wants to be at the bottom, but people need to know who is at the bottom (and also at the top) to figure out where they, themselves, are located.

Are you an immigrant or refugee yourself, or do you know someone who is? Perhaps you have had an experience—regardless of geographic place—where *you* were the outsider who did not speak the language and did not know how to behave like a native. If so, take a moment and recall what you felt like. Think about whether these feelings were pleasant or not. Try to name your feelings; for example, did you feel excited or fearful, challenged or frustrated? Did you experience anxiety or anticipation? If you have never had this type of experience, talk to someone who has. Ask that person to explain to you how he or she felt. The more you or the person you spoke with felt fear, anxiety, or frustration, the less belonging was felt. These are the feelings of cultural *discomfort*. The more excitement, anticipation, and challenge felt, the more culturally flexible you (or the other person) are. People's personalities vary; some people are more "naturally" curious and risk-taking. They tend to do well in new cultural environments. Others are more shy and/or settled in their ways, and they tend to have more challenges adapting to new cultural contexts (Holmes 2011).

However, there are greater patterns to *acculturation* among immigrants and refugees than just individual variations. The literature in this area is so huge it would take many books to discuss, but none of the studies I have seen (and I've spent about 20 years studying them) make all of the connections I would like you to make here. What are those connections? First, culture (as I have said so many times) is about interrelating seamlessly with others so that we experience our interactions comfortably. Culture is about comfort. Therefore, when we do not share culture we typically feel discomfort. Discomfort is your tip-off to being outside your cultural comforts; you can try to retreat back into your comforts or you can try to expand your comfort zones. I favor expansion over contraction.

Second, and as you know from reading this book, one of the reasons it is difficult—but not impossible—to adapt to new cultural circumstances is that in childhood our cultural comforts become part of our brain's very structure. To change what we do, we have to change those neural circuits that were built up to help us avoid having to spend a lot of brainpower paying attention to the everyday aspects of life. When you enter a cultural discomfort zone, your brain snaps to attention because there are a lot of unusual things that don't fit nicely into your subconscious expectations. Therefore, your brain spends a lot more of its energy trying to figure things out (imagine listening to a language you don't know) and that's very taxing and tiring. So cultural change is very much about breaking habits, climbing out of our cultural ruts, and this is hard to do. Third, children's brains are more flexible, which is why they are so adept at learning new languages and cultural contexts, whereas adults overwhelmingly find learning "new tricks" harder. But all brains retain flexibility, and the more we flex these cultural "muscles," the more we expand our cultural comforts and the less we feel discomforts. This leads me back to studies of immigrant acculturation (adaptation, integration, assimilation).

The rule of thumb is that if you move to a very different cultural context (where the spoken and body language, customs, rituals, etc., vary from what you learned as a baby) before adolescence, you are much more likely to find broad cultural belonging in the new cultural circumstances (as well as retaining what you learned before—so long as that language and customs are still practiced in your home). If you recall what you learned before about the brain's development (think pruning), you will now know why this is true. In early childhood, children package each experience as connections in their brains, but neural connections that are not being used are pruned out of the way. This translates into a lot of early learning that eventually becomes the child's cultural habits. This is also the time when children who are exposed to a new language and customs pick them up easily and "naturally" without any real instruction needed (though classes can help speed up the process). My husband, Miguel, arrived into the United States from Cuba at age 8; in 6 months, he was so fluent in English that his relatives frequently took him out of school to translate for them whenever they needed his help. Indeed, immigrating to a new country before adolescence is recognized as such a special phenomenon among immigration scholars that we have a distinctive name for these children: the "1.5 generation." Why 1.5? Well, the 1.0 generation is those people who themselves immigrate, while the 2.0 generation consists of the children of immigrants (the second generation is born in the new country). Children who are in the 1.5 generation are, technically, immigrants because they cross a border into a new country, but they act more like children of immigrants culturally, so that's why they are 1.5.

People who immigrate as adults are very culturally comfortable with their homeland's language, habits, customs, rituals, and so on. Moreover, their brains have gone through more pruning and their non-neocortex neurons' axons have been fully myelinated (sheathed), making them less flexible. As adults, the circuits in our brains have become highways and superhighways transporting these comforts and expectations for others' behavior. Adult immigrants, like adults in general, can change and adapt, but it's just harder; and for immigrants crossing into cultural contexts with different languages, values, and customs, the difficulty to adapt may seem insurmountable—especially if they have little or no time to devote to learning the language and cultural nuances of the host country. Moreover, their brains constantly compare their new experiences against their cultural comforts, which is exhausting mentally. And then there are the emotions of adapting. Immigrants, especially in adulthood, tend to feel like fish out of water—and what happens to us when we feel culturally discomforted? We often feel stressed. Stress is not conducive to learning; it is conducive to protecting our comforts. Immigrants just like the native born *can* embrace their cultural discomforts (next section), but more often than not, they do not enjoy the right conditions for adapting quickly—time to devote solely to learning new cultural competencies and close relations to people who the immigrants can learn from without feeling stupid or intimidated. Without those conditions, much more readily available to younger immigrants than to adults, the "natural" tendency is to avoid cultural discomforts and try to find cultural comforts, wherever they may be. Among immigrants, this means moving to neighborhoods where co-ethnics live, eating comfort foods, continuing to speak the same language, joining the same community of faith, not venturing out into the greater society unless absolutely necessary, and so on. These actions are completely reasonable from a culture as comfort perspective.

Of course, the greater society does not see what these immigrants are doing as seeking cultural comforts during times of huge cultural stress but, rather, as not being willing to integrate into society. Yet, as we discussed at length in Chapter 4 of this book, people want to integrate. Feeling discomforted is stressful, so we need and seek comfort. Too much stress is not only bad emotionally, it takes a physical toll and taxes our brains. My mother-in-law, bless her soul, is a great case in point. Born into a peasant family in rural Cuba, she had almost no chance to better her life except to follow the coattails of the man she fell in love with (but who was abusive) and travel away from all she had ever known to be with him in New York City. Imagine arriving in a new country in your 20s, not speaking the language and with no formal education. She could not even read or write in Spanish. The day she arrived, her husband was supposed to meet her but her flight was delayed due to a huge snowstorm. He got tired of waiting for her at the airport, didn't know when she would arrive, and decided to return home to his apartment where he had some drinks and then fell asleep. This was 1956. When she finally arrived in the airport, there was no husband anywhere. All she had was his address because he had no phone. What was she to do? Imagine her panic! New York at that time had few Spanish speakers. So she literally collapsed crying. A kind soul approached her and, in Spanish, asked her what was wrong and my mother-in-law told her story of woe. At that time, the few Spanish-speaking people in Manhattan lived clustered in the same area and, thankfully for my mother-in-law, this woman lived nearby and took her to the address that was scrawled on the piece of paper she carried. When she finally arrived, her husband was still sleeping!

Now, my mother-in-law had no time to study English or even acquire basic literacy; she had to work, and work she did. She learned some English but, in her more than six decades in the United States, it is still halting. She still cooks only Cuban food and lives in Miami where Cubans are everywhere, so that she has to engage few if any discomforting cultural contexts. What can be said about her acculturation? She learned to live, survive, raise two children, and navigate life from New York to Florida but she never really assimilated. Should society expect her to? The research indicates that her case is far from unusual and, in fact, is the norm for adult immigrants who arrive without knowing the language and with little education or training to help them adapt.

The first generation of immigrants, much like the case of my mother-in-law, will acculturate or adapt to varying degrees to the cultural contexts they arrive into, but researchers have found that the true test of integration is with their children (Kasinitz et al. 2004; Levitt & Waters 2002; Portes & Rumbaut 2001; Stepick 1998). Whether studying them in Europe, Australia, the Middle East, Canada, or the U.S., whether studying today's immigrants or yesterday's, scholars find that the key to cultural integration of immigrants (they measure integration by ethnic group, not by individuals) is the second, not the first, generation. This makes sense, as children are more culturally flexible. Do you remember the example of how kids, when faced with listening to adults speak pidgin (the mixture of two different languages), will invent their own new language complete with grammar? Well, children come into the world needing clear patterns and they typically find them; when they do not, they can even create their own. So keep this in mind as I describe a bit about the second generation's experiences with acculturation.

Children begin life in very small-scale societies—interacting with just a few to several dozen different people. Thus, they usually begin to learn cultural patterns from people who are largely culturally comfortable with each other. In the "old" way of talking about culture (which I'm trying to break out of), you might say they "share" the same culture. (But that treats culture as a *thing* we possess.) Any child who interacts with more than one person has to figure out what is common and what is different from interacting with other people. The child is looking for cultural patterns that order his world. There will always be some variation in how people act toward a child—even among food foragers who, as we have seen, live in very small, close-knit societies where everyone knows each other face-to-face and thus tend to be very similar culturally. Now, imagine a child who learns the cultural patterns of his home and is used to dealing with his family members, but at the age of 6 months is taken to daycare. He has to integrate into that cultural environment too. And then there is another different environment when he visits his relatives' homes, accompanies his father to the store, etc. So babies are regularly exposed to different cultural environments and learn these without any problems. The environments have some similarities and also some differences from each other. For example, while his home life is full of rituals (like feeding, diapering, nap times, bath times, etc.), his daycare life will have many of those rituals but they will be experienced somewhat differently and the physical context will shift. Still, imagine that the basic rituals' patterns of behavior will remain pretty much the same between home and daycare. The caregivers will speak the same language, probably hold the baby in similar ways, and also feed him similar foods in similar ways. All this helps expand his cultural comforts beyond home.

Take a moment and imagine the child of immigrants whose language, customs, and rituals are different from the greater society. This child will acquire these cultural comforts just like all children do as they figure out and reproduce them. But now imagine this child as a baby going off to daycare or as a kindergartner going off to elementary school. Imagine that the language of the school is completely new, as are the food and the daily rituals of interactions, behavior, body language, and so forth. Very young children will experience some degree of "culture shock" because of these dissimilarities; but given the flexibility of their brains, they will integrate just fine within weeks or months, depending on the degree of cultural differences present and on their personality characteristics. To illustrate, let me refer to a newspaper article I read some years ago about elementary schoolchildren in Queens, New York (Williams 1994). The article described that at the start of the school year, children brought their lunches from home and these lunches varied just like the kids' backgrounds. Dozens of different languages were spoken at home among these children—it was probably the most diverse elementary school in the country, if not the world. However, after only a few weeks the kids' lunches went from sushi or beef patties or sandwiches made on pitas to peanut butter-and-jelly sandwiches—the quintessential "American" lunch food. Such is the social desire and pressure to fit in among children.

Another factor that will influence immigrant children's integration (or acculturation) is *the degree to which they are accepted culturally into their new context*. Recall from Chapter 5 that even quite young children have been busy learning the social status hierarchies

This Child of Immigrant Parents Probably Crosses More Cultural Discomforts When Going to School from Home than Many of His Playmates. Why? He's Becoming Multicultural, but Will He Celebrate This or Just Want to Be Like "Normal" Kids?

operative in their small worlds, and they will impose those cultural boundaries on each other. Boys try to establish themselves as superior to girls, racial majority kids often do the same in regard to minorities, and so on. For example, Aviva, the daughter of immigrants, is from a country stereotyped as low status in the new country—such as Mexicans in the United States, Turks in Germany, or Pakistanis in Dubai. Aviva may become totally culturally fluent in her new context, but still never be accepted as truly belonging because others do boundary work against her. Alternatively, she may become so integrated into the cultural comforts of her own ethnic group that she never truly interfaces (beyond physically) with the broader society. This is particularly true in situations where children grow up surrounded by other immigrants who continue to *do* their cultural comforts day in and day out. If the neighborhood receives new immigrants from the same homeland continuously, then these newcomers will cleave toward their cultural comforts and help reproduce them for the next generation. The consequence of so much effort to maintain immigrants' cultural comforts is that when Aviva grows up, she may not feel comfortable leaving her neighborhood because to step beyond it is just too strange for her.

The scenarios I am painting here are very real consequences of living as an immigrant—not only today but historically as well. There is no one outcome for these second-generation children; rather, as many researchers have found, these children experience "segmented assimilation" (Portes & Zhou 1993). In the best-case scenario, second-generation children grow up to have multiple languages and cultural fluencies. They can shift effortlessly from the cultural comforts of home to those of the broader society's institutions (like schools, universities, workplaces). They are accepted and feel integrated and comfortable. More often, however, children of immigrants will grow up to feel "betwixt and between" different "cultures." They won't feel as though they totally belong to any place. They won't feel they are completely accepted in the new country and when they go "home" to their parents' homeland, they may also be told that they are different. They begin to wonder if they have a culture at all because they understand culture to be a possession and that everyone should have one culture. They hunger to belong somewhere *completely*; a great deal of recent literature about the immigrant experience reflects these feelings of being betwixt and between different cultural worlds, never quite comfortable anywhere.

I readily admit that this situation is uncomfortable for many people, but I also argue that it is more uncomfortable because we have come to expect ourselves to have only one culture. If we agree that we are all multicultural and not mono- or bicultural, then we are all betwixt and between cultural contexts; we just need to help ourselves to see this as a gift rather than as a problem. We need to come to embrace our cultural flexibilities and to feel opportunity, not dis*ease*, when encountering cultural discomforts. Given that we all belong to different groups whose cultural comforts are not exactly the same—our family, friends, neighborhoods, clubs, work teams, and so on—if we focus more on *how we as humans create belonging*, I believe these somewhat alienated second-generation children can grow up seeing themselves as important cultural bridges. However, to do so will necessitate some creative ideas for rituals to help this group feel they truly belong. Cultural isolation constructs differences, but the emotional distance produced by these differences can be bridged through imaginative interactions (i.e., rituals) that build connections between people from different cultural backgrounds. Earlier in the book we observed how people who start out different can be quickly and tightly bonded through intense rituals, particularly initiations and rites of passage (such as military boot camp).

There is yet another, third, outcome for second-generation immigrant youth that scholars have documented. In this scenario the youth feel least a part of the broader society, sometimes owing to cultural isolation but much more often because the broader society rejects them as not worthy of belonging. So these youth grow up culturally, psychologically, and emotionally alienated. However, though they share some of the feelings of the second group discussed earlier, the difference is that this group of second-generation immigrant youth *also rejects the greater society*. They don't *want to belong to it*. In his widely cited acculturation model, John W. Berry (1980) refers to this alternative as "separation." Youth subconsciously know they cannot belong, and they turn that rejection into their own rejection of the very society that excludes them. They then build their own cultural context; they cultivate their own cultural comforts that tend to be oppositional to those practiced by other youth. Recall that as people culturally create "us," they also create "others." The stronger the boundaries separating "us" from "them," the harder it is for people to move across these boundaries. The boundary work is just too intense.

A good example of this type of tight-knit, youth cultural context is the gang. Gangs apply my point that culture is about order to a very advanced degree. I do not want to imply that second-generation immigrant youth who are disaffected all become gang members, but some do, as do some native-born youth without immigrant parents. The issue here is not your background or heritage; the issue is your feeling of belonging, of fitting in, and of having a stake in the greater society. If those feelings are weak, and if you have grown up without a strong sense of the broader society's cultural rules (or if you feel confusion about which rules to follow, as is often the case for youth raised between cultural comforts), then the gang is a great temptation because what it does exceedingly well is build belonging. However, once you go through the rituals of belonging into gang membership (and especially if they involve committing a crime, because committing a violent crime arguably transforms a person from being innocent or pure into being permanently impure), then it is difficult if not impossible to leave the gang. Gangs tend to have very distinctive and noticeable symbols—tattoos, colors, clothing, graffiti—that they use to mark membership and their territory. They want to be recognized as different. And as you probably know, gangs compete for social status in local hierarchies. In other words, gangs represent cultural contexts of belonging in very stark ways; though they may not be cultural contexts we want to encourage, we should still see that they can help us understand what culture is better.

This section of the chapter has been focusing on getting to know your cultural comforts because the more we are aware of these comforts—and how we grow to have them—the more we can handle cultural discomforts constructively. That's the subject of the next section. As you get ready for that, I want to underscore a key point that I've been making implicitly in this chapter and now want to make explicit: No person—native or immigrant—is born culturally integrated into society. We *all* have to acquire culture. No one is born with culture. No one is therefore born integrated. Childhood is about becoming integrated into our first cultural contexts, but we continue to integrate into new cultural comforts throughout life. Therefore, *the experience of immigrants should not be treated as fundamentally different from that of natives.* People who immigrate as adults should not be blamed for "not assimilating" but encouraged to integrate to the degree they can. Natives should not be blamed for "not assimilating" into culturally discomforting contexts but should be encouraged to integrate across as many contexts as possible. This is our great gift as a cultural species and yet we shortchange ourselves when we treat culture as a thing and ourselves as monocultural.

We also must understand that cultural integration is not easy because culture is about habits. If it is difficult to stop "bad habits" such as biting your fingernails, smoking, drinking too much, or abusing drugs it's because these are habits that have become wired into our brains. So, too, are our cultural comforts. And we need to understand that to be comfortable, we need to keep practicing culture. I once was fluent in being a teenager but I no longer can fit in fluidly with teenagers. When I lived in Colombia I was much more culturally comfortable there than I would be now if I returned. Culture is about continual practice. Yes, it's a bit like learning to ride a bike in that once you learn it's not as difficult to ride, even if you have not ridden for a long time. But unlike riding a bike, feeling culturally comfortable takes more practice because while we're away from a bike, riding a bike does not change but when we're away from a culture, cultural practices do change. This is all the more reason to not shy away from your cultural discomforts but to embrace them as opportunities to continually grow personally and culturally.

EMBRACING YOUR CULTURAL DISCOMFORTS

As humans, we are all creatures of cultural habits. We love our cultural comforts because, subconsciously, they make the world intelligible, known and thus highly predictable. We know there is a future and we know that we can only control it to some extent. That puts a premium on being able to predict the future. We like predictions, though we rarely think about them—except when we cannot predict something. For example, we may watch the news for a weather report to know if we need to bring an umbrella or a coat or when a big storm threatens our area. Thank goodness for being able to predict the weather. When pregnant for the first time, women often worry if their pregnancies are normal. That's precisely why, for years and years, the book *What to Expect When You're Expecting* has been the go-to manual for pregnant women in the United States. The book walks you through pregnancy month by month and answers the little questions that people have, such as whether or not it's normal to feel a baby kick one week but not the next, for your feet to swell, and so on. Being pregnant for the first time is quite mysterious even if you've read all about it, and you don't want anyone to think you or your baby are abnormal, so you need a source to help you not only predict what is going to happen, but to also judge whether what *is* happening to you is normal.

Prediction is enormously valuable in economics as well. The stock market is all about trying to predict whether or not to invest in stocks, bonds, or commodities such as gold. To do this well, you need to predict what other people will invest in. Fortunately, since people's behavior is patterned (even when it's the behavior of millions of people acting around the world), with profound knowledge of people's cultural comforts, plus some good math, psychology, and other social science knowledge and skills, you can do pretty well investing in the stock market—so long as people are not panicking. When people get anxious, they are much less predictable. And when we feel outside our cultural comforts, we tend to be anxious. Think of this feeling of anxiousness as the telltale sign that our brains cannot predict what's going to happen. In particularly uncertain times, our brains spend much more time than normal trying to predict and this is stressful. This is one of the reasons

why many people, today as well as yesterday, consult prophets, fortune tellers, and diviners in the belief that these people have greater predictive powers than everyone else. Recently, I went to see a world-famous mystic who intuited the energy in a room of people. She was able to "know" very personal details about members of the audience. What was particularly interesting to me was that while adults wanted to connect to deceased people who had "passed over" into the spirit world, the children wanted the mystic to predict their futures. If only we could know the future, we think, then we would not feel so anxious about it. The more we feel change, too, the more we want to know what the changes will bring. So our brains hunger for predictions.

What I have been trying to get across in this book is that culture creates predictability because we are not born to be random; we create cultural patterns so that others can feel at ease with us and we with them. And we constantly communicate these patterns to others. We just need to listen more carefully to the messages others send out.

The best-case scenario is someone whose cultural contexts are not changing too much and who

People All Over the World Seek More Knowledge about the Future. We Consult Specialists to Help Us—Including Fortunetellers Like this One Reading Cards in Morocco as Well as Weather Forecasters, Financial Planners, and Astrologists Who Write Our Horoscopes. Whom Do You Go to? What Is It About Our Brains that Incites Our Desires to Predict the Future?"

is culturally fluent in those contexts, his brain doesn't have to do many calculations to predict what people in his environment will do. Let's call him Benjamin to personalize him. Benjamin is feeling calm and comfortable. He does not see (nor does he need to see) that culture is about predictability. We now know that culture is about how we humans impose order on our own cultural flexibility which makes it more predictable. Now let's change his context to make it more chaotic. Let's start with a "natural" disaster. "Good" disasters are those we predict and thus can plan for. So they make excellent "cultural" disasters since we do have some control over what happens. We may not be able to control the weather, but when we can predict it we at least can control how we act. Think about the difference between a huge snowstorm or rainstorm that was predicted over the course of a few days, or even a hurricane threatening the shoreline. These storms can be scary to experience, but at least Benjamin would have warning and could prepare. Now imagine Benjamin is in Los Angeles and a 7.0-magnitude earthquake hits. Imagine that, just by chance, Benjamin is outside when the quake hits. He feels the ground shaking and his mind jumps to "This is an earthquake!" He knows what it is but he is powerless over it and he has had no chance to prepare. What do people do during predicted storms? They hunker down in their homes with plenty of food and wait for the bad weather to move by. What do people do in big earthquakes? They panic, they scream, they run outside. The human social environment jumps from cultural order into disorder, into chaos. People can predict neither the disaster's impact nor what other people will do. In that cultural context, people feel scared and anxious. Order breaks down and confusion and chaos race in.

Sudden, huge natural disasters and human-made disasters such as war are the ultimate chaos producers. During such disasters, most people panic; and to handle this panic, soldiers and police train for them. For example, Navy SEALs have to practice overcoming panic in a pool when they are on the brink of drowning. Why? They were put into these extreme situations so that they would remain disciplined and in control during emotionally sensational times and life-threatening situations. When others panic, then, the SEALs function. They are the ultimate predictable humans. That is what all militaries want—disciplined people who will do exactly as they have been trained and ordered to do under the most extreme, unpredictable conditions.

I recall very clearly the day that I had this insight into culture as predictability. I was in graduate school studying anthropology at Columbia University and living in Washington Heights, a neighborhood of Manhattan above Harlem. At that time in the 1980s, the "Heights" was the epicenter of the crack cocaine trade. Why it became the epicenter has to do with the fact that the Cross-Bronx Expressway (a section of Highway I-95 connecting New Jersey with Manhattan and the Bronx in New York City as well as Westchester, New York, and then Connecticut) ran through the northernmost section of our neighborhood. This geographic location proved ideal for drug dealers to sell crack to people all over the metropolitan region. All buyers had to do was to get off I-95 for a few moments in the Heights, pick up whatever they wanted nearby, and then return home on the highway. Those of us who lived there, however, endured the epidemic's effects, including nightly gun battles and weekly murders. Our sidewalks were carpeted with crushed plastic crack vials, our streets were littered with burnt-out cars that had been vandalized, and addicts wandered our so-called parks. The most dangerous part of life there was not the dealers' guns, however, but the addicts. Why? Well, as I learned by living there, you could basically avoid the areas where you would be most likely to be shot at the most risky times, but you could not predict what the addicts would do. One day I was really upset by a car that pulled out in front of me while I was crossing the street and—I don't know what possessed me to do it but I was pretty wild back then (you had to be to live in that neighborhood)—I hammered the car's hood with my fist and yelled at the driver for almost killing me. My neighbors, almost all Dominicans who referred to me as the Spanish-speaking *Americana*, later scolded me for doing this. "What were you thinking?" said one. "You could have gotten yourself killed! What if that person was an addict?" That's when I realized something. I realized that I had become culturally fluent in the Heights—excellent at interpreting my surroundings and at predicting what all these people in my neighborhood did, *except* the addicts, of course. They were inherently unpredictable and, because of that, they were the most dangerous. Suddenly, it clicked in my head the association between culture and predictability. It has stuck with me ever since.

Living in Washington Heights was an adventure in culturally adapting to a discomfort zone. Thankfully, when I arrived there in the early 1980s I was already fluent in Spanish from my year of adapting to another place that had been very culturally discomforting—the capital city of Colombia, Bogotá. I was just 19 when I took a leave of absence from college and ventured to Colombia, despite the fact I spoke almost no Spanish and had never lived in a city, let alone a huge metropolis of over 6 million. But the fact that I challenged myself to adapt to this culturally discomforting context was the outcome of years of work by my parents. A very shy child growing up, I benefited from the fact that my parents forced me to engage cultural discomforts from an early age. I hated it then and resisted their pressure to send me away during summers to camp; I also dug my heels in when we moved when I was going into junior high. I learned not only to adapt, but I learned that as an outsider to someone else's comforts you really "see" what they do not see. You learn to analyze cultural contexts from a privileged (yes, privileged) location as an outsider. Of course I didn't want to be an outsider; like kids in general I wanted to fit in and to make friends more than exercising my analytical muscles! My natural tendency was to retreat from cultural discomforts, just like it is for people in general. When we feel culturally uncomfortable, we tend to just leave those circumstances and return to our cultural comforts. The more you dislike change, the more likely you are to avoid discomforts because change involves having to adapt. After being encouraged to adapt to new cultural discomforts numerous times, I gradually got over being so shy and disliking change. Now I find stability a bit boring and really thrive on change. If that were not true, it would be hard to be an anthropologist because we are, professionally, outsiders learning to become insiders.

There is a broader lesson in my own experience that I share with my children and grandchildren now. You may know it from the common saying that what children need is "roots and wings." You give them roots so that they are firmly grounded and have a sense of belonging—these are their cultural comforts. But you also give them wings so that they can go off and explore and see the world. By allowing them to grow wings, you encourage them to embrace their cultural discomforts, to grow culturally, to flex their cultural muscles as much as possible. Too strongly rooted people rarely fly free. Tethered to the tried and true, they often feel that their sense of self, their "culture," is being threatened by others. On the other hand, people whose wings are too strong have less appreciation for why most of us need to feel grounded. So, as with all things in life, there needs to be a balance between roots and wings, a balance that is different for each person given our individual personalities. Still, as the quintessentially cultural species in all of creation, we should not clip our children's wings in order to keep them close to their roots. This has perhaps never been truer than in the 21st century of cross-cultural contact. We all need to be multicultural—to extend our wingspans and our flight paths—to understand each other and thus promote getting along better, or we will likely see even more conflict than the horrors that characterized the 20th century. We cannot thwart culture wars until we change our views on the "nature" of culture.

My challenge to you in ending this book is, then, to *discover your cultural comforts and those of others . . . and to embrace your cultural discomforts as opportunities to grow, adapt, and collaborate*, not as things to fear. Discomforting feelings are our signals that we are entering opportunities for cultural growth. Humans evolved into a cultural species so that we could change and adapt when we encountered newness. Embrace this gift, don't shy from it! Additionally, teach your children well. Encourage them to grow deep roots but also strong wings. Children can learn any language, any cultural context, any customs and idiosyncrasies—but only if they are exposed to them sufficiently and in ways that encourage them to learn. So wherever you find yourself and those you love, seek out whatever opportunities you can given your circumstances to find and embrace cultural discomforts. You don't have to travel far away, for people are as diverse in our backyards as they are across the globe. Visit a different neighborhood and meet people there; venture into a different place of worship; walk a few kilometers in someone else's shoes; if you're a man, try out a part of a woman's world and vice versa. Learn a new instrument; interact online behind the safety of your avatar; watch a movie about people different from yourself. Invent a bonding ritual or modify one you already know. Examine the ways that your group symbolizes itself and what boundary work it does. Are "others" welcomed in or kept out? How and why? Whom do you and your group dislike? Invite these "others" to share a meal or an event with you; person-to-person, face-to-face contact is an effective antidote to prejudices and hatreds. Humanize those who have been dehumanized. Work toward reaching cultural comfort when you or others feel cultural discomfort and you'll find that once you get over the initial fear, embarrassment, or anxiety (if any) you will make a new human connection, a small step toward building yours and others' cultural muscles. Make it a movement—your small steps joining mine, and mine with others' until we have so many people in motion that we will not be able to avoid connecting.

APPLYING *CULTURE AS COMFORT*

Take a moment to contemplate how you can apply what you have learned in *Culture as Comfort*. This is not a silly exercise. What you have learned here should be useful to you to solve problems you encounter in your own life and also in our interconnected world. On the next page you will encounter the book's final Planned Pause. Please prepare your responses to the questions mindfully.

Now it is time for you to think about ways that *you* can apply what you have learned here. How can you discover your cultural comforts and embrace your discomforts? How can you encourage others to flex their cultural muscles as well? As our lives are full of many shifting cultural contexts, your list can and should be long. But if each of us figures out one or two ways to go forward and we share these—which is what my website www.cultureascomfort.com is for, then we can quickly build a wide-ranging wiki of evolving ideas.

PLANNED PAUSE 6-2

"HOW I WILL EXPAND MY CULTURAL COMFORTS"

In the space provided below, you have two tasks to complete:

1. *Taking stock: To evaluate whether or not your views on culture have changed by reading this book, please return to the first Planned Pause in which you wrote down your thoughts about culture. As you read your response, how does it strike you? Have your ideas changed? If so, explain the changes. If not, explain why not.*

2. *Now apply the thesis of* Culture as Comfort—*that we can all continue to expand our cultural comforts over the course of our lives—and discuss one or two ways that you wish to grow culturally and what your plan is for making that growth possible. Make sure you identify an area in which you need to grow culturally (even if you don't want to or feel afraid to grow in this way), and explain why you need to grow in that way as part of your Planned Pause response. Then, using the tools you've learned in this book for creating and expanding culturally comfortable contexts (e.g., interactions with "others," rituals, symbols, trade, boundary work, etc.) sketch out a plan of action for how you will go about expanding your comforts.*

Conclusion

So now that you have some of your own ideas as well as some of mine, go back into your cultural spaces and *do culture more mindfully*. Be aware of what you do and think, what others do and think, of what you want to keep the same and what you want to change in yourself and in the world. Recall always that we do not *have* culture itself, but we *do* culture to ourselves and to others. This is the human gift that we short-change when we stick within our cultural comforts, failing to embrace opportunities to expand those comforts even if they cause us unease at the beginning. Discomfort is a sign that we can grow and change. As always, unlocking the proverbial secrets about people can be used for a wide variety of purposes—both positive and negative. While for some time you have heard that people are "naturally" competitive, that's not nearly as true as it is for other species. Our *social* species evolved very specially; we evolved to collaborate—to extend our hands and hearts out to others and to have them collaborate and comfort us in kind. We *can* be distinctive from one another; we *can* retain our uniqueness at the same time that we interact with others who are, to varying degrees, different

from us. Distinction is intimately related to being human (Bourdieu 1984); using those distinctions to generate unequal social statuses is not. Am I saying that we all have to accept each other's ways? No. I do advocate cultural relativism, but by that I mean that before you judge others' ways, *at least do your best to understand their ways from their perspective.* You want others to respect you and your ways, so offer that same respect to others as well. And when "they" tell you what rules and values they follow, understand these rules as the very cultural order that we all need. You may not agree with their rules and values, but you now know that we all find comfort in these because they create for us a *feeling* of belonging and stability in an ever-changing cultural world. Learn your cultural dialect well, but also learn others'. That is the best hope we can have for preserving ourselves and our precious Earth into the future. Try to turn the Culture Wars into cultural comprehension. So go out and do culture ever more mindfully and respectfully. Culture is an interactive verb—to cultivate—not a possession to defend from others. Cultivate yourself, cultivate others. To you I now entrust this perspective and its future.

BIBLIOGRAPHY

Aboud, Frances. 1988. *Children and prejudice.* New York: Blackwell.

Allen, Nicholas J. 2008. "Tetradic theory and the origin of human kinship systems." Pp. 96–112 in *Early human kinship: from sex to social reproduction,* edited by Nicholas J. Allen, Hilary Callan, Robin Dunbar, and Wendy James. Malden, MA and Oxford: Royal Anthropological Institute and Blackwell Publishing.

Alleyne, Mervyn C. 2002. *Construction and representation of race and ethnicity in the Caribbean and the world.* Kingston: University of the West Indies Press.

Amen, Daniel. 1998. *Change your brain, change your life.* New York: Three Rivers Press of Random House.

Anderson, Benedict. 1991. *Imagined communities: reflections on the origins and spread of nationalism.* London: Verso.

Bader-Rusch, Andrea. 2003. "In the beginning was the word: language and the womb." Pp. 101–108 in *The multilingual mind: issues discussed by, for, and about people living with many languages,* edited by Tracey Tokuhama-Espinosa. Westport, CT: Praeger.

Barnard, Alan. 2008. "The co-evolution of language and kinship." Pp. 232–243 in *Early human kinship: from sex to social reproduction,* edited by Nicholas J. Allen, Hilary Callan, Robin Dunbar, and Wendy James. Oxford: Royal Anthropological Institute and Blackwell Publishing.

Barrett, Martyn. 2005. "Children's understanding of, and feelings about, countries and national groups." Pp. 251–285 in *Children's understanding of society,* edited by Martyn Barrett and Eithne Buchanan-Barrow. Hove and New York: Psychology Press.

Barrett, Martyn. 2007. *Children's knowledge, beliefs and feelings about nations and national groups.* East Sussex and New York: Psychology Press.

Barrett, Martyn, and Eithne Buchanan-Barrow. 2005. *Children's understanding of society.* Hove and New York: Psychology Press.

Barth, Fredrick. 1975. *Ritual and knowledge among the Baktaman of New Guinea.* New Haven, CT: Yale University Press.

Begley, Sharon. 2007. *Train your mind, change your brain.* New York: Ballantine Books.

Benedict, Ruth. 1959. *Patterns of culture.* Boston: Houghton Mifflin.

Berry, John W. 1980. "Acculturation as varieties of adaptation." Pp. 9–25 in *Acculturation theory, models, and some new findings,* edited by Amado Padilla. Boulder, CO: Westview Press.

Bickerton, Derek. 1981. *Roots of Language.* Ann Arbor, MI: Karoma.

Bjorklund, David F. 2000. *Children's thinking: developmental function and individual differences.* Belmont, CA: Wadsworth/Thomson Learning.

Bloemraad, Irene. 2006. *Becoming a citizen: incorporating immigrants and refugees in the United States and Canada.* Berkeley: University of California Press.

Bloom, Paul. 2009. "Natural Happiness." *The New York Times Magazine,* April 15 Retrieved (www.nytimes.com/2009/04/19/magazine/19wwln-lede-t.html).

Bloom, Paul. 2011. *How pleasure works: the new science of why we like what we like.* New York and London: W.W. Norton & Company, Inc.

Bourdieu, Pierre. 1984. *Distinction: a social critique of the judgment of taste.* Cambridge, MA: Harvard University Press.

Bowlby, John. 1988. *A secure base: parent-child attachment and healthy human development.* New York: Basic Books.

Bowles, Samuel. 2009. "Did warfare among ancestral hunter-gatherers affect the evolution of human social behaviors?" *Science* 324(5932):1293–1298.

Bowles, Samuel, and Herbert Gintis. 2011. *A cooperative species: human reciprocity and its evolution.* Princeton: Princeton University Press.

Boyd, Robert, and Peter J. Richerson. 2005. *The origin and evolution of cultures.* Oxford and New York: Oxford University Press.

Boyd, Robert, and Peter J. Richerson. 2006. "Culture and the evolution of the human social instincts." Pp. 453–77 in *Roots of human sociality*, edited by Stephen C. Levinson. London and New York: Berg Publishers.

Brooks, David. 2011. *The social animal: the hidden sources of love, character, and achievement.* New York: Random House.

Brown, Melissa J. 2008. "Introduction: developing a scientific paradigm for understanding culture." Pp. 3–16 in *Explaining culture scientifically*, edited by Melissa Brown. Seattle, WA: University of Washington Press.

Brubaker, Rogers, and Frederick Cooper. 2000. "Beyond 'identity'." *Theory and Society* 29(1):1–47.

Bruner, Jerome S., Rose R. Olver, and Patricia Marks Greenfield. 1966. *Studies in Cognitive Growth.* Oxford: Wiley.

Burns, Tracy C., Katherine A. Yoshida, Karen Hill, and Janet F. Werker. 2007. "The development of phonetic representation in bilingual and monolingual infants." *Applied Psycholinguistics* 28:455–474.

Burns, Tracy C., Janet F. Werker, and Karen McVie. 2003. "Development of phonetic categories in infants raised in bilingual and monolingual environments." in *Proceedings of the 27th Annual Boston University Conference on Language Development*, edited by B. Beachley, A. Brown, and F. Conlin. Somerville, MA: Cascadilla Press.

Bussey, Kay, and Albert Bandura. 1999. "Social cognitive theory of gender development and differentiation." *Psychological Review* 106:676–713.

Chase, Ivan D. 1980. "Social process and hierarchy formation in small groups: a comparative perspective." *American Sociological Review* 45(6):905–924.

Collins, Randall. 2004. *Interaction ritual chains.* Princeton and Oxford: Princeton University Press.

Connolly, Paul. 1998. *Racism, gender identities and young children.* London and New York: Routledge.

de Waal, Frans. 2005. *Our inner ape: a leading primatologist explains why we are who we are.* New York: Riverhead Books.

de Waal, Frans. 2009. *The age of empathy: nature's lessons for a kinder society.* New York: Harmony Press.

Diamond, Jared. 2005. *Guns, germs, and steel: the fates of human societies.* New York and London: W.W. Norton & Company, INC.

Domínguez D., Juan F., E. Douglas Lewis, Robert Turner, and Gary F. Egan. 2009. "The brain in culture and culture in the brain: a review of core issues in neuroanthropology." *Progress in Brain Research* 178:43–64.

Domínguez Duque, Juan F., Robert Turner, E. Douglas Lewis, and Gary F. Egan. 2010. "Neuroanthropology: a humanistic science for the study of the culture–brain nexus." *Social Cognitive and Affective Neuroscience* 5(2-3):138–147.

Donald, Merlin. 1991. *Origins of the modern mind: three stages in the evolution of culture and cognition.* Cambridge, MA: Harvard University Press.

Douglas, Mary. 1984. *Purity and danger: an analysis of the concepts of pollution and taboo.* London and Boston: Ark Paperbacks.

Dunbar, Robin. 1993. "The coevolution of neocortical size, group size and language in humans." *Behavioral and Brain Sciences* 16:681–735.

Dunbar, Robin. 2003. "The social brain: mind, language, and society in evolutionary perspective." *Annual review of anthropology* 32:163–181.

Dunbar, Robin. 2004. *The human story: a new history of mankind's evolution*. London: Faber and Faber.

Dunbar, Robin. 2008. "Kinship in Biological Perspective." Pp. 131–150 in *Early human kinship: from sex to social reproduction*, edited by Nicholas J. Allen, Hilary Callan, Robin Dunbar, and Wendy James. Malden, MA and Oxford: Blackwell Publishers Ltd.

Dunbar, Robin. 2010. *How many friends does one person need? Dunbar's number and other evolutionary quirks*. London: Faber and Faber.

Dunbar, Robin, and Louise Barrett, eds. 2007. *Oxford handbook of evolutionary psychology*. Oxford and New York: Oxford University Press.

Durkin, Kevin. 2005. "Children's understanding of gender roles in society." Pp. 135–167 in *Children's understanding of society*, edited by Martyn Barrett and Eithne Buchanan-Barrow. Hove and New York: Psychology Press.

Ekman, Paul, and Wallace V. Friesen. 2003. *Unmasking the face: a guide to recognizing emotions from facial clues*. Los Altos, CA: Malor Books.

Eliot, Lise. 1999. *What's going on in there? how the brain and the mind develop in the first five years of life*. New York: Bantam Books.

Eysenck, Hans Jurgen. 2006. *The biological basis of personality*. New Brunswick, NJ: Transaction Publishers.

Ferree, Myra Marx, and Beth B. Hess. 1987. *Analyzing gender: a handbook of social science research*. Newbury Park, CA: Sage Publications.

Fiske, Alan Page. 2004. "Relational models theory 2.0." Pp. 3–24, in *Relational models theory: a contemporary overview*, edited by Nick Haslam. Mahway, NJ: Lawrence Erlbaum Associates.

Fiske, Susan T., and Shelley E. Taylor. 2008. *Social cognition*. New York: McGraw Hill.

Fogel, Alan. 1993. *Developing through relationship: origins of communication, self, and culture*. Chicago: University of Chicago Press.

Friedl, Ernestine. 1975. *Women and men: an anthropologist's view*. New York: Holt, Rinehart and Winston.

Gardner, Howard. 1983. *Frames of mind: the theory of multiple intelligences*. New York: Basic Books.

van Gennep, Arnold. 1960. *The rites of passage*. Chicago: University of Chicago Press.

Giddens, Anthony. 1979. *Central problems in social theory: action, structure and contradiction in social analysis*. Berkeley and Los Angeles: University of California Press.

Gieryn, Thomas F. 1983. "Boundary-work and the demarcation of science from non-science: strains and interests in professional interests of scientists." *American Sociological Review* 48:781–795.

Ginsburg, Rebecca. 2008. "The view from the back step: white children learn about race in Johannesburg's suburban homes." Pp. 193–212 in *Designing modern childhoods: history, space, and the material culture of children*, edited by Marta Gutman and Ning De Coninck-Smith. New Brunswick, NJ: Rutgers University Press.

Glass, Ira. 2010. "NUMMI." *This American Life*. Radio Broadcast. Retrieved July 11, 2012 (http://www.thisamericanlife.org/radio-archives/episode/403/nummi).

Glick, Peter, and Susan T. Fiske. 1996. "The ambivalent sexism inventory: differentiating hostile and benevolent sexism." *Journal of Personality and Social Psychology* 70(3):491–512.

Goleman, Daniel. 2006. *Social intelligence: the new science of human relationships*. New York: Bantam Books.

Gopnik, Alison. 2009. *The philosophical baby: what children's minds tell us about truth, love, and the meaning of life.* New York: Farrar, Straus and Giroux.

Gottlieb, Alma. 2004. *The afterlife is where we come from: the culture of infancy in West Africa.* Chicago: University of Chicago Press.

Greenwald, Anthony G., and Linda Hamilton Krieger. 2006. "Implicit bias: scientific foundations." *California Law Review* 94(4):945–967.

Hahn-Holbrook, Jennifer, Colin Holbrook, and Jesse Bering. 2010. "Snakes, spiders, strangers: how the evolved fear of strangers may misdirect efforts to protect children from harm." Pp. 263–289 in *Protecting children from violence: evidence-based interventions,* edited by James Lampinen and Kathy Sexton-Radek. New York: Psychology Press.

Haith, Marshall M., and Janette B. Benson. 1998. "Infant cognition." Pp. 199–254 in *Handbook of child psychology: volume 2: cognition, perception, and language,* edited by William Damon. Hoboken, NJ: John Wiley & Sons Inc.

Hall, Edward T. 1990. *The silent language.* New York: Anchor Books.

Harwood, Robin L., Joan G. Miller, and Nydia Lucca Irizarry. 1995. *Culture and attachment: perceptions of the child in context.* New York and London: The Guilford Press.

Hewlett, Barry S., and Michael E. Lamb. 2005a. "Emerging issues in the study of hunter-gatherer children." Pp. 3–18 in *Hunter-gatherer childhoods: evolutionary, developmental & cultural perspectives,* edited by Barry S. Hewlett and Michael E. Lamb. New Brunswick, NJ and London: Aldine Transaction.

Hewlett, Barry S., and Michael E. Lamb. 2005b. *Hunter-gatherer childhoods: evolutionary, developmental & cultural perspectives.* New Brunswick, NJ and London: Aldine Transaction.

Hirschfeld, Lawrence. 2005. "Children's understanding of racial groups." Pp. 199–221 in *Children's understanding of society,* edited by Martyn Barrett and Eithne

Buchanan-Barrow. Hove and New York: Psychology Press.

Hobsbawm, E. J., and David J. Kertzer. 1992. "Ethnicity and Nationalism in Europe Today." *Anthropology Today* 8(1):3–8.

Hobsbawn, Eric J., and Terence O. Ranger. 1983. *The invention of tradition.* Cambridge and New York: Cambridge University Press.

Hofstede, Geert. 1980. *Culture's consequences: international differences in work-related values.* Beverly Hills, CA: Sage Publications.

Hofstede, Geert, and Robert R. McCrae. 2004. "Personality and culture revisited: linking traits and dimensions of culture." *Cross-Cultural Research* 38(1):52–88.

Holmes, Hannah. 2011. *Quirk: brain science makes sense of your peculiar personality.* New York: Random House.

Holmes, Robyn M. 1995. *How young children perceive race.* Thousand Oaks, CA: Sage.

Hrdy, Sarah Blaffer. 2009. *Mothers and others: the evolutionary origins of mutual understanding.* Cambridge, MA and London: Harvard University Press.

Huber, Brad, and William Breedlove. 2007. "Evolutionary theory, kinship, and childbirth in cross-cultural perspective." *Cross-Cultural Research* 41(2):196–219.

Jahoda, Gustav. 1963. "The development of children's ideas about country and nationality." *British Journal of Educational Psychology* 33(1):47–60.

Jahoda, Gustav, and I.M. Lewis. 1988. "Child development in psychology and anthropology." Pp. 1–34 in *Acquiring culture: cross cultural studies in child development,* edited by Gustav Jahoda and I.M. Lewis. London and New York: Croom Helm.

James, Wendy. 2008. "Why 'kinship'? New questions on an old topic." Pp. 3–20 in *Early human kinship: from sex to social reproduction,* edited by Nicholas J. Allen, Hilary Callan, Robin Dunbar, and Wendy James. Malden, MA and Oxford: Royal Anthropological Institute and Blackwell Publishing.

Johanson, Donald C., and Maitland A. Edey. 1981. *Lucy, the beginnings of humankind.* New York: Simon and Schuster.

Johnson, Spencer. 1998. *Who moved my cheese? an amazing way to deal with change in your work and in your life.* New York: G.P. Putnam's Sons.

Kasinitz, Philip, John. H. Mollenkopf, and Mary C. Waters, eds. 2004. *Becoming New Yorkers: ethnographies of the new second generation.* New York: The Russell Sage Foundation.

Kaufman, Sharon R., and Lynn M. Morgan. 2005. "The anthropology of the beginnings and ends of life." *Annual Review of Anthropology* 34(1):317–341.

Kelly, Raymond C. 2000. *Warless societies and the origin of war.* Ann Arbor, MI: University of Michigan Press.

Kitayama, Shinobu, and Ayse K. Uskul. 2011. "Culture, mind, and the brain: current evidence and future directions." *Annual Review of Psychology* 62:419–449.

Konner, Melvin. 2004. "The ties that bind." *Nature* 429(6993):705.

Kroeber, Alfred L., and Clyde Kluckhohn. 1963. *Culture: a critical review of concepts and definitions.* New York: Vintage.

Kuper, Adam. 1999. *Culture: the anthropologists' account.* Cambridge, MA: Harvard University Press.

Lamont, Michèle, and Virág Mólnar. 2002. "The study of boundaries in the social sciences." *Annual Review of Sociology* 28:167–195.

Lancy, David F. 2010. *The anthropology of childhood: cherubs, chattel, changelings.* Cambridge: Cambridge University Press.

Layton, Robert. 2008. "What can ethnography tell us about human social evolution?" Pp. 113–127 in *Early human kinship: from sex to social reproduction,* edited by Nicholas J. Allen, Hilary Callan, Robin Dunbar, and Wendy James. Oxford: Royal Anthropological Institute and Blackwell Publishing.

Lee, Richard B. 1972. "!Kung spatial organization: an ecological and historical perspective." *Human Ecology* 1(2):125–147.

Lee, Richard B. 1979. *The !Kung San: men, women and work in a foraging society.* New York: Cambridge University Press.

Lende, Daniel, and Gregory Downey, eds. 2012. *The encultured brain: an introduction to neuroanthropology.* Cambridge, MA: MIT Press.

LeVine, Robert A., and Rebecca S. New. 2008. *Anthropology and child development: a cross-cultural reader.* Malden, MA and Oxford: Blackwell Publishing.

LeVine, Robert A., and Karin Norman. 2001. "The infant's acquisition of culture: early attachment reexamined in anthropological perspective." Pp. 83–104 in *The psychology of cultural experience,* edited by Carmella C. Moore and Holly F. Mathews. Cambridge and New York: Cambridge University Press.

LeVine, Robert A., and Karin Norman. 2008. "Attachment in anthropological perspective." Pp. 127–142 in *Anthropology and child development: a cross-cultural reader,* edited by Robert A. LeVine and Rebecca A. New. Malden, MA and Oxford: Blackwell Publishing.

Levinson, Stephen C. 2006. "On the human 'interaction engine'." Pp. 39–69 in *Roots of human sociality,* edited by N.J. Enfield and Stephen C. Levinson. Oxford and New York: Berg.

Levitt, Peggy, and Mary C. Waters. 2002. *The changing face of home: the transnational lives of the second generation.* New York: Russell Sage Foundation.

Levy, Gary, and Robert A. Haaf. 1994. "Detection of gender-related categories by 10-month-old infants." *Infant Behavior and Development* 17(4):457–459.

Lichtenstein, Jessie. 2011. "Next-Generation Scientists." *The New York Times Magazine,* March 25.

López, Gerardo. 2003. "The (racially neutral) politics of education: a critical race theory perspective." *Educational Administration Quarterly* 39(1):68–94.

Maccoby, Eleanor E. 1998. *The two sexes: growing up apart, coming together.* Cambridge, MA and London: Harvard University Press.

Maccoby, Eleanor E. 2002. "Gender and group process: a developmental perspective." *Current Directions in Psychological Science* 11(2):54–58.

Macrae, C. Neil, and Galen V. Bodenhausen. 2000. "Social cognition: thinking categorically about others." *Annual Review of Psychology* 51:93–120.

Macrae, C. Neil, Alan B. Milne, and Galen V. Bodenhausen. 1994. "Stereotypes as energy-saving devices: A peek inside the cognitive toolbox." *Journal of Personality and Social Psychology* 66(1):37–47.

Marshall, Lorna. 1961. "Sharing, talking, and giving: relief of social tensions among !Kung Bushmen." *Africa* 31(3):231–249.

Martin, Carol Lynn, Diane N. Ruble, and Joel Szkrybalo. 2002. "Cognitive theories of early gender development." *Psychological Bulletin* 128(6):903–933.

Massey, Douglas S. 2007. *Categorically unequal: the American stratification system.* New York: Russell Sage Foundation.

McElreath, Richard, Robert Boyd, and Peter J. Richerson. 2003. "Shared norms and the evolution of ethnic markers." *Current Anthropology* 44(1):122–130.

Mehler, Jacques, Josiane Bertoncini, and Michèle Barrière. 1978. "Infant recognition of mother's voice." *Perception* 7:491–497.

Meltzoff, Andrew N, Patricia K. Kuhl, Javier Movellan, and Terrence J. Sejnowski. 2009. "Foundations for a new science of learning." *Science* 325(5938):284–288.

Miller, Jake. 2012. "Dawn of social networks." *Focus: news from Harvard medical, dental and public health schools,* January 25 Retrieved March 24, 2012 (http://www.focushms.com/features/dawn-of-social-networks/).

Mitchell, Lisa M, and Eugenia Georges. 1998. "Baby's first picture: the cyborg fetus of ultrasound imaging." Pp. 105–124 in *Cyborg babies: from techno-sex to techno-tots,* edited by Robbie Davis-Floyd and Joseph Dumit. New York and London: Routledge.

Montgomery, Heather. 2009. *An introduction to childhood: anthropological perspectives on children's lives.* Malden, MA and Oxford: Wiley-Blackwell.

Nederveen Pieterse, Jan. 2007. *Ethnicities and global multiculture: pants for an octopus.* New York: Rowman & Littlefield Publishers, Inc.

Nettle, Daniel, and Robin Dunbar. 1997. "Social markers and the evolution of reciprocal exchange." *Current Anthropology* 38(1):93–99.

Nowak, Martin A. 2011. *SuperCooperators: altruism, evolution, and why we need each other to succeed.* New York: Free Press.

Paley, Vivian Gussin. 1984. *Boys & girls: superheroes in the doll corner.* Chicago and London: University of Chicago Press.

Pascual-Leone, Alvaro, Amir Amedi, Felipe Fregni, and Lotfi B. Merabet. 2005. "The plastic human brain cortex." *Annual Review of Neuroscience* 28:377–401.

Portes, Alejandro, and Rubén Rumbaut. 2001. *Legacies: the story of the immigrant second generation.* Berkeley and New York: University of California Press and Russell Sage Foundation.

Portes, Alejandro, and Min Zhou. 1993. "The new second generation: segmented assimilation and its variants." *Annals of the American Academy of Political and Social Science* 530(Nov):74–96.

Price, T. Douglas, and Ofer Bar-Yosef. 2011. "The origins of agriculture: new data, new ideas." *Current Anthropology* 52(S4):S163–S174.

Raeff, Catherine, and Janette B. Benson. 2003. "Introduction: interaction and development." Pp. 1–9 in *Social cognitive development in the context of individual, social, and cultural processes,* edited by Catherine Raeff and Janette B. Benson. London and New York: Routledge.

Ramachandran, V.S. 2011. *The tell-tale brain: a neuroscientist's quest for what makes us human.* New York: Norton.

Ratey, John J. 2002. *A user's guide to the brain.* New York: Vintage Books.

Richerson, Peter J., and Robert Boyd. 2005. *Not by genes alone: how culture transformed human evolution.* Chicago: University of Chicago Press.

Richter, Linda, and Arie W. Kruglanski. 2004. "Motivated closed mindedness and the emergence of culture." Pp. 101–21 in *The psychological foundations of culture,* edited by Mark Schaller and Christian S. Crandall. Mahwah, NJ: Lawrence Erlbaum Associates.

Ricks, Thomas. 1997. *Making the corps.* New York: Scribner.

Rizzolatti, G., L. Fadiga, L. Fogassi, and V. Gallese. 1996. "Premotor cortex and the recognition of motor actions." *Cognitive Brain Research* 3(2):131–141.

Rogoff, Barbara. 2003. *The cultural nature of human development.* Oxford and New York: Oxford University Press.

Rosaldo, Michelle Zimbalist, and Louise Lamphere, eds. 1974. *Woman, culture, and society.* Stanford, CA: Stanford University Press.

Rozin, Paul, Jonathan Haidt, and Clark R. McCauley. 2008. "Disgust." Pp. 757–776 in *Handbook of emotions,* edited by Michael Lewis and Jeannette M. Haviland-Jones. New York: Guilford Press.

Saffran, Jenny R., Richard N. Aslin, and Elissa L. Newport. 1996. "Statistical learning by 8-month-old infants." *Science* 274(5294):1926–1928.

Scheper-Hughes, Nancy. 1992. *Death without weeping: the violence of everyday life in Brazil.* Berkeley CA University of California Press.

Scourfield, Jonathan, Bella Dicks, Mark Drakeford, and Andrew Davies. 2006. *Children, place and identity: nation and locality in middle childhood.* London and New York: Routledge.

Senghas, Ann. 1995. "Children's contribution to the birth of Nicaraguan sign language." Boston: PhD Thesis, Massachusetts Institute of Technology.

Seung, Sebastian. 2012. *Connectome: how the brain's wiring makes us who we are.* Boston and New York: Houghton Mifflin Harcourt.

Shaw, Marie E., and Mark A. Hector. 2010. "Listening to military members returning from Iraq and/or Afghanistan: a phenomenological investigation." *Professional Psychology: Research and Practice* 41(2):128–134.

Sherif, Muzafer, O.J. Harvey, B. Jack White, William R. Hood, and Carolyn W. Sherif. 2010. *The robbers cave experiment: intergroup conflict and cooperation.* Middletown, CT: Wesleyan University Press.

Siegel, Daniel J. 1999. *The developing mind: how relationships and the brain interact to shape who we are.* New York: The Guilford Press.

Siegler, Robert S. 1996. *Emerging minds: the process of change in children's thinking.* New York and Oxford: Oxford University Press.

Small, Meredith F. 1998. *Our babies, ourselves: How biology and culture shape the way we parent.* New York: Anchor Books.

Smedley, Audrey. 2007. *Race in North America: origin and evolution of a worldview.* Boulder, CO: Westview Press.

Sroufe, L. Alan, Byron Egeland, Elizabeth A. Carlson, and W. Andrew Collins. 2005. *The development of the person: the Minnesota study of risk and adaptation from birth to adulthood.* New York: Guilford Press.

Stepick, Alex. 1998. *Pride against prejudice: Haitians in the United States.* Boston: Allyn & Bacon.

Stryker, Rachael. 2010. *The road to Evergreen: adoption, attachment therapy, and the promise of family.* Ithaca, NY: Cornell University Press.

Taylor, Janelle. 2008. *The public life of the fetal sonogram technology, consumption, and the politics of reproduction.* New Brunswick, NJ: Rutgers University Press.

Thalenberg, Eileen. 2003. *The baby human.* Discovery health channel.

Thorne, Barrie. 1993. *Gender play: girls and boys in school.* New Brunswick, NJ: Rutgers University Press.

Tilly, Charles. 2001. "Justice and categorical inequality." *Theory, Culture and Society* 18(4):129–133.

Todorov, Alexander, Susan T. Fiske, and Deborah A. Prentice, eds. 2011. *Social neuroscience: toward understanding the underpinnings of the social mind.* Oxford and New York: Oxford University Press.

Tomasello, Michael. 1999. *The cultural origins of human cognition.* Cambridge, MA: Harvard University Press.

Tomasello, Michael. 2008. "How are humans unique?" *New York Times Magazine,* May 25 Retrieved July 11, 2011 (http://www.nytimes.com/2008/05/25/magazine/25wwln-essay-t.html?8br).

Toren, Christina. 1988. "Children's perceptions of gender and hierarchy in Fiji." Pp. 225–270 in *Acquiring culture: cross cultural studies in child development,* edited by Gustav Jahoda and I.M. Lewis. London: Routledge.

Trevarthen, Colwyn, Kenneth Aitken, Despina Papoudi, and Jacqueline Robarts. 1998. *Children with autism: diagnosis and interventions to meet their needs.* 2nd ed. London: Jessica Kingsley Publishers.

Turner, Victor. 1967. *The forest of symbols: aspects of Ndembu ritual.* Ithaca, NY: Cornell University Press.

Turner, Victor. 1977. *The ritual process: structure and anti-structure.* Ithaca, NY: Cornell University Press.

Van Ausdale, Debra, and Joe R. Feagin. 2001. *The first R: how children learn race and racism.* New York: Rowman & Littlefield Publishers, Inc.

van der Elst, Dirk. 2003. *Culture as given, culture as choice.* Prospect Heights, IL: Waveland Press, Inc.

Vygotsky, Lev S. 1978. *Mind in society: the development of higher psychological processes.* Cambridge: Harvard University Press.

Warin, Jo. 2000. "The Attainment of self-consistency through gender in young children." *Sex Roles* 42(3-4):209–231.

Warner, W. Lloyd, and Leo Srole. 1976. *The social systems of American ethnic groups.* Westport, CT: Greenwood Press.

Weisner, Thomas S., and Ronald Gallimore. 1977. "My brother's keeper: child and sibling caretaking." *Current Anthropology* 18(2):169–190.

Wenger, Martha. 2008. "Children's work, play, and relationships among the Giriama of Kenya." Pp. 289–306 in *Anthropology and child development: a cross-cultural reader,* edited by Robert A. LeVine and Rebecca S. New. Malden, MA and Oxford: Blackwell Publishing.

Werker, Janet F., John H. V. Gilbert, Keith Humphrey, and Richard C. Tees. 1981. "Developmental aspects of cross-language speech perception." *Child Development* 52(1):349–355.

Whiting, Beatrice B., and Carolyn P. Edwards. 1988. *Children of different worlds: the formation of social behavior.* Cambridge, MA: Harvard University Press.

Williams, Lena. 1994. "What's for lunch? American." *The New York Times,* October 26, C1.

Wilson, Timothy D. 2004. *Strangers to ourselves: discovering the adaptive unconscious.* Cambridge, MA: Belknap Press of Harvard University Press.

Zimbardo, Phillip. 2007. *The Lucifer effect: understanding how good people turn evil.* New York: Random House.

CREDITS

PHOTO CREDITS

Chapter 1: Page 5: Frank Greenaway/Dorling Kindersley; page 8: Florida Division of Cultural Affairs; Artwork by Tim Leatzon **Chapter 2:** Page 13: Ruth Jenkinson/Dorling Kindersley; page 18: Vanessa Davies/Dorling Kindersley; page 20: Vanessa Davies/Dorling Kindersley; page 24: Ruth Jenkinson/Dorling Kindersley; page 27: Detail Heritage/Alamy; page 31: Sophia E. Dominguez-Mahler **Chapter 3:** Page 37: *Jeopardy!*/Landov; page 38: Kalim/Shutterstock; page 41: F. D. Giddings/PHOTOTAKE/Alamy Limited; page 42: Sophia E. Dominguez-Mahler; page 44: Martin Richardson/Rough Guides/Dorling Kindersly; page 48: Dorling Kindersley **Chapter 4:** Page 56: Rohan Preston/MCT/Newscom; page 59: Niels Poulsen/Alamy; page 61: Anthony Thorne; page 63: World of Warcraft. Copyright Blizzard Entertainment®. Blizzard Entertainment is a trademark or registered trademark of Blizzard Entertainment, Inc. in the U.S. and/or other countries. All rights reserved; page 64: Pearson Education; page 66: Samuel Lewis/ImageReflex; page 72: JEAN-PHILIPPE KSIAZEK/AFP/Getty Images/Newscom; page 73: David R. Frazier Photolibrary, Inc./Alamy **Chapter 5:** Page 77: Sarah J. Mahler; page 78: AF archive/Alamy; page 79: Ulrich Doering/Alamy; page 80: Spencer Grant/PhotoEdit; page 88: Randy Faris/Corbis Super/Alamy; page 90: Rafael Mustafa; page 99: David H. Wells / Danita Delimont/ Alamy **Chapter 6:** Page 104: Dave King/Dorling Kindersley; page 106: Vanessa Davies/ Dorling Kindersley; page 109: david pearson/Alamy; page 119: Janine Wiedel/Alamy; page 122: Alan Keohane/ Dorling Kindersley **Cover:** Joanne Pedro

TEXT CREDITS

Chapter 2: Page 20: Ramachandran, V.S. The Tell Tale Brain. Copyright © by W.W. Norton. Reprinted by permission. **Chapter 3:** Page 35: KAIL, ROBERT V., CHILDREN AND THEIR DEVELOPMENT, 6th Ed., © 2012. Reprinted and Electronically reproduced by permission of Pearson Education, Inc., Upper Saddle River, New Jersey; page 40: ARNETT, JEFFREY JENSEN, HUMAN DEVELOPMENT: A CULTURAL APPROACH, 1st Ed., © 2013. Reprinted and Electronically reproduced by permission of Pearson Education, Inc., One Lake Street, Upper Saddle River, NJ 07458. **Chapter 5:** Page 75: "You've Got To Be Carefully Taught" by Richard Rodgers and Oscar Hammerstein II Copyright © 1949 by Richard Rodgers and Oscar Hammerstein II. Copyright Renewed. International Copyright Secured. All Rights Reserved. Used by Permission of Williamson Music, A Division of Rodger & Hammerstein: An Imagem Company.

INDEX